Computer Accounting

with

QuickBooks Online

Computer Accounting

with

QuickBooks Online

First Edition

Donna Kay, MBA, PhD, CPA, CITP

McGraw Hill Education

COMPUTER ACCOUNTING WITH QUICKBOOKS™ ONLINE

Published by McGraw-Hill Education, 2 Penn Plaza, New York, NY 10121. Copyright © 2019 by McGraw-Hill Education. All rights reserved. Printed in the United States of America. No part of this publication may be reproduced or distributed in any form or by any means, or stored in a database or retrieval system, without the prior written consent of McGraw-Hill Education, including, but not limited to, in any network or other electronic storage or transmission, or broadcast for distance learning.

Some ancillaries, including electronic and print components, may not be available to customers outside the United States.

This book is printed on acid-free paper.

1 2 3 4 5 6 QVS 22 21 20 19 18

ISBN 978-1-260-25842-4
MHID 1-260-25842-4

Portfolio Manager: *Steve Schuetz*
Product Developer: *Alexandra Kukla*
Marketing Manager: *Michelle Williams*
Content Project Manager: *Dana M. Pauley*
Buyer: *Susan K. Culbertson*
Design: *Egzon Shaqiri*
Content Licensing Specialist: *Beth Thole*
Cover Image: *©Diego Grandi/Shutterstock*
Compositor: *SPi Global*

All credits appearing on page or at the end of the book are considered to be an extension of the copyright page.

The Internet addresses listed in the text were accurate at the time of publication. The inclusion of a website does not indicate an endorsement by the authors or McGraw-Hill Education, and McGraw-Hill Education does not guarantee the accuracy of the information presented at these sites.

Preface

Computer Accounting with QuickBooks Online

Donna Kay

WELCOME TO LEARNING QUICKBOOKS ONLINE!

Give yourself a competitive advantage – learn a leading online financial app for entrepreneurs using *Computer Accounting with QuickBooks Online*. Designed using the most effective way to learn QuickBooks Online, this text streamlines learning QuickBooks Online because it focuses on you—the learner.

Proven instructional techniques are incorporated throughout the text to make your mastery of QuickBooks Online as effortless as possible. Using a hands-on approach, this text integrates understanding accounting with mastery of QuickBooks Online. Designed for maximum flexibility to meet your needs, *Computer Accounting with QuickBooks Online* can be used either in a QuickBooks Online course or independently at your own pace.

Why learn QBO with *Computer Accounting with QuickBooks Online* by Donna Kay?

- **By design, this text makes learning QuickBooks Online efficient and effective.**

- **Tight Write.** Do you have time to read extra unnecessary words? If you are like most students you are pressed for time. So this text will save you time using tight writing - what you need to know without unnecessary extra words.

- **Streamlined Learning.** Simplify and streamline learning QuickBooks Online with **XPM**. What is XPM?
  - e**X**plore
  - **P**ractice
  - **M**aster

    e**X**plore QuickBooks Online using the chapter with walkthrough screen captures. Don't worry about making mistakes while we eXplore, letting us focus on learning how to navigate and use QBO.

    Practice entering information and transactions into QBO with end-of-chapter exercises.

    Master QBO with QBO projects. The projects cover QBO tasks from setting up a new QBO company and entering transactions to generating QBO reports.

- **www.mhhe.com/KayQBO1e** website offers updates, help and support links, video links and more.

- **Connect.** Enter assignments into Connect, receive interactive feedback to facilitate learning, and have it auto graded with feedback.

What kind of study tools does *Connect* offer?

- **SmartBook.** As a student engages with SmartBook, the reading experience continually adapts by highlighting content based on what the student knows and doesn't know. This means students are more engaged with course content, can better prioritize their time, and come to class prepared.

- **Assignment Materials.** After completing assignments in QuickBooks Online students can enter key elements of their solution into Connect for grading. Based on instructor settings, they can receive instant feedback either while working on the assignment or after the assignment is submitted for grade. Assignable materials include: exercises, projects, practice quizzes, and test bank materials.

- **Insight.** The analytic tools within Connect provide at-a-glance information regarding class performance and assignment effectiveness.

Good luck with QuickBooks Online and best wishes for your continued success,

Donna Kay

McGraw-Hill Connect® is a highly reliable, easy-to-use homework and learning management solution that utilizes learning science and award-winning adaptive tools to improve student results.

Homework and Adaptive Learning

- Connect's assignments help students contextualize what they've learned through application, so they can better understand the material and think critically.
- Connect will create a personalized study path customized to individual student needs through SmartBook®.
- SmartBook helps students study more efficiently by delivering an interactive reading experience through adaptive highlighting and review.

Connect's Impact on Retention Rates, Pass Rates, and Average Exam Scores

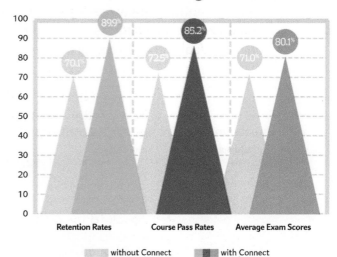

without Connect   with Connect

Over **7 billion questions** have been answered, making McGraw-Hill Education products more intelligent, reliable, and precise.

Using **Connect** improves retention rates by **19.8** percentage points, passing rates by **12.7** percentage points, and exam scores by **9.1** percentage points.

73% of instructors who use **Connect** require it; instructor satisfaction **increases** by 28% when **Connect** is required.

Quality Content and Learning Resources

- Connect content is authored by the world's best subject matter experts, and is available to your class through a simple and intuitive interface.
- The Connect eBook makes it easy for students to access their reading material on smartphones and tablets. They can study on the go and don't need internet access to use the eBook as a reference, with full functionality.
- Multimedia content such as videos, simulations, and games drive student engagement and critical thinking skills.

Robust Analytics and Reporting

©Hero Images/Getty Images

- Connect Insight® generates easy-to-read reports on individual students, the class as a whole, and on specific assignments.

- The Connect Insight dashboard delivers data on performance, study behavior, and effort. Instructors can quickly identify students who struggle and focus on material that the class has yet to master.

- Connect automatically grades assignments and quizzes, providing easy-to-read reports on individual and class performance.

Impact on Final Course Grade Distribution

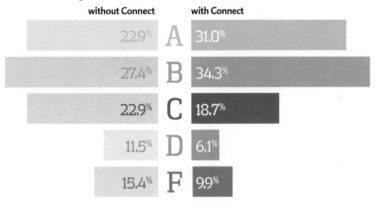

without Connect		with Connect
22.9%	A	31.0%
27.4%	B	34.3%
22.9%	C	18.7%
11.5%	D	6.1%
15.4%	F	9.9%

More students earn **As** and **Bs** when they use **Connect**.

Trusted Service and Support

- Connect integrates with your LMS to provide single sign-on and automatic syncing of grades. Integration with Blackboard®, D2L®, and Canvas also provides automatic syncing of the course calendar and assignment-level linking.

- Connect offers comprehensive service, support, and training throughout every phase of your implementation.

- If you're looking for some guidance on how to use Connect, or want to learn tips and tricks from super users, you can find tutorials as you work. Our Digital Faculty Consultants and Student Ambassadors offer insight into how to achieve the results you want with Connect.

QuickBooks Online Certification

QuickBooks Online Certification is certification that is obtained by passing the QuickBooks Online Certification Examination.

The QBO Certification Exam consists of four sections and 95 questions, with an average time of 2 hours to complete. To pass the Exam, you must obtain a minimum score of 80% on each section. If you obtain less than 80% on a section, you receive four attempts to retake a section of the exam to obtain your certification.

The QBO Certification Exam is updated each year so you are certified for one year.

For more information about preparing for QuickBooks Online Certification, go to https://quickbooks.intuit.com/accountants/training-certification/.

Meet the Author

Donna Kay is a former professor of Accounting and Accounting Systems & Forensics, teaching both undergraduate and graduate accounting. Dr. Kay earned her BS and MBA degrees from Southern Illinois University at Edwardsville before receiving a PhD from Saint Louis University, where she conducted action research on the perceived effectiveness of instructional techniques for learning technology. Dr. Kay designs her textbooks to incorporate the most effective instructional techniques based on research findings, making your learning journey as effective as possible.

Named in Who's Who Among American Women, Dr. Kay holds certifications as both a Certified Public Accountant (CPA) and Certified Informational Technology Professional (CITP) and is an active member of the American Institute of Certified Public Accountants (AICPA).

Donna Kay is also the author of *Computer Accounting with QuickBooks,* a leading textbook for learning QuickBooks Desktop software.

Visit Dr. Kay's website www.my-quickbooksonline.com to learn more about her books and support materials for the texts.

Acknowledgments

To make this text possible, special thanks to:

- MHE QuickBooks Online team Steve, Kevin, Allie, Dana, and Daryl
- Becky Cornell for her cheerful, careful accuracy checking and editing
- Brian Behrens for always being in my corner with greatly appreciated support
- Matt, Steve, and Sherry
- Faust, Silvia, Lucas, Garret, Winston, and Carlos
- James, JR, Rick, Luis, Rene, Lisa, and Grazielle
- Romeo, George, Jose, Fred, and Nadia
- Maria, Julie, Honey, Kathy, Karen, Eugene, Gerry, Eddie, Frank, and Nancy
- Carole, Mimi, Kelly, Herb, Maureen, and Voitek
- Andre, Lynne, Tony, Paulny, Jean, Lumenes, Bichotte, and William
- TJ and Baxter
- Sam, Cathy, and Carl

- All the QuickBooks educators who share ideas, comments, suggestions, and encouragement. Special recognition to:
  - Mary Ann Hurd, Sauk Valley Community College
  - Jennifer Johnson, University of Texas at Dallas
  - Sophia Ju, Edmonds Community College
  - Craig Miller University of Minnesota, Crookston
  - Jeanette Ramos-Alexander, New Jersey City University
  - Susan C. Robbins, Pensacola State College
  - Nancy Schrumpf, Parkland College
  - Stephanie Swaim, North Lake College
  - James Tappen, SUNY Rockland Community College
  - W. Brian Voss, Austin Community College–Eastview
  - Laurence Zuckerman, SUNY Fulton Montgomery Community College

QuickBooks® and QuickBooks® Online Plus are registered trademarks of Intuit Inc.

MookieTheBeagle.com © 2017 Carl K. Yazigi. All Rights Reserved. Used with Permission.

MookieTheBeagle.com™, Mookie The Beagle™, and the Mookie character, names and related indicia are trademarks of Carl K. Yazigi and used with permission.

Contents

Computer Accounting with QuickBooks Online

Donna Kay

Chapter 1

QuickBooks Online Navigation and Settings

QuickBooks® Online Plus (QBO) is a cloud-based financial system for entrepreneurs. We use a web browser to access QBO instead of using software installed on a computer like QuickBooks® Desktop (QBDT). So the advantage of QBO is that we can access QBO from any desktop and laptop computer that has an Internet connection.

> **QuickBooks Online (QBO)** refers to the QuickBooks system accessed through a web browser with data stored in the cloud. **QuickBooks Desktop (QBDT)** refers to QuickBooks software that is installed on your desktop or laptop computer.

QBO is updated on an ongoing basis. So we may go into QBO and see that screens may appear somewhat differently than the screen captures here.

> **Updates to the text** are posted at www.My-QuickBooksOnline.com > QuickBooks Online > scroll down to view **Updates.**

Learning QuickBooks Online requires integrating knowledge of accounting, financial systems, and financial technology. Don't become discouraged if you find that you need to go over the same material more than once. That is normal. Learning how accounting and financial technology is interrelated takes repetition. To make learning QBO easier, we will use an XPM (eXplore, Practice, Master) approach. First, we will eXplore using the Chapter illustrations, then we will Practice using Exercises at the end of the chapter, and finally we will Master QBO by completing the Project at the end of each chapter.

QuickBooks® and QuickBooks® Online Plus are registered trademarks of Intuit Inc.

Section 1.1

QBO SAMPLE COMPANY TEST DRIVE

To access the QBO Sample Company, complete the following steps.

1. Open a web browser. (Note: Intuit recommends using Google Chrome.)

2. Go to the Sample Company at https://qbo.intuit.com/redir/ testdrive

3. Follow onscreen instructions for security verification. If a message about cookies or blocking pop-up windows appears, follow the onscreen instructions.

> Note: Although the Sample Company link should work, if for some reason the previous link for the Sample Company does not work with your browser, **using Google search type in "qbo.intuit.com Sample Company." Select the entry to Test Drive Sample Company.**

Craig's Design and Landscaping Services, the QBO Sample Company, should appear on the screen.

> The Sample Company **will reset each time it is reopened. So make certain to allow enough time to complete all chapter activities before closing the Sample Company. Otherwise, you will lose the work you have entered when you reopen the Sample Company.**

> We use the Sample Company **for practice throughout the chapter and exercises. In Project 1.1 at the end of this chapter, we will set up a new QBO client company.**

Section 1.2

QBO NAVIGATION

The QBO Navigation Bar is located on the left side of the screen. The Navigation Bar permits us to quickly access commonly used QBO screens

1. **Dashboard** provides on overview and summary of key information for your QuickBooks Online company

2. **Banking** transactions relate to bank and credit card accounts and transactions

3. **Sales** transactions relate to customer and sales transactions (money in)

4. **Expenses** transactions relate to vendors and expense transactions (money out)

5. **Employee** transactions relate to employee and payroll transactions (money out)

6. **Reports** that summarize the output of our QBO financial system

7. **Taxes** relate to sales taxes and, if QuickBooks Online payroll is used, payroll taxes

8. **Accounting** displays the Chart of Accounts

9. **My Accountant** is used to connect to your accountant. Project 1.1 contains instructions on how you can connect your QuickBooks Online company with your instructor

Section 1.3

QBO TOOLS

Three useful QBO tools are:

1. **Gear** icon
2. **Create (+)** icon
3. **Search** icon

GEAR ICON

The Gear icon located in the upper right of the QBO screen lists various tasks.

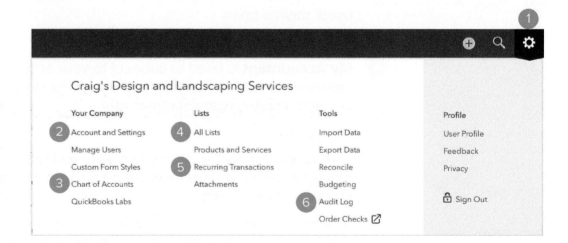

1. Select the **Gear** icon to display the options
2. Select **Account and Settings** to update company settings
3. Select **Chart of Accounts** to view and update the list of accounts our company uses

(4) Select **All Lists** to view lists such as Chart of Accounts, Recurring Transactions, and Products and Services

(5) Select **Recurring Transactions** to view the list of transactions that are saved for future reuse

(6) Select **Audit Log** to view the list of transactions entered

CREATE (+) ICON

The Create (+) icon located in the upper right of the QBO screen lists various transactions we can create.

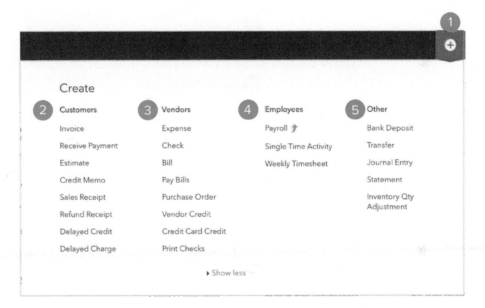

(1) Select the **Create (+)** icon to display options for entering transactions

(2) **Customers** transactions include create an invoice, receive payment, create an estimate, create a credit memo, and create a sales receipt

(3) **Vendors** transactions include create an expense, enter a check, create a bill, pay bills, create a purchase order, and create a credit card credit

(4) **Employees** transactions include entering payroll and tracking time worked using single time activity and weekly timesheet

(5) **Other** transactions include create a bank deposit, record a bank transfer, and create a journal entry

SEARCH ICON

The Search icon located in the upper right of the QBO screen permits us to search for amounts, dates, display names and more to locate transactions. Advanced Search permits us to further define our search. The Search feature is useful if we want to review a transaction after it has been entered or we need to update a transaction.

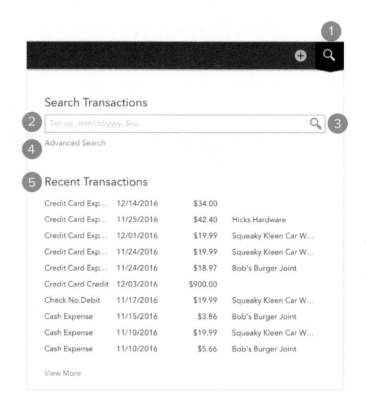

1. Select the **Search** icon
2. Enter **Search** criteria, such as $ Amount, Transaction No. or Date
3. Select **Search**
4. Select **Advanced Search** to enter more detailed search criteria
5. Select from **Recent Transactions** to view more detail

Section 1.4

QBO HELP AND SUPPORT

QBO Help and Support resources include:

- QBO Help and Support feature
- www.my-quickbooksonline.com for addition resources including Intuit QBO videos

To use the QBO Help and Support feature:

1. Select the **?** icon
2. Enter the question
3. Select **Search**
4. Select from **Top help topics**
5. For additional assistance select **Contact us for help** and search for the question

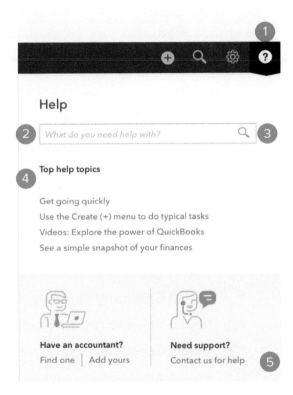

Section 1.5

QBO SETTINGS

When setting up a new QBO company, we want to align QBO with our company legal and tax information. During setup, we must specify the legal entity form used by our company, such as sole proprietorship, partnership, LLC, or corporation. In addition, the tax form that our company uses will affect the accounts we need in QBO. For more information about legal entity form and tax forms, see Accounting Essentials at the end of this chapter.

Two aspects of QBO settings are:

- Company Settings
- QBO Chart of Accounts

COMPANY SETTINGS

To access Your Company Settings:

① Select **Gear** icon

② Select **Account and Settings**

③ Select **Company** to review Company information

④ Select **Sales** to review Company Sales preferences

⑤ Select **Expenses** to review Company Expenses preferences

⑥ Select **Advanced** to review Company Advanced preferences

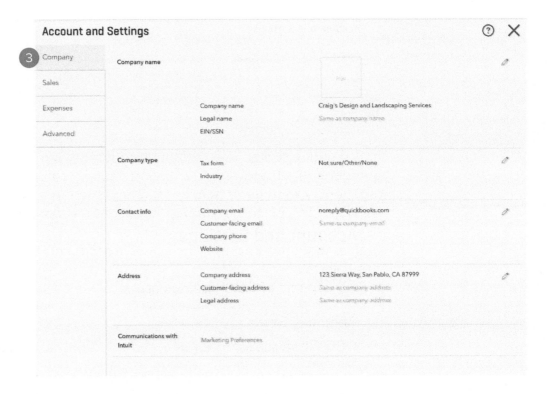

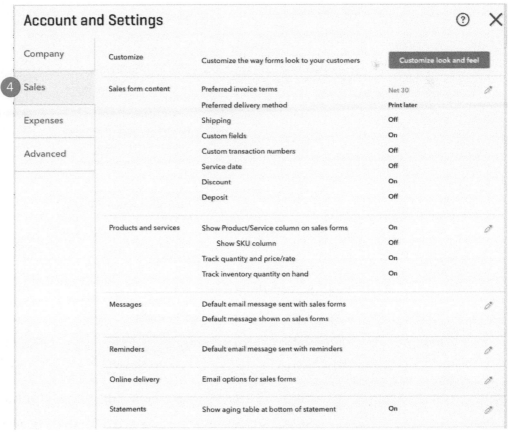

Account and Settings

Company	**Bills and expenses**	Show Items table on expense and purchase forms	On	✎
		Track expenses and items by customer	On	
Sales		Make expenses and items billable	On	
		Default bill payment terms		
⑤ Expenses				
	Purchase orders	Use purchase orders	On	✎
Advanced				
	Messages	Default email message sent with purchase orders		✎

Account and Settings

Company	Accounting	First month of fiscal year	January	✎
		First month of income tax year	Same as fiscal year	
		Accounting method	Accrual	
Sales		Close the books	Off	
	Company type	Tax form	Not sure/Other/None	✎
Expenses				
	Chart of accounts	Enable account numbers	Off	✎
		Discount account	Discounts given	
⑥ **Advanced**		Billable expense income account	Billable Expense Income	
	Categories	Track classes	Off	✎
		Track locations	Off	
	Automation	Pre-fill forms with previously entered content	On	✎
		Automatically apply credits	On	
		Automatically invoice unbilled activity	Off	
		Copy estimates to invoices	On	
		Automatically apply bill payments	On	
	Time tracking	Add Service field to timesheets	On	✎
		Make Single-Time Activity Billable to Customer	On	
	Currency	Home Currency	United States Dollar	✎
		Multicurrency	Off	
	Other preferences	Date format	MM/dd/yyyy	✎
		Number format	123,456.00	
		Customer label	Customers	
		Warn if duplicate check number is used	On	
		Warn if duplicate bill number is used	Off	
		Sign me out if inactive for	1 hour	

QBO CHART OF ACCOUNTS

The Chart of Accounts is a list of all the accounts for a company. Accounts are used to sort and track information. For example, a business needs one account for cash, another account to track amounts customers owe (Accounts Receivable), and another account to track inventory.

QBO automatically creates a Chart of Accounts (COA) when we set up a new company. Then we may customize the COA, adding and deleting accounts as necessary to fit our client's specific needs.

In the next chapter we cover how to customize QBO COA to meet client needs and specific business requirements. Since one of the primary reasons most businesses are using QBO is to organize financial information for tax return preparation, when we customize the QBO COA, we want to make sure the QBO COA aligns with the company's tax return.

To view the Chart of Accounts:

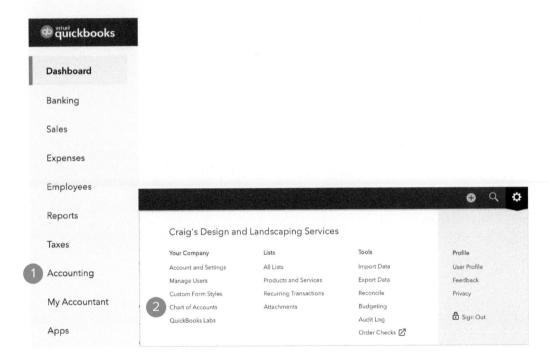

1   From the Navigation Bar, select **Accounting** to display the COA *or*

2   From the **Gear** icon, select **Chart of Accounts** to display the COA

3   If necessary, select See your Chart of Accounts. To run the COA report, from the Chart of Accounts window, select **Run Report**.

④ To view more detail about a specific account in the COA, from the Chart of Accounts window, select **View register** for the specific account. A register shows every transaction for an account and the running balance.

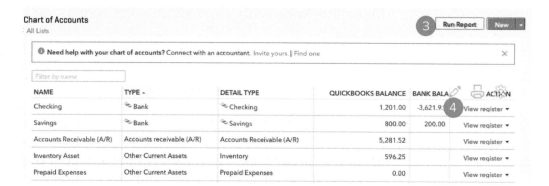

Section 1.6

QBO SatNav

QBO SatNav is our satellite navigation for QuickBooks Online, assisting us in navigating QBO

Just like we use a smartphone to zoom in for detail and zoom out for the big picture, when learning QBO, we may need to adjust our thinking to zoom out to see the big picture of the entire financial system or at other times adjust our thinking to zoom in to view details in QBO.

QBO SatNav is designed to assist us in zooming out and zooming in. QBO SatNav divides QBO into three processes:

1. **QBO Settings.** This includes Company Settings and the Company Chart of Accounts. QBO Settings are covered in Chapters 1 and 2.

2. **QBO Transactions.** This includes recording transactions in QBO. Transaction types can be categorized as Banking, Customers & Sales, Vendors & Expenses and Employees & Payroll. In basic terms, recording transactions involves recording money in and money out.

   Transactions are exchanges between the QBO company and other parties, such as customers, vendors, and employees. Typically in a transaction, the company gives something and receives something in exchange. QBO is used to keep a record of what is given and what is received in the transaction. QBO Transactions are covered in Chapters 3, 4, 5, 6, 7, and 8.

3. **QBO Reports.** QBO reports are the output of the system. Reports typically provide information to decision makers. For example, accounting information is used to prepare:

   - Financial statements, such as Income Statement, Balance Sheet, and Statement of Cash Flows, for creditors and investors.

   - Tax returns for federal and state tax agencies.

   - Management reports for company managers and owners to use when making business decisions. Such decisions include: Will we have enough cash to pay our bills on time? Are we collecting customer payments when due?

   QBO Reports are covered in Chapters 9 and 10.

This QBO SatNav will be used in each chapter to illustrate which aspect of QBO the chapter will focus on. If you start to feel lost in QBO, return to this QBO SatNav to assist in navigating QBO.

The portion of the QBO SatNav that is the focus of the chapter will be highlighted in yellow. For example, the project at the end of this chapter will focus on the Company Settings, so Company Settings in the SatNav is highlighted.

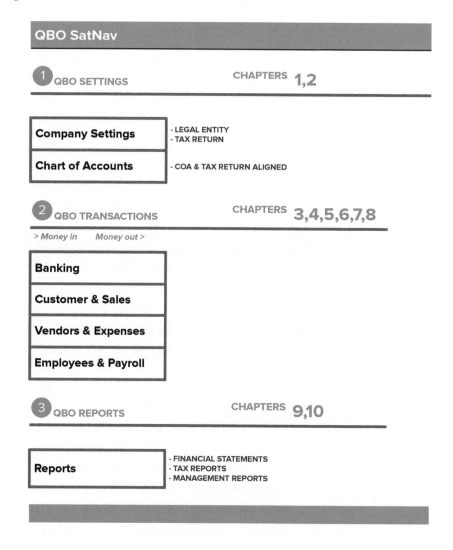

Section 1.7

ACCOUNTING ESSENTIALS

Legal, Tax, and Financial Questions

Accounting Essentials summarize important foundational accounting knowledge that may be useful when using QBO

Why do we care about the legal entity and tax form used by our business when setting up an accounting system?

The type of legal entity a business uses impacts the equity accounts we need and the tax form our business files. The tax form our business must file also impacts the type of financial information we need to track in our financial system. Bottom line: It's all interrelated. If we are going to set up a financial system that meets our client's needs, then we need to understand how the legal and tax implications impact the financial system.

What is a legal entity?

How our business legal entity was organized (Sole Proprietorship, Partnership, Limited Liability Partnership (LLP), Limited Liability Company (LLC), C Corporation, S Corporation, or Non-Profit affects which tax form and tax lines we use. There are advantages and disadvantages to each type of legal entity. Currently, many entrepreneurs use the LLC form to offer tax advantages and also limit liability of the owners.

How does the legal entity affect which business tax return we file?

The legal entity used to organize a business affects which tax return the business files.

- If the legal entity is a sole proprietorship, Schedule C attached to Form 1040
- If the legal entity is a partnership (LLP), Form 1065
- If the legal entity is a C corporation, Form 1120
- If the legal entity is an LLC, then the business chooses how the business wants to be treated for tax purposes

What business tax return does an LLC file?

It depends. If a business is an LLC (Limited Liability Company), then the business has a choice to make regarding how the business wants to be treated for tax purposes. For tax purposes, assuming an LLC meets necessary tax requirements, an LLC can elect to be treated as:

- Sole proprietorship and file Schedule C attached to owner's Form 1040
- Partnership and file Form 1065
- S Corporation and file Form 1120S (See www.irs.gov for more information about requirements to elect the S Corporation option for tax purposes.)

How do we know which business tax return needs to be filed?

Business tax returns to file are:

1. Sole proprietorships file Schedule C attached to owner's Form 1040
2. Partnerships file Form 1065
3. C corporations file Form 1120
4. S corporations file Form 1120S

Business Type	Tax Form
Sole Proprietorship	Form 1040 Schedule C
Partnership	Form 1065
C Corporation	Form 1120
S Corporation	Form 1120S

How does our business tax return affect our financial system?

When setting up the financial system and accounts for our business, it is often helpful to review the tax form that our business must use. Then our company's accounts can be customized to track information needed for our tax form. Basically, we can align our accounts with the tax return, so information in our accounts feeds into the lines on the tax return. This can reduce the amount of extra work needed at year end to obtain information for the business tax return. The tax form used by the type of organization is listed previously and the forms and tax lines can be viewed at www.irs.gov.

PRACTICE QUIZ 1

Q1.1

Which of the following does not appear on the QuickBooks Online Navigation Bar?

a. Accounting

b. Employees

c. Owners

d. Sales

Q1.2

Which of the following categories does not appear on the QuickBooks Create (+) screen?

a. Banking

b. Customers

c. Employees

d. Vendors

Q1.3

How do you access QBO Account and Settings?

a. Create (+) icon

b. Gear icon

c. Search icon

d. Help icon

Q1.4

What are two ways that we can access and view the Chart of Accounts in QBO?

a. From the Navigation Bar select Accounting

b. From the Create (+) icon select Other > Chart of Accounts

c. From the Gear icon select Chart of Accounts

d. From the Home Page select Chart of Accounts

Q1.5

Which of the following could be considered three main processes of using QuickBooks Online?

a. QBO Settings, QBO Transactions, QBO Reports

b. QBO Sales, QBO Expenses, QBO Reports

c. QBO Chart of Accounts, QBO Exchanges, QBO Settings

d. QBO Sales Transactions, QBO Banking Transactions, QBO Reports

Q1.6

QBO transactions include which of the following?

a. Sales

b. Expenses

c. Banking

d. All of the above

Q1.7

Financial statements include which of the following two?

a. Income statement

b. Statement of cash flows

c. Cash flow forecast

d. Physical inventory worksheet

Q1.8

Which of the following legal entities can use QuickBooks Online?

a. Sole proprietorship

b. Partnership

c. S corporation

d. All of the above

Q1.9

Match the following legal entities with the federal tax return the entity files?

1. Form 1040 Schedule C

2. Form 1120

3. Form 1065

4. Form 1120S

a. Partnership _____

b. C Corporation _____

c. S Corporation _____

d. Sole Proprietorship _____

Q1.10

Which federal tax return does an LLC (Limited Liability Company) file?

a. Form 1040 Schedule C

b. Form 1065

c. Form 1120S

d. It depends upon how the LLC chooses to be treated for tax purposes

Q1.11

QuickBooks Online Settings to set up a new company include which of the following two?

a. Chart of Accounts

b. Reconciliation Settings

c. Company Settings

d. Tax Settings

EXERCISES 1

We use the QBO Sample Company, Craig's Design and Landscaping Services for practice throughout the exercises. The Sample Company will reset each time it is reopened. So make certain to allow enough time to complete exercises before closing the Sample Company. Otherwise, you will lose the work you have entered when you reopen the Sample Company.

To access the QBO Sample Company, complete the following steps.

1. Open a web browser. (Note: Intuit recommends using Google Chrome.)

2. Go to the https://qbo.intuit.com/redir/testdrive

3. Follow onscreen instructions for security verification.

Craig's Design and Landscaping Services should appear on the screen.

E1.1 Company Settings: Company

Go to Craig's Design and Landscaping Company > Gear icon > Account and Settings > Company. Answer the following questions about the Company Settings.

1. What is the setting for Tax Form ?

2. What is the setting for Company email?

3. What is the setting for Company address?

E1.2 Company Settings: Sales

Go to Craig's Design and Landscaping Company > Gear icon > Account and Settings > Sales. Answer the following questions about the Sales Settings.

1. What is the setting for Preferred invoice terms?
2. What is the setting for Service Date?
3. What is the setting for Discount?
4. What is the setting for Show Product/Service column on sales forms?
5. What is the setting for Show SKU column?
6. What is the setting for Track quantity and price/rate?
7. What is the setting for Track inventory quantity on hand?

E1.3 Company Settings: Expenses

Go to Craig's Design and Landscaping Company > Gear icon > Account and Settings > Expenses. Answer the following questions about the Expenses Settings.

1. What is the setting for Show Items table on expense and purchase forms?
2. What is the setting for Track expenses and items by customer?
3. What is the setting for Make expenses and items billable?
4. What is the setting for Use purchase orders?

E1.4 Company Settings: Advanced

Go to Craig's Design and Landscaping Company > Gear icon > Account and Settings > Advanced. Answer the following questions about the Advanced Settings.

1. First month of fiscal year?
2. First month of tax year?
3. Accounting method?
4. Enable account numbers?
5. Pre-fill forms with previously entered content?
6. Automatically apply bill payments?
7. Add Service field to timesheets?
8. Make Single-Time Activity Billable to Customer?
9. Home Currency?
10. Warn if duplicate check number is used?

E1.5 Chart of Accounts

Go to Craig's Design and Landscaping Services Navigation Bar > Accounting. Answer the following questions about the Chart of Accounts.

<u>**Account Types**</u>

- **Bank**
- **Accounts Receivable (A/R)**
- **Other Current Assets**
- **Fixed Assets**
- **Accounts Payable (A/P)**
- **Credit Card**
- **Other Current Liabilities**
- **Long-Term Liabilities**
- **Equity**
- **Income**
- **Cost of Goods Sold**
- **Expenses**
- **Other Income**
- **Other Expense**

What is the Account Type for the following accounts?

1. Checking account
2. Visa
3. Accounts Receivable (A/R)
4. Advertising
5. Prepaid Expenses
6. Pest Control Services

E1.6 Chart of Accounts

Go to Craig's Design and Landscaping Services Navigation Bar > Accounting. Answer the following questions about the Chart of Accounts.

In the following Chart of Accounts, what is the name of each column?

Column 1?

Column 2?

Column 3?

Column 4?

Column 5?

Column 6?

E1.7 Register

Go to Craig's Design and Landscaping Services Navigation Bar > Accounting > select View Register for the Checking account in the Chart of Accounts. Answer the following questions about the Checking Register.

In the following Chart of Accounts, what is the name of each column?

Column 1?

Column 2?

Column 3?

Column 4?

Column 5?

Column 6?

E1.8 Transactions

Match the following categories found on the Create (+) window with the following transactions.

- **Customers**
- **Vendors**

- **Employees**
- **Other**

1. Bank Deposit
2. Single Time Activity
3. Expense
4. Sales Receipt
5. Payroll
6. Journal Entry
7. Purchase Order
8. Estimate
9. Pay Bills
10. Check
11. Receive Payment
12. Invoice

E1.9 QBO SatNav

Match these three main QBO processes with the following items.

- **QBO Settings**
- **QBO Transactions**
- **QBO Reports**

1. Income Statement
2. Identify form of legal entity used by the business
3. Exchange of cash for sale of product with customer
4. Statement of Cash Flows
5. Exchange of credit card payment for purchasing of product from vendor
6. Balance Sheet

E1.10 QBO Tools

Match these two QBO tools with the following items.

- **Gear icon**
- **Create (+) icon**

1. Invoice
2. Recurring Transactions
3. Purchase Order
4. Settings
5. Check
6. All Lists
7. Bank Deposit
8. Audit Log
9. Credit Card Credit
10. Sales Receipt
11. Quickbooks Labs
12. Receive Payment
13. Chart of Accounts
14. Weekly Timesheet
15. Manage Users
16. Journal Entry
17. Pay Bills

PROJECT 1.1

BACKSTORY

Mookie The Beagle™ Concierge, a pet care service, was founded by CK Walker, a young professional who was searching for a way to meet his demanding work and travel commitments while caring for his pet beagle, Mookie.

CK discovered that he was not the only working professional trying to balance pet care and work commitments. So CK started Mookie The Beagle Concierge to provide caring staff who go beyond the typical doggie day care, providing water and food (even organic and home cooked), exercising the pet with scheduled walks and playtime, providing pet training, administering required medication, taking the pet to scheduled and unscheduled vet visits that often fall during the work day when a professional cannot take time off, and providing other pet healthcare and support services as needed.

Drawing upon a local university veterinarian program, CK hired vet students with pet care training and flexibility in their schedules. Working as independent contractors, the students were a good fit for providing high quality, relatively low-cost pet care on a flexible basis. If intensive pet care is needed, such as when a client has out-of-town travel, two or three vet students rotate schedules to accommodate the pet's needs.

CK designed and developed a Mookie The Beagle Concierge mobile app which permits clients to schedule pet care service. Mookie The Beagle Concierge app also tracks complicated medication schedules, showing who administered the medication and when. The app permits the client to view and speak to the pet in real time. In addition, the app connects to the vet's office for follow-up questions, provides pet parent texting to Mookie The Beagle Concierge staff, and offers an on-call button to alert staff of urgent issues.

In short, Mookie The Beagle Concierge takes pet care to the next level, providing convenience and pet care support that permits professionals to maintain busy work and travel schedules while being reassured their valued pet is receiving the best care.

Mookie The Beagle Concierge picked QuickBooks Online to maintain its financial records and asks us to assist in setting up QBO. After reviewing Mookie The Beagle Concierge user requirements for a financial system, we agree to provide QBO consulting services. In addition, we will train CK in QuickBooks Online so he can take over some QBO tasks in the future.

Complete the following for Mookie The Beagle Concierge.

QBO SatNav

Project 1.1 focuses on the QBO Settings, specifically the QBO Company Settings shown in the following partial QBO SatNav.

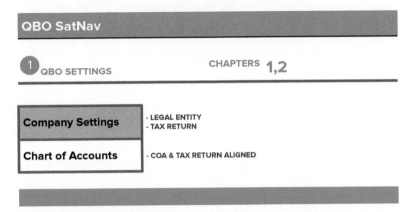

HOW TO USE THE QBO+ ACCESS CODE

The first time you use QBO, you will need to use your QBO Access Code that accompanies your text. After the first time you set up your account using the access code, you can log into QBO using your User ID and Password.

This text **uses QBO+ with an access code that accompanies the text.**

To log into QBO for the first time using your Access Code, using a web browser go to the QBO sign up page at https://quickbooks.intuit.com/start/retail_sui. Then complete the following steps.

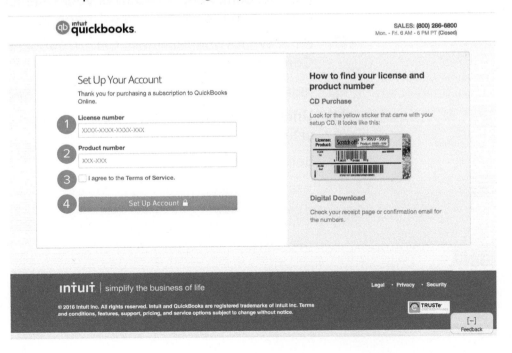

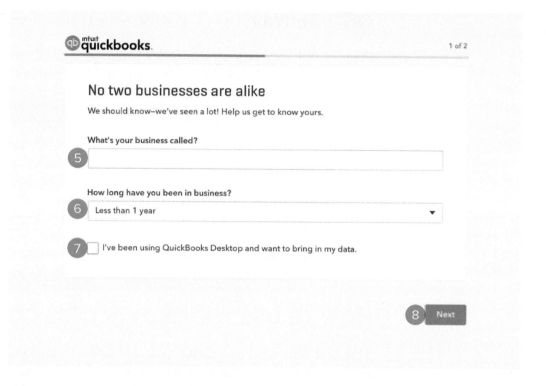

① Enter the **License number**

② Enter the **Product number**

③ Select **I agree to the Terms of Service**

④ Select **Set Up Account.** Follow the onscreen instructions to set up your account. Keep a record of your User ID and Password used to set up your account. You will need this later.

⑤ Enter What's Your Business Called? **Mookie The Beagle Concierge**

⑥ Select How long have you been in business? **Less than 1 year**

⑦ **Uncheck** I've been using QuickBooks Desktop and want to bring in my data

⑧ Select **Next**

9 When What can we take off your plate? appears, select **Invoice customers**

10 Select **Track expenses**

11 Select **Track inventory**

12 Select **Retail sales**

13 Select **Manage bills**

14 Select **Track sales tax**

15 Select **Pay employees**

16 Select **Track time**

17 Select **All set.** The QBO Mookie The Beagle Concierge screen should appear.

HOW TO LOG INTO QBO+

After completing using the QBO Access Code, the next time we log into QBO, we will complete the following steps.

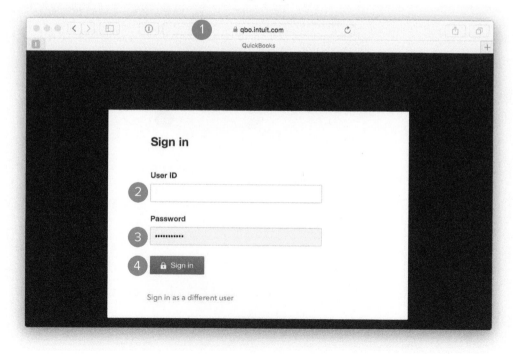

1. Using a web browser go to qbo.intuit.com

2. Enter **User ID** (the email address you used to set up your QBO Account)

3. Enter **Password** (the password you used to set up your QBO Account)

4. Select **Sign in**

If you are <u>not</u> using a public or shared computer, **to speed up login, you can save your login to your desktop and select Remember Me. If you are using a public computer or shared computer, do not save to your desktop and unselect Remember Me.**

The new QBO company **we create in Project 1.1 will carry all work forward into future chapters and projects. So it is important to check and crosscheck your work to verify it is correct before clicking the Save button. Any errors entered are carried forward in the QBO company you use for text projects.**

INVITE YOUR ACCOUNTANT (INSTRUCTOR)

Next, invite your accountant (in this case your instructor) to join your QuickBooks Online. This permits your accountant (instructor) to view your QBO company when using QuickBooks Online Accountant. Basically, through QBO you will send your accountant (instructor) an email and the accountant (instructor) clicks on the link in the email to join your QBO company.

To invite your accountant (instructor) to join your QBO Company:

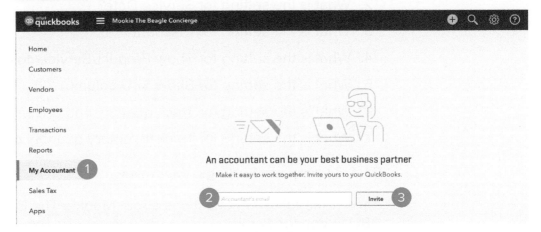

1. From the Navigation Bar select **My Accountant**

2. Enter **your Instructor's email address**

3. Select **Invite**

> **If your instructor receives an error message** when accepting your QBO Invite, completely delete the invite from your QBO Company. (Do not click Resend.) Then recreate the invite. Typically this fixes this known issue with invites. If it does not fix the issue after you delete the invite and recreate it, then contact your Instructor or Intuit Support.

P1.1.1 Set Up QBO

Complete QBO set up for Mookie The Beagle™ Concierge using the following information.

1. To select the Tax Form complete the following.
   a. Select **Gear** icon > **Account and Settings**
   b. Select **Company** tab > **Edit pencil** on right in Company Type section
   c. Select Tax Form **Small business corporation, two or more owners (Form 1120S)**
   d. Select **Save**
   e. What Is the Company name?

P1.1.2 Company Settings: Sales

Answer the following questions about Mookie The Beagle Concierge's QBO Sales Settings.

1. What is the setting for Preferred invoice terms?
2. What is the setting for Service Date?
3. What is the setting for Discount?
4. What is the setting for Show Product/Service column on sales forms?
5. What is the setting for Show SKU column?
6. What is the setting for Track quantity and price/rate?
7. What is the setting for Track inventory quantity on hand?

P1.1.3 Company Settings: Expenses

Answer the following questions about Mookie The Beagle Concierge's QBO Expenses Settings.

1. What is the setting for Show Items table on expense and purchase forms?
2. What is the setting for Track expenses and items by customer?
3. What is the setting for Make expenses and items billable?

4. Change the setting for Make expenses and items billable to **On.**

5. What is the setting for Use purchase orders?

6. Change the setting for Use purchase orders to **On.**

P1.1.4 Company Settings: Advanced

Answer the following questions about Mookie The Beagle Concierge's QBO Advanced Settings.

1. First month of fiscal year?

2. First month of tax year?

3. Accounting method?

4. Close the books?

5. Tax form?

6. Enable account numbers?

7. Pre-fill forms with previously entered content?

8. Automatically apply bill payments?

9. Add Service field to timesheets?

10. Make Single-Time Activity Billable to Customer?

11. Home Currency?

12. Warn if duplicate check number is used?

P1.1.5 Chart of Accounts

Display Mookie The Beagle Concierge's Chart of Accounts that QBO automatically created by selecting **Navigation Bar > Accounting.**

What is the QBO Account Type for the following accounts appearing in Mookie The Beagle Concierge's Chart of Accounts?

QBO Account Types

- **Bank**
- **Accounts Receivable (A/R)**
- **Other Current Asset**
- **Fixed Asset**
- **Accounts Payable (A/P)**
- **Credit Card**
- **Other Current Liabilities**

- **Long-Term Liabilities**
- **Equity**
- **Income**
- **Cost of Goods Sold**
- **Expenses**
- **Other Income**
- **Other Expense**

> QBO is continually rolling out new features so it is possible your Chart of Accounts may not look the same as the accounts listed here. If an account is not listed in your Chart of Accounts, then just identify the appropriate account type.

1. Prepaid Expenses
2. Uncategorized Asset
3. Undeposited Funds
4. Retained Earnings
5. Billable Expense Income
6. Discounts
7. Gross Receipts
8. Refunds-Allowances
9. Sales
10. Shipping, Delivery Income
11. Uncategorized Income
12. Cost of labor - COS
13. Freight & delivery - COS
14. Other Costs - COS
15. Purchases - COS
16. Subcontractors - COS
17. Supplies & materials - COGS
18. Advertising
19. Bad Debts
20. Bank Charges
21. Commissions & Fees

22. Disposal Fees
23. Dues & Subscriptions
24. Freight & Delivery
25. Insurance
26. Insurance - Disability
27. Insurance - Liability
28. Interest Expense
29. Job Materials
30. Legal & Professional Fees
31. Meals and Entertainment
32. Office Expenses
33. Other General and Admin Expenses
34. Promotional
35. Rent or Lease
36. Repair & Maintenance
37. Shipping and Delivery Expense
38. Stationery & Printing
39. Subcontractors
40. Supplies
41. Taxes & Licenses
42. Tools
43. Travel
44. Travel Meals
45. Uncategorized Expense
46. Utilities

www.my-quickbooksonline.com

Go to www.My-QuickBooksOnline.com for additional resources including QBO Help, QBO Videos, and more.

Chapter 2

QBO Chart of Accounts

Businesses use QuickBooks Online for many reasons, but one of the main reasons is usually to track information for tax return preparation. To provide information the client needs to prepare a tax return requires customizing the QBO Chart of Accounts to align with the tax return.

Section 2.1

QBO SatNav

QBO SatNav is our satellite navigation for QuickBooks Online, assisting us in navigating QBO

This chapter focuses on the QBO Settings, specifically the QBO Chart of Accounts shown in the following partial QBO SatNav.

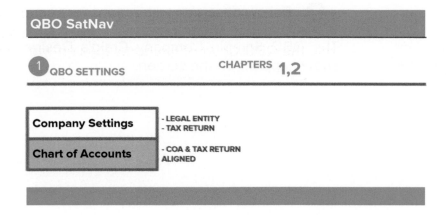

Section 2.2

QBO SAMPLE COMPANY LOGIN

To log into the QBO Sample Company:

1. Open a web browser. (Note: Intuit recommends using Google Chrome.)
2. Go to https://qbo.intuit.com/redir/testdrive
3. Follow onscreen instructions for security verification.

The QBO Sample Company Craig's Design and Landscaping Services should appear on the screen.

Section 2.3

QBO SAMPLE COMPANY CHART OF ACCOUNTS

The Chart of Accounts is a list of accounts and account numbers. A company uses accounts to record transactions in the accounting system. Accounts (such as the Cash account or Inventory account) permit us to sort and track information.

QuickBooks will automatically create a Chart of Accounts when we set up a new company. Then we can customize the Chart of Accounts, adding and deleting accounts as necessary to suit our company's specific needs. QuickBooks also permits us to use subaccounts. Subaccounts are useful in tracking additional detail. For example, a parent account might be Insurance Expense. The two subaccounts might be Disability Insurance Expense and Liability Insurance Expense. By having two subaccounts we can easily track how much a company spends on each type of insurance, as well as for insurance in total.

In Project 2.1, we will set up our own QBO Client Company, but for now we will use the Sample Company to view and edit a sample Chart of Accounts.

> Your text uses the Sample Company **for practice throughout the chapter and exercises. The Sample Company will reset each time it is reopened. So make certain to allow enough time to complete all chapter activities before closing the Sample Company. Otherwise, you will lose the work you have entered.**

VIEW QBO CHART OF ACCOUNTS

To display the Chart of Accounts (COA):

1 Select **Accounting**

2 The following **Chart of Accounts** should appear

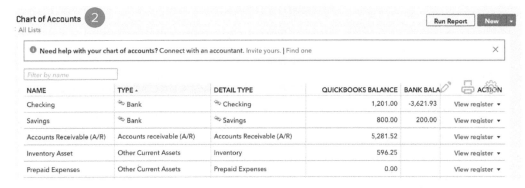

NAME	TYPE ▲	DETAIL TYPE	QUICKBOOKS BALANCE	BANK BALA	ACTION
Checking	Bank	Checking	1,201.00	-3,621.93	View register ▾
Savings	Bank	Savings	800.00	200.00	View register ▾
Accounts Receivable (A/R)	Accounts receivable (A/R)	Accounts Receivable (A/R)	5,281.52		View register ▾
Inventory Asset	Other Current Assets	Inventory	596.25		View register ▾
Prepaid Expenses	Other Current Assets	Prepaid Expenses	0.00		View register ▾

DISPLAY QBO COA ACCOUNT NUMBERS

Account numbers are used to uniquely identify accounts. Usually account numbers are used as a coding system to also identify the account type. For example, a typical numbering system for accounts might be as follows.

Account Type	Account No.
Asset accounts	10000 - 19999
Liability accounts	20000 - 29999
Equity accounts	30000 - 39999
Revenue (income) accounts	40000 - 49999
Expense accounts	50000 - 59999

To display account numbers in the COA:

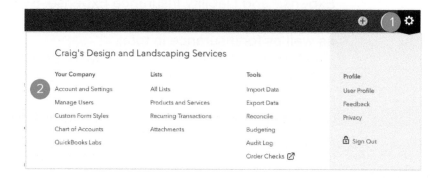

1. Select the **Gear** icon to display options
2. Select **Account and Settings**
3. Select **Advanced**
4. For Chart of Accounts, select the **Edit Pencil,** then select **Enable account numbers**
5. Select **Show account numbers**
6. Select **Save**
7. Select **X** to close **Account and Settings**

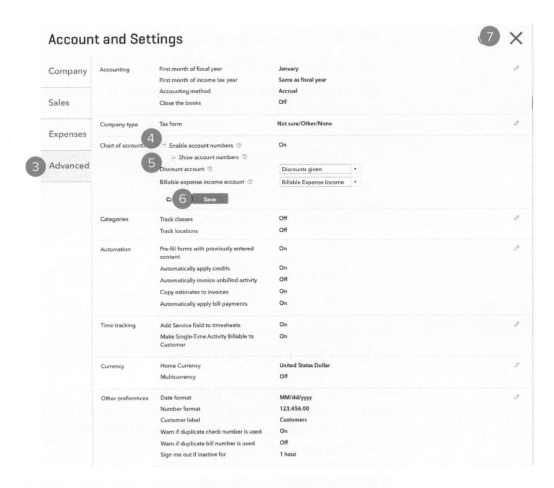

To enter account numbers in the Chart of Accounts:

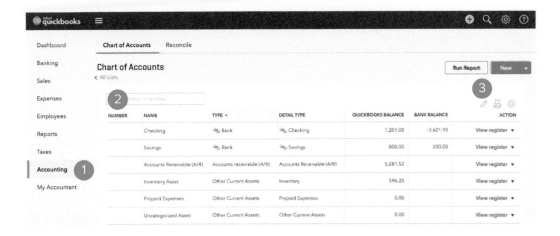

1 Select **Accounting** in the Navigation Bar

2 If necessary, select See your Chart of Accounts. Notice that the Chart of Accounts now displays a **NUMBER** column.

③ Select the **Edit pencil** icon

④ Enter **Account Numbers** in the NUMBER column

⑤ Typically we would select Save. In this case, select **Cancel.**

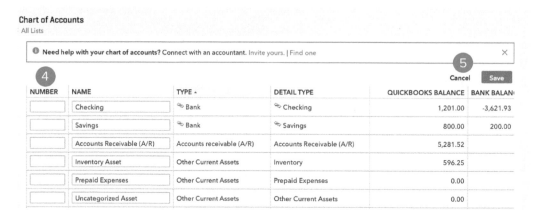

VIEW QBO REGISTERS

Registers display more detailed information about accounts. A register displays all transactions for an account and a running balance.

To view more detail about the Checking account, we can view the Checking account register as follows:

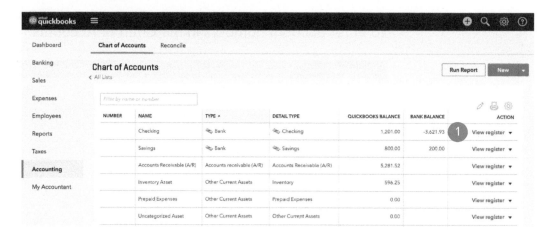

① From the Chart of Accounts window, select **View register**

② The Checking account register shows every transaction in the account and a running **balance** is displayed on the right

③ Select **Back to Chart of Accounts** to close the Register and return to the Chart of Accounts

Bank Register Checking

Back to Chart of Accounts

Bank Balance
$-3,621.93

ENDING BALANCE
$1,201.00 Reconcile

Go to: 1 of 1 < First Previous 1-44 of 44 Next Last >

▽ ▾ All

DATE ▾	REF NO. TYPE	PAYEE ACCOUNT	MEMO	PAYMENT	DEPOSIT	✓		BALANCE
Add check ▾								
12/03/2016	CC-Credit	Mastercard		$900.00				$1,201.00
11/22/2016	Cash Purch	Tania's Nursery Job Expenses:Job Materials:Plants and Soil		$23.50				$2,101.00
11/19/2016	76 Expense	Pam Seitz Legal & Professional Fees		$75.00				$2,124.50
11/19/2016	75 Check	Hicks Hardware -Split-		$228.75				$2,199.50
11/19/2016	Deposit	-Split-			$868.15			$2,428.25
11/18/2016	Cash Purch	Chin's Gas and Oil Automobile:Fuel		$63.15				$1,560.10

Section 2.4

HOW TO ALIGN QBO CHART OF ACCOUNTS WITH TAX RETURN

QBO automatically creates a COA when we set up a new company. Then we can customize the COA, adding and deleting accounts as necessary to fit our company's specific needs. In many cases, we are using QBO to track information for tax return preparation. So to streamline the process, it only makes sense to align the QBO Chart of Accounts with our company's tax return.

When setting up a Chart of Accounts for a business, it is often helpful to review the tax form that the business will use. Then a company's Chart of Accounts can be customized to track information needed for the tax form.

Our goal is to see that the QBO Chart of Accounts feeds into the tax return lines. So first, we need to know which business tax return the company files. The tax form used by form of organization is listed as follows. For example, if the business is a S Corporation, then for federal income taxes the business files Form 1120S.

Form of Organization	Tax Form
Sole Proprietorship	Form 1040 Schedule C
Partnership	Form 1065
C Corporation	Form 1120
S Corporation	Form 1120S

To view various tax return forms for businesses with the tax lines on each form, go to the Internal Revenue Service website: www.irs.gov.

Section 2.5

EDIT QBO COA

We can customize the Chart of Accounts by adding, deleting, and editing accounts as needed to meet a company's specific and changing needs.

ADD QBO ACCOUNTS

To add a new account to the Chart of Accounts:

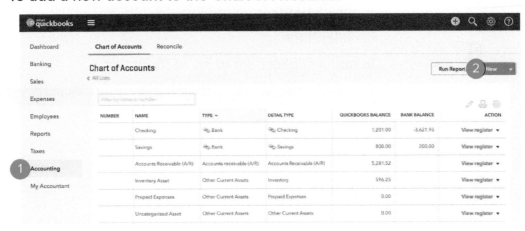

① From the Navigation Bar, select **Accounting**

② From the Chart of Accounts window, select **New**

③ From the Account window, select Category Type **Bank**

④ Select Detail Type **Saving**

⑤ Enter Name **Savings**

⑥ If not a subaccount, verify that Is sub-account is **Unchecked**

⑦ Normally we would select Save and Close, but in this case select **Cancel.** We will enter new accounts in the exercises at the end of the chapter.

ADD QBO SUBACCOUNTS

Subaccounts are subcategories of an account. For example, the Sample Company has a Utilities Expense account with two subaccounts:

- Gas and Electric

- Telephone

To add a subaccount to an account:

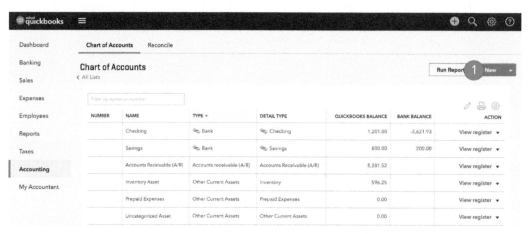

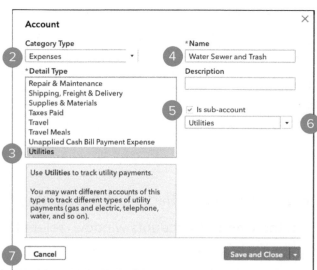

① From the Chart of Accounts window, select **New**

② From the Account window, select Category Type **Expenses**

③ Select Detail Type **Utilities**

④ Enter Name **Water Sewer and Trash**

⑤ **Check** Is sub-account

⑥ From the drop-down list select **Utilities**

⑦ Select **Save and Close**

EDIT QBO ACCOUNTS

We can edit an account in QBO to update the account name. To change the name of an account:

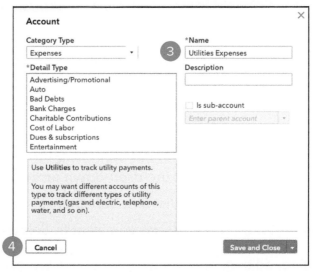

① From the Chart of Accounts window for the Utilities account, select the **drop-down arrow** next to Run report

② From the drop-down list that appears, select **Edit**

③ Update Account Name to **Utilities Expenses**

④ Normally we would select Save and Close, but in this case select **Cancel.** We will update accounts in the exercises at the end of the chapter.

DELETE QBO ACCOUNTS

Occasionally we may want to delete unused accounts from the Chart of Accounts. We can only delete accounts that are not being used. For example, if an account has been used to record a transaction and has a balance, it cannot be deleted. If an account has subaccounts associated with it, that account cannot be deleted.

To delete an account:

① From the Chart of Accounts window for the Water Sewer and Trash account, select the **drop-down arrow** next to Run report

② From the drop-down list that appears, select **Delete**

③ When asked Are you sure you want to delete this? select **Yes**

By adding, editing, and deleting accounts, we can customize the QBO Chart of Accounts to align with the business tax return. This can save countless hours when preparing tax reports, reduce errors, and streamline tax return preparation.

Section 2.6

ACCOUNTING ESSENTIALS

Chart of Accounts

Accounting Essentials summarize important foundational accounting knowledge you may find useful when using QBO

What is the primary objective of accounting?

- The primary objective of accounting is to provide information for decision making. Businesses use a financial system, such as QuickBooks Online, to capture, track, sort, summarize, and communicate financial information.

How is financial information for decision making provided?

- Financial reports summarize and communicate information about a company's financial position and business operations.

What is the difference between financial reports and financial statements?

- Financial statements are standardized financial reports that summarize information about past transactions. Financial statements are provided to external users and internal users for decision making. External users include bankers, creditors, and investors.
- Internal users include managers and employees of the business.

What are the main financial statements for a business?

- The primary financial statements for a business are:
  - **Balance Sheet** summarizes what a company *owns* and *owes* on a particular date.
  - **Profit & Loss Statement** (also referred to as P & L or Income Statement) summarizes the income a company has earned and the expenses incurred to earn the income.
  - **Statement of Cash Flows** summarizes cash inflows and cash outflows for operating, investing, and financing activities of a business.

What is a Chart of Accounts?

- **Chart of Accounts (COA)** is a list of all the accounts and account numbers for a business. Accounts are used to sort and track accounting information. For example, a business needs one account for cash, another account to track amounts customers owe (Accounts Receivable), and yet another account to track inventory.

Why Use Accounts?

- We use **accounts** to record transactions in our accounting system. Accounts (such as the Checking account or Insurance Expense account) permit us to sort, organize, summarize, and track information.
- We can add **subaccounts** for even better tracking. Example: We could add subaccounts Rental Insurance Expense and Liability Insurance Expense as subaccounts to our Insurance Expense account. We have additional detail of subaccounts Rental Insurance and Liability Insurance Expense and the subaccounts roll up into the total for the parent account, Insurance Expense.

What are the Different Types of Accounts?

- We can group accounts into the following different account types:

Balance Sheet accounts			Profit and Loss accounts	
Assets	**Liability**	**Equity**	**Income**	**Expense**
Bank account	Accounts Payable	Capital Investment	Sales	Supplies Expense
Accounts Receivable	Credit Cards Payable	Retained Earnings	Consulting Fees	Rent Expense
Equipment	Loans Payable		Interest Income	Utilities Expense

What are Balance Sheet Accounts?

- The Balance Sheet is a financial statement that summarizes what a company owns and what it owes.
- Balance Sheet accounts are accounts that appear on the company's Balance Sheet.
- Three types of accounts appear on the Balance Sheet:

1. Assets
2. Liabilities
3. Owners' (or Stockholders') Equity

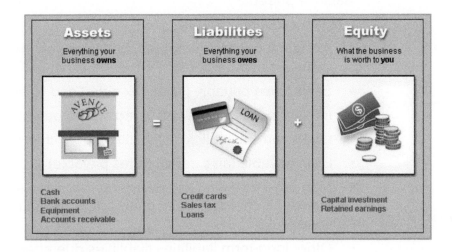

1. **Assets** are resources that a company owns. These resources are expected to have future benefit.

   Asset accounts include:

   * Cash
   * Accounts receivable (amounts to be *received* from customers in the future)
   * Inventory
   * Other current assets (assets likely to be converted to cash or consumed within one year)
   * Fixed assets (property used in the operations of the business, such as equipment, buildings, and land)
   * Intangible assets (such as copyrights, patents, trademarks, and franchises)

   > **How Do We Know if an Account is an Asset?**
   >
   > Ask:
   > Will our enterprise receive a *future benefit* from the item?
   >
   > Answer:
   > If we will receive *future benefit,* the account is probably an *asset.* For example, prepaid insurance has future benefit.

2. **Liabilities** are amounts a company owes to others. Liabilities are obligations. For example, if a company borrows $10,000 from the bank, the company has an obligation to repay the $10,000 to the bank. Thus, the $10,000 obligation is shown as a liability on the company's Balance Sheet.

Liability accounts include:

- Accounts payable (amounts that are owed and will be paid to suppliers in the future)
- Sales taxes payable (sales tax owed and to be paid in the future)
- Interest payable (interest owed and to be paid in the future)
- Other current liabilities (liabilities due within one year)
- Loan payable (also called notes payable)
- Mortgage payable (The difference between a note payable and a mortgage payable is that a mortgage payable has real estate as collateral.)
- Other long-term liabilities (liabilities due after one year)

> **How Do We Know if an Account is a Liability?**
>
> Ask:
> Is our enterprise *obligated* to do something, such as pay a bill or provide a service?
>
> Answer:
> If we have an *obligation,* the account is probably a *liability.*

3. **Equity accounts** (or stockholders' equity for a corporation) represent the net worth of a business. Equity is calculated as assets (resources owned) minus liabilities (amounts owed).

Different types of business ownership include:

- Sole proprietorship (an unincorporated business with one owner)
- Partnership (an unincorporated business with more than one owner)
- Corporation (an incorporated business with one or more owners)

Owners' equity is increased by:

- Investments by owners. For a corporation, owners invest by buying stock.
- Net profits retained in the business rather than distributed to owners

Owners' equity is decreased by:

- Amounts paid to owners as a return for their investment. For a sole proprietorship or partnership, these are called withdrawals or distributions. For a corporation, they are called dividends.

- Losses incurred by the business

How Do We Calculate Equity?

Equity = Assets − Liabilities

Assets
− Liabilities
= Equity

What we *own* minus what we *owe* leaves equity.

What are Profit and Loss Accounts?

- The Profit and Loss Statement (also called the Income Statement or P&L Statement) reports the results of a company's operations, listing income and expenses for a period of time.

- Profit and Loss accounts are accounts that appear on a company's Profit and Loss Statement.

- QBO uses two different types of Profit and Loss accounts:

  1. Income accounts
  2. Expense accounts

1. **Income** accounts record sales to customers and other revenues earned by the company. Revenues are the prices charged customers for products and services provided.

   Examples of Income accounts include:

   - Sales or revenues
   - Fees earned
   - Interest income
   - Rental income
   - Gains on sale of assets

2. **Expense** accounts record costs that have expired or been consumed in the process of generating income. Expenses are the costs of providing products and services to customers.

Examples of Expense accounts include:

- Cost of goods sold expense
- Salaries expense
- Insurance expense
- Rent expense
- Interest expense

How Do We Calculate Net Income?

Net Income = Income (Revenue) − Expenses (including CGS)

Income (Revenue)
− Expenses (including CGS)
= Net Income (Net Profit or Net Earnings)

Net income is calculated as income (or revenue) less cost of goods sold and other expenses. Net income is an attempt to match or measure efforts (expenses) against accomplishments (revenues).

3 Names for the Same Thing: Net Income is also referred to as Net Profit or Net Earnings.

What are Permanent Accounts?

- In general, Balance Sheet accounts are considered **permanent accounts** (with the exception of the Withdrawals or Distributions account which is closed out each year).
- Balances in permanent accounts are carried forward from year to year. Thus, for a Balance Sheet account, such as Checking, the balance at December 31 is carried forward and becomes the opening balance on January 1 of the next year.

What are Temporary Accounts?

- Profit and Loss accounts are called **temporary accounts** because they are used to track account data for a temporary period of time, usually one year.
- At the end of each year, temporary accounts are closed (the balance reduced to zero). For example, if a Profit and Loss account, such as Advertising Expense, had a $13,000 balance at December 31, the $13,000 balance would be closed or transferred to owners' equity at year-end. The opening balance on January 1 for the Advertising Expense account would be $0.00.

PRACTICE QUIZ 2

Q2.1

Select two from the following to display the Chart of Accounts (COA):

  a. From the Navigation Bar select Accounting

  b. From the Navigation Bar select Customers > Chart of Accounts

  c. From the Create (+) icon, select Chart of Accounts

  d. From the Gear icon, select Chart of Accounts

Q2.2

In QBO, the Chart of Accounts displays which of the following two?

  a. QuickBooks Balance

  b. Bank Balance

  c. All account transactions

  d. None of the above

Q2.3

The Chart of Accounts displays:

  a. Account Name

  b. Type

  c. Detail Type

  d. All of the above

Q2.4

Why would a company want to use account numbers on its Chart of Accounts?

  a. To be able to check the current account balance quickly

  b. To uniquely identify each account on the Chart of Accounts

  c. To confuse users of the Chart of Accounts

  d. None the above

Q2.5

To display account numbers on the Chart of Accounts in QBO:

a. From the Navigation Bar select Transactions > Chart of Accounts > Enable Account numbers > Show account numbers

b. From the Create (+) icon select Other > Chart of Accounts > Account Numbers

c. From the Gear icon select Chart of Accounts > Account Numbers

d. From the Gear icon select Account and Settings > Advanced > Enable account numbers > Show account numbers

Q2.6

Registers in QBO:

a. Display more detailed information about accounts

b. Display all transactions for the account

c. Display a running balance for the account

d. All of the above

Q2.7

To view a register:

a. Display the Chart of Accounts, select View Register

b. From the Navigation Bar, select Register

c. From the Gear icon, select Register

d. From the Create (+) icon, select Register

Q2.8

Match the following legal entities with the federal tax return the entity files.

1. Form 1040 Schedule C

2. Form 1120

3. Form 1065

4. Form 1120S

a. Partnership _____

b. C Corporation _____

c. S Corporation _____

d. Sole Proprietorship _____

Q2.9

To edit an account in the Chart of Accounts:

a. Display the Chart of Accounts, select Edit

b. Display the Chart of Accounts, select Run Report drop-down arrow, select Edit

c. From Create (+) icon, select Chart of Accounts, select Edit

d. None of the above

Q2.10

To delete an account in the Chart of Accounts:

a. Display the Chart of Accounts, select Delete

b. Display the Chart of Accounts, select Run Report drop-down arrow, select Delete

c. From Create (+) icon, select Chart of Accounts, select Delete

d. None of the above

Q2.11

An example of an asset account is:

a. Mortgage Payable

b. Sales Taxes Payable

c. Equipment

d. None of the above

Q2.12

Income accounts for a company are used to track:

a. Sales to customers and other revenue earned

b. Costs that have expired or been consumed

   c. Cost of items sold to customers

   d. Purchases from vendors

Q2.13

What are assets?

   a. Net worth of a company

   b. Amounts paid to owners

   c. Resources that a company owns with future benefit

   d. Amounts owed to others and are future obligations

Q2.14

Accounts used for only one year are called:

   a. Temporary accounts

   b. Short-term assets or liabilities

   c. Supply accounts

   d. Estimate accounts

EXERCISES 2

> We use the QBO Sample Company, Craig's Design and Landscaping Services **for practice throughout the exercises. The Sample Company will reset each time it is reopened. So make certain to allow enough time to complete exercises before closing the Sample Company. Otherwise, you will lose the work you have entered when you reopen the Sample Company.**

To access the QBO Sample Company, complete the following steps.

① Open a web browser. (Note: Intuit recommends using Google Chrome.)

② Go to https://qbo.intuit.com/redir/testdrive

③ Follow onscreen instructions for security verification.

Craig's Design and Landscaping Services should appear on your screen.

E2.1 COA: Types of Accounts

Using the QBO Sample Company to Craig's Design and Landscaping Services, select **Navigation Bar > Accounting.** Indicate the QBO

Account Category Type for each of the following accounts appearing in Craig's COA.

QBO Account Category Types

- **Bank**
- **Accounts Receivable (A/R)**
- **Other Current Asset**
- **Fixed Asset**
- **Accounts Payable (A/P)**
- **Credit Card**
- **Other Current Liabilities**
- **Long-Term Liabilities**
- **Equity**
- **Income**
- **Cost of Goods Sold**
- **Expenses**
- **Other Income**
- **Other Expense**

1. Bank Charges
2. Meals and Entertainment
3. Accounts Receivable (A/R)
4. Maintenance and Repair
5. Landscaping Services: Job Materials
6. Equipment Rental
7. Accounts Payable (A/P)
8. Mastercard
9. Savings
10. Loan Payable
11. Inventory Asset
12. Opening Balance Equity
13. Retained Earnings
14. Interest Earned
15. Design Income
16. Landscaping Services

17. Landscaping Services: Labor

18. Undeposited Funds

19. Cost of Goods Sold

20. Notes Payable

21. Legal and Professional Fees

22. Rent or Lease

23. Utilities

24. Billable Expense Income

E2.2 Aligning COA and Tax Return

Typically when customizing the Chart of Accounts for businesses, we want to verify that the accounts on the Chart of Accounts correspond to expenses shown on the tax return the business files.

Assume that Craig's Design and Landscaping Services files the following IRS Schedule C, Form 1040 for its business operations.

SCHEDULE C (Form 1040)	Profit or Loss From Business (Sole Proprietorship)	
Department of the Treasury Internal Revenue Service (99)	► Information about Schedule C and its separate instructions is at www.irs.gov/schedulec. ► Attach to Form 1040, 1040NR, or 1041; partnerships generally must file Form 1065.	

Name of proprietor — Social security number (SSN)

A Principal business or profession, including product or service (see instructions)   B Enter code from instructions ►

C Business name. If no separate business name, leave blank.   D Employer ID number (EIN), (see instr.)

E Business address (including suite or room no.) ►
   City, town or post office, state, and ZIP code

F Accounting method: (1) ☐ Cash   (2) ☐ Accrual   (3) ☐ Other (specify) ►

G Did you "materially participate" in the operation of this business during 2016? If "No," see instructions for limit on losses   ☐ Yes ☐ No

H If you started or acquired this business during 2016, check here   ► ☐

I Did you make any payments in 2016 that would require you to file Form(s) 1099? (see instructions)   ☐ Yes ☐ No

J If "Yes," did you or will you file required Forms 1099?   ☐ Yes ☐ No

Part I   Income

1	Gross receipts or sales. See instructions for line 1 and check the box if this income was reported to you on Form W-2 and the "Statutory employee" box on that form was checked ► ☐	1
2	Returns and allowances	2
3	Subtract line 2 from line 1	3
4	Cost of goods sold (from line 42)	4
5	**Gross profit.** Subtract line 4 from line 3	5
6	Other income, including federal and state gasoline or fuel tax credit or refund (see instructions)	6
7	**Gross income.** Add lines 5 and 6 ►	7

Part II   Expenses. Enter expenses for business use of your home only on line 30.

8	Advertising	8	18	Office expense (see instructions)	18
9	Car and truck expenses (see instructions)	9	19	Pension and profit-sharing plans	19
10	Commissions and fees	10	20	Rent or lease (see instructions):	
11	Contract labor (see instructions)	11	a	Vehicles, machinery, and equipment	20a
12	Depletion	12	b	Other business property	20b
13	Depreciation and section 179 expense deduction (not included in Part III) (see instructions)	13	21	Repairs and maintenance	21
			22	Supplies (not included in Part III)	22
			23	Taxes and licenses	23
14	Employee benefit programs (other than on line 19)	14	24	Travel, meals, and entertainment:	
			a	Travel	24a
15	Insurance (other than health)	15	b	Deductible meals and entertainment (see instructions)	24b
16	Interest:		25	Utilities	25
a	Mortgage (paid to banks, etc.)	16a	26	Wages (less employment credits)	26
b	Other	16b	27a	Other expenses (from line 48)	27a
17	Legal and professional services	17	b	Reserved for future use	27b

For the following accounts from Craig's Chart of Accounts, identify the corresponding Line number on the Schedule C.

Craig's COA   **IRS Schedule C**

1. Cost of Goods Sold   Schedule C Line _____

2. Advertising   Schedule C Line _____

3. Legal and Professional Fees   Schedule C Line _____

4. Maintenance and Repair   Schedule C Line _____

5. Office Expenses   Schedule C Line _____

6. Rent or Lease   Schedule C Line _____

7. Taxes and Licenses   Schedule C Line _____

8. Utilities   Schedule C Line _____

2.3 Display and Enter Account Numbers

Using the QBO Sample Company, Craig's Design and Landscaping Company, complete the following.

1. Turn on Account Numbers as follows.

   a. To turn on account numbers, from the **Gear** icon, select **Account and Settings > Advanced > Check Enable account numbers > Check Show account numbers > Save.**

   b. To display COA, from the **Navigation Bar,** select **Accounting.**

   c. On the Chart of Accounts, what is the name of the column displaying the account numbers?

2. Enter Asset Account Numbers as follows.

   a. From COA window select **Edit pencil.**

   b. Asset accounts will be numbered in the 1000s. Starting with 1001 for the first Asset account, **enter** accounts numbers consecutively for the following Asset accounts.

      • Checking
      • Savings
      • Accounts Receivable (A/R)
      • Inventory Asset
      • Prepaid Expenses

3. Enter Liability Account Numbers as follows.

   a. If needed, from the COA window, select **Edit pencil.**

   b. Liability accounts will be numbered in the 2000s. Starting with 2001 for the first Liability account, **enter** account numbers consecutively for the following Liability accounts.

      • Accounts Payable (A/P)
      • Mastercard
      • Visa
      • Arizona Dept. of Revenue Payable
      • Board of Equalization Payable
      • Loan Payable
      • Notes Payable

4. Enter Equity Account Numbers as follows.

   a. If needed, from the COA window, select **Edit pencil.**

   b. Equity accounts will be numbered in the 3000s. Starting with 3001 for the first Equity account, **enter** account numbers consecutively for the following Equity accounts.

      • Opening Balance Equity
      • Retained Earnings

5. Enter Income Account Numbers as follows.

   a. If needed, from the COA window, select **Edit pencil.**

   b. Income accounts will be numbered in the 4000s. Starting with 4001 for the first Income account, **enter** account numbers consecutively for the following Income accounts.

      • Billable Expense Income
      • Design Income
      • Fees Billed
      • Landscaping Services
      • Other Income
      • Pest Control Services
      • Sales of Product Income
      • Services

6. Enter Expense Account Numbers as follows.

    a. If needed, from the COA window, select **Edit pencil.**

    b. Expense accounts will be numbered in the 5000s. Starting with 5001 for the first Expense account, **enter** account numbers consecutively for the following Expense accounts.

       *   Cost of Goods Sold
       *   Advertising
       *   Automobile
       *   Bank Charges
       *   Commissions & Fees
       *   Disposal Fees
       *   Dues & Subscriptions
       *   Equipment Rental
       *   Insurance
       *   Job Expenses
       *   Legal & Professional Fees
       *   Maintenance & Repair
       *   Meals and Entertainment
       *   Office Expenses
       *   Promotional Expenses
       *   Purchases
       *   Rent or Lease
       *   Stationary & Printing
       *   Supplies
       *   Taxes & Licenses
       *   Travel
       *   Travel Meals
       *   Utilities

E2.4 COA: Add Accounts

Using the QBO Sample Company, Craig's Design and Landscaping Company, complete the following.

In order to align better with the IRS Form 1040 Schedule C, Craig would like you to add accounts to its QBO Chart of Accounts.

To add accounts to the COA, from the **Navigation Bar,** select **Accounting > New.**

1. Add Interest Expense account.

    a. Select Category Type: **Expenses**

    b. Select Detail Type: _____

    c. Enter Name: **Interest Expense**

    d. Leave Number **blank**

    e. Leave Description **blank**

    f. Leave Is sub-account **unchecked**

    g. Select **Save and New**

2. Add Other Expenses account.

    a. Select Category Type: _____

    b. Select Detail Type: _____

    c. Enter Name: **Other Expenses**

    d. Leave Number **blank**

    e. Leave Description **blank**

    f. Leave Is sub-account **unchecked**

    g. Select **Save and Close**

E2.5 COA: Add SubAccounts

Using the QBO Sample Company, Craig's Design and Landscaping Company, complete the following.

In order to align better with the IRS Form 1040 Schedule C, Craig would like you to add two subaccounts to the Rent or Lease account in its QBO Chart of Accounts.

To add subaccounts to the COA, from the **Navigation Bar,** select **Accounting > New.**

1. Add Vehicles, machinery, and equipment subaccount.

    a. Select Category Type: _____

    b. Select Detail Type: **Equipment Rental**

    c. Enter Name: **Vehicle, machinery, and equipment**

    d. Leave Number **blank**

    e. Leave Description **blank**

   f. **Check** Is sub-account

   g. Enter Parent Account _____

   h. Select **Save and New**

2. Add Other business property subaccount.

   a. Select Category Type: _____

   b. Select Detail Type: **Rent or Lease of Buildings**

   c. Enter Name: **Other business property**

   d. Leave Number **blank**

   e. Leave Description **blank**

   f. **Check** Is sub-account

   g. Enter Parent Account _____

   h. Select **Save and Close**

E2.6 COA: Edit Accounts

Using the QBO Sample Company, Craig's Design and Landscaping Company, complete the following.

In order to align better with the IRS Form 1040 Schedule C, Craig would like you to edit two accounts in its QBO Chart of Accounts.

To edit account names in the COA, from the **Navigation Bar,** select **Accounting** > select **Edit pencil.**

Another way to edit accounts when you need to update more than just the account name **is to select the specific account > drop-down arrow by View register or Run report > Edit.**

---

1. Edit name of Maintenance and Repairs account to Repairs and Maintenance.

   a. Select **Save**

   b. After saving, what account is listed immediately before the Repairs and Maintenance account?

2. Edit name of Legal and Professional Fees account to Legal and Professional Services.

   a. Select **Save**

   b. After saving, what three subaccounts are listed immediately after the Legal and Professional Services account?

E2.7 COA: Delete Accounts

Using the QBO Sample Company, Craig's Design and Landscaping Company, complete the following.

In order to align better with the IRS Form 1040 Schedule C, Craig would like you to delete an account in its QBO Chart of Accounts.

To delete an account in the QBO COA, from the **Navigation Bar,** select **Accounting** > select the **specific account** > **drop-down arrow by View register or Run report** > **Delete.**

1. Delete the account Penalties and Settlements.

    a. When asked Are you sure you want to delete this?, select **Yes**

    b. Now what is the last account listed in Craig's QBO Chart of Accounts?

2. Delete the account Other Portfolio Income.

    a. When asked Are you sure you want to delete this?, select **Yes**

    b. Now what are the last three accounts listed in Craig's QBO Chart of Accounts?

E2.8 Definitions

Match the following Account Types with the appropriate definition.

<u>Account Types</u>

- **Assets**
- **Liabilities**
- **Equity**
- **Revenues**
- **Expenses**

1. What we own less what we owe equals this

2. Prices charged customers for products and services

3. Resources that we own that have future benefit

4. Obligations or amounts that we owe to others

5. Costs of providing products and services to customers

E2.9 Account Types

For each of the following accounts on Craig's Design and Landscaping Services Chart of Accounts, identify Account Type and Financial Statement on which it appears.

Account Types

- **Asset**
- **Liability**
- **Equity**
- **Income**
- **Expense**

Financial Statements

- **Balance Sheet**
- **Profit and Loss**

	Account Type	Financial Statement
1. Design Income		
2. Savings		
3. Accounts Receivable (A/R)		
4. Rent or Lease		
5. Prepaid Expenses		
6. Notes Payable		
7. Inventory Asset		
8. Opening Balance Equity		
9. Utilities		
10. Undeposited Funds		
11. Accounts Payable (A/P)		
12. MasterCard		
13. Visa		
14. Loan Payable		
15. Sales of Product Income		

Account Type   Financial Statement

16. Legal and Professional Fees

17. Advertising

18. Meals and Entertainment

19. Retained Earnings

20. Checking

21. Landscaping Services

22. Pest Control Services

23. Cost of Goods Sold

24. Automobile: Fuel

25. Bank Charges

26. Interest Earned

PROJECT 2.1

Project 2.1 is a continuation of Project 1.1. You will use the QBO client company you created for Project 1.1. Keep in mind the QBO company for Project 2.1 does not reset and carries your data forward, including any errors. So it is important to check and crosscheck your work to verify it is correct before clicking the Save button.

BACKSTORY

Mookie The Beagle™ Concierge, a concierge pet care service, provides convenient, high-quality pet care. CK, the founder of Mookie The Beagle Concierge, has asked us to customize the Chart of Accounts to assist in streamlining tax preparation. Mookie The Beagle Concierge, an S corporation, files US federal tax form 1120S, which can be viewed at www.irs.gov.

Complete the following for Mookie The Beagle Concierge.

QBO SatNav

Project 2.1 focuses on the QBO Settings, specifically the QBO Chart of Accounts shown in the following partial QBO SatNav.

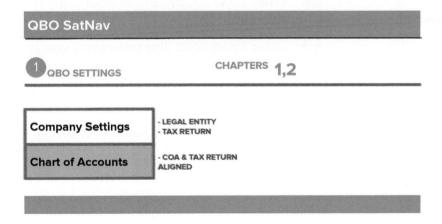

HOW TO LOG INTO QBO+

To log into QBO, complete the following steps.

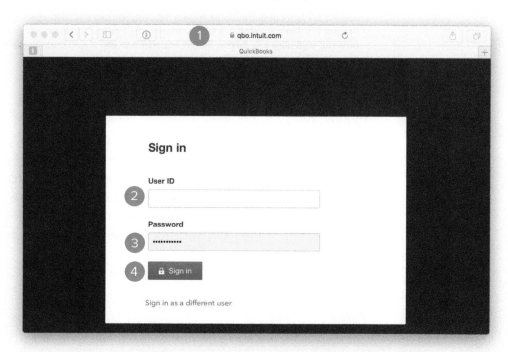

① Using a web browser go to qbo.intuit.com

② Enter **User ID** (the email address you used to set up your QBO Account)

③ Enter **Password** (the password you used to set up your QBO Account)

④ Select **Sign in**

> If you are <u>not</u> using a public or shared computer, **to speed up login, you can save your login to your desktop and select Remember Me. If you are using a public computer or shared computer, do not save to your desktop and unselect Remember Me.**

> The new QBO company **we created in Project 1.1 will carry all work forward into future chapters. So it is important to check and crosscheck your work to verify it is correct before clicking the Save button. Any errors entered are carried forward in the QBO company you create for text projects.**

P2.1.1 Aligning the COA with the Tax Return

Typically when customizing the Chart of Accounts for businesses, we want to verify that the accounts on the Chart of Accounts correspond to expenses shown on the tax return the business files.

Mookie The Beagle Concierge files the following IRS Form 1120S for its business operations.

For the following accounts from Mookie The Beagle Concierge's QBO COA, identify the corresponding Line number on Form 1120S.

QBO COA	IRS FORM 1120S
1. Rents	Form 1120S Line _____
2. Advertising	Form 1120S Line _____
3. Repairs and maintenance	Form 1120S Line _____
4. Interest	Form 1120S Line _____
5. Bad debts	Form 1120S Line _____
6. Taxes and licenses	Form 1120S Line _____

P2.1.2 COA: Add Accounts

Complete the following to add the following Asset accounts to Mookie The Beagle Concierge's Chart of Accounts.

> QBO is continually rolling out new features so it is possible your Chart of Accounts may not look the same. If your COA does not have the following accounts, add them to your COA as follows.

To add accounts to the COA, from the **Navigation Bar,** select **Accounting > New.**

1. Add Checking account.

   a. Select Category Type: **Bank**

   b. Select Detail Type: _____

   c. Enter Name: **Checking**

   d. Leave Description **blank**

   e. Leave Is sub-account **unchecked**

   f. Select **Save and New**

2. Add Accounts Receivable account.

   a. Select Category Type: _____

   b. Select Detail Type: _____

   c. Enter Name: **Accounts Receivable (A/R)**

   d. Leave Description **blank**

   e. Leave Is sub-account **unchecked**

   f. Select **Save and New**

3. Add Inventory account.

   a. Select Category Type: _____

   b. Select Detail Type: _____

   c. Enter Name: **Inventory**

   d. Leave Description **blank**

   e. Leave Is sub-account **unchecked**

   f. Select **Save and Close**

P2.1.3 COA: Add Accounts

Complete the following to add the following Liability and Equity accounts to Mookie The Beagle Concierge's Chart of Accounts.

> QBO is continually rolling out new features so it is possible your Chart of Accounts may not look the same. If your COA does not have the following accounts, add them to your COA as follows.

To add accounts to the COA, from the **Navigation Bar,** select **Accounting > New.**

1. Add Accounts Payable account.
   a. Select Category Type: _____
   b. Select Detail Type: _____
   c. Enter Name: **Accounts Payable (A/P)**
   d. Leave Description **blank**
   e. Leave Is sub-account **unchecked**
   f. Select **Save and New**

2. Add VISA Credit Card account.
   a. Select Category Type: _____
   b. Select Detail Type: _____
   c. Enter Name: **VISA Credit Card**
   d. Leave Description **blank**
   e. Leave Is sub-account **unchecked**
   f. Select **Save and New**

3. Add Owner Contributions account.
   a. Select Category Type: **Equity**
   b. Select Detail Type: _____
   c. Enter Name: **Owner Contributions**
   d. Leave Description **blank**
   e. Leave Is sub-account **unchecked**
   f. Select **Save and New**

4. Add Owner Distributions account.

   a. Select Category Type: **Equity**

   b. Select Detail Type: _____

   c. Enter Name: **Owner Distributions**

   d. Leave Description **blank**

   e. Leave Is sub-account **unchecked**

   f. Select **Save and Close**

P2.1.4 COA: Add SubAccounts

Complete the following to add subaccounts to Mookie The Beagle Concierge's Chart of Accounts.

> QBO is continually rolling out new features so it is possible your Chart of Accounts may not look the same. If your COA does not have the following a Prepaid Expense account and the following Prepaid Expenses subaccounts, add Prepaid Expenses to your COA and then add the following subaccounts.

To add subaccounts to the COA, from the **Navigation Bar,** select **Accounting > New.**

1. After adding or verifying your COA has a Prepaid Expenses account, add Prepaid Expenses: Supplies subaccount.

   a. Select Category Type: **Other Current Assets**

   b. Select Detail Type: _____

   c. Enter Name: **Supplies**

   d. Leave Description **blank**

   e. **Check** Is sub-account

   f. Enter Parent Account **Prepaid Expenses**

   g. Select **Save and New**

2. Add Prepaid Expenses: Insurance subaccount.

   a. Select Category Type: _____

   b. Select Detail Type: _____

   c. Enter Name: **Insurance**

   d. Leave Description **blank**

   e. **Check** Is sub-account

   f. Enter Parent Account **Prepaid Expenses**

   g. Select **Save and Close**

P2.1.5 COA: Delete Accounts

Complete the following to delete accounts Mookie The Beagle Concierge will not be using from the Chart of Accounts.

> QBO is continually **rolling out new features so it is possible your Chart of Accounts may not look the same. If your COA has the following accounts, delete them from your COA as follows.**

To delete an account in the QBO COA, from the **Navigation Bar,** select **Accounting** > select the **specific account** > **drop-down arrow by View register or Run report** > **Delete.**

1. Delete the account Penalties and Settlements.

   a. When asked Are you sure you want to delete this?, select **Yes**

   b. Now what is the last account listed in the QBO Chart of Accounts?

2. Delete the account Other Portfolio Income.

   a. When asked Are you sure you want to delete this?, select **Yes**

   b. Now what are the last two accounts listed in the QBO Chart of Accounts?

P2.1.6 Display and Enter Account Numbers

Complete the following for Mookie The Beagle Concierge.

> QBO is continually **rolling out new features so it is possible your Chart of Accounts may not have the same accounts as listed below. If your COA does not have the following accounts, add the appropriate accounts to your COA before adding the account numbers.**

1. Turn on Account Numbers as follows.

   a. To turn on account numbers, from the **Gear** icon, select **Account and Settings** > **Advanced** > **Check Enable account numbers** > **Check Show account numbers** > **Save.**

   b. To display COA, from the **Navigation Bar,** select **Accounting.**

   c. On the Chart of Accounts, what is the name of the column displaying the account numbers?

2. Enter Asset Account Numbers as follows.

   a. From COA window select **Edit pencil.**

   b. Asset accounts will be numbered in the 1000s. Starting with 1001 for the first Asset account, **enter** accounts numbers consecutively for the following Asset accounts.

- Checking
- Accounts Receivable (A/R)
- Inventory
- Prepaid Expenses
- Prepaid Expenses: Insurance
- Prepaid Expenses: Supplies
- Uncategorized Asset
- Undeposited Funds

3. Enter Liability Account Numbers as follows.

   a. If needed, from the COA window, select **Edit pencil.**

   b. Liability accounts will be numbered in the 2000s. Starting with 2001 for the first Liability account, **enter** account numbers consecutively for the following Liability accounts.

      - Accounts Payable (A/P)
      - VISA Credit Card

4. Enter Equity Account Numbers as follows.

   a. If needed, from the COA window, select **Edit pencil.**

   b. Equity accounts will be numbered in the 3000s. Starting with 3001 for the first Equity account, **enter** account numbers consecutively for the following Equity accounts.

      - Opening Balance Equity
      - Owner Contributions
      - Owner Distributions
      - Retained Earnings

5. Enter Income Account Numbers as follows.

   a. If needed, from the COA window, select **Edit pencil.**

   b. Income accounts will be numbered in the 4000s. Starting with 4001 for the first Income account, **enter** account numbers consecutively for the following Income accounts.

      - Sales
      - Uncategorized Income

6. Enter Expense Account Numbers as follows.

    a. If needed, from the COA window, select **Edit pencil.**

    b. Expense accounts will be numbered in the 5000s. Starting with 5001 for the first Expense account, **enter** account numbers consecutively for the following Expense accounts.

       - Purchases - COS
       - Subcontractors - COS
       - Supplies & Materials - COGS
       - Advertising
       - Bank Charges
       - Insurance
       - Insurance: Disability
       - Insurance: Liability
       - Interest Expense
       - Legal & Professional Fees
       - Meals and Entertainment
       - Office Expenses
       - Other General and Admin Expenses
       - Promotional Expenses
       - Rent or Lease
       - Repair & Maintenance
       - Shipping and Delivery Expense
       - Stationary & Printing
       - Subcontractors
       - Supplies
       - Taxes & Licenses
       - Tools
       - Travel
       - Travel Meals
       - Utilities
       - Interest Earned

P2.1.7 COA

Complete the following for Mookie The Beagle Concierge.

Display the COA by selecting **Navigation Bar > Accounting.**

Indicate the QBO Account Category Type using the following QBO Account Category Type for each of the following accounts appearing in Mookie The Beagle Concierge's COA.

QBO Account Category Types

- **Bank**
- **Accounts Receivable (A/R)**
- **Other Current Assets**
- **Fixed Assets**
- **Accounts Payable (A/P)**
- **Credit Card**
- **Other Current Liabilities**
- **Long-Term Liabilities**
- **Equity**
- **Income**
- **Cost of Goods Sold**
- **Expenses**
- **Other Income**
- **Other Expense**

1. Checking
2. Accounts Receivable (A/R)
3. Inventory
4. Prepaid Expenses
5. Prepaid Expenses: Insurance
6. Prepaid Expenses: Supplies
7. Accounts Payable (A/P)
8. VISA Credit Card
9. Owner Contributions
10. Owner Distributions

11. Retained Earnings

12. Sales

13. Subcontractors - COS

14. Advertising

15. Bank Charges

16. Insurance - Liability

17. Interest Expense

18. Legal and Professional Fees

19. Meals and Entertainment

20. Office Expenses

21. Rent or Lease

22. Subcontractors

23. Supplies

24. Utilities

25. Interest Earned

P2.1.8 Account Types

The following accounts are from Mookie The Beagle Concierge's Chart of Accounts. For each account identify Account Type and Financial Statement on which it appears.

Account Types

- **Asset**
- **Liability**
- **Equity**
- **Income**
- **Expense**

Financial Statements

- **Balance Sheet**
- **Profit and Loss**

Account Type | **Financial Statement**

1. Sales

2. Checking

3. Accounts Receivable (A/R)

4. Rent or Lease

5. Prepaid Expenses

6. Prepaid Expenses: Supplies

7. Supplies

8. Prepaid Expenses: Insurance

9. Insurance: Liability

10. Undeposited Funds

11. Accounts Payable (A/P)

12. VISA Credit Card

13. Interest Earned

14. Interest Expense

15. Subcontractors - COS

16. Legal and Professional Fees

17. Advertising

18. Meals and Entertainment

19. Retained Earnings

20. Owner Contributions

21. Owner Distributions

22. Office Expenses

23. Utilities

www.my-quickbooksonline.com

Go to www.My-QuickBooksOnline.com for additional resources for you including QBO Help, QBO Videos, and more.

Chapter 3

QBO Transactions

One objective of our QBO financial system is to collect information about transactions. Transactions are simply exchanges between our business and other parties, such as customers, vendors, and employees. We need to keep a record of all transactions. QBO offers us a streamlined way to keep track of those transactions.

After we set up QBO Company Settings and the QBO Chart of Accounts, we're ready to enter transactions into QBO. Transactions increase and decrease accounts so that's why it's important for us to have our Chart of Accounts created before we enter transactions.

When working with clients, we have to determine the types of transactions that the client will need to record. Then we plan how to save time and minimize errors when entering those transactions, especially ones that are recurring.

This chapter introduces different types of transactions and later chapters will look at each type of transaction in greater detail.

Section 3.1

QBO SatNav

QBO SatNav is your satellite navigation for QuickBooks Online, assisting you in navigating QBO

This chapter provides an overview of QBO transactions, shown in the following QBO SatNav.

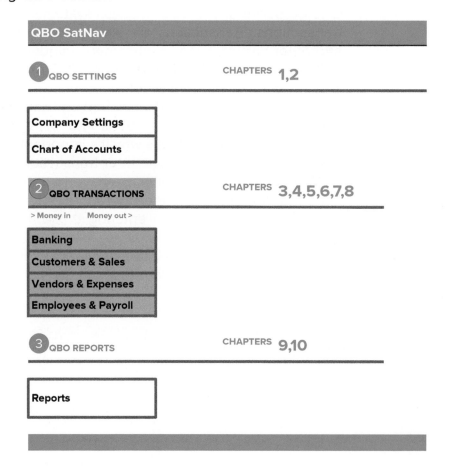

Section 3.2

QBO LOGIN TO SAMPLE COMPANY

To log into the QBO Sample Company:

1   Open a web browser. (Note: Intuit recommends using Google Chrome.)

2   Go to https://qbo.intuit.com/redir/testdrive

3   Follow onscreen instructions for security verification.

Craig's Design and Landscaping Services should appear on your screen.

> **We use the Sample Company** for practice throughout the chapter and exercises. The Sample Company will reset each time it is reopened. So make certain to allow enough time to complete all chapter activities before closing the Sample Company. Otherwise, you will lose the work you have entered when you reopen the Sample Company.

Section 3.3

QBO LISTS

As a company conducts business operations, the company enters into transactions with customers, vendors, and employees. Before entering these transactions in QBO, we typically want to make sure our QBO Lists are up to date.

WHAT ARE QBO LISTS?

QBO Lists are a time saving feature so that we do not have to continually re-enter the same information for accounts, customers, vendors, and so on, each time we enter a new transaction. Lists permit us to collect information that we will reuse so we do not have to re-enter it.

Some of the lists we might use when entering transactions include:

- Chart of Accounts
- Customers List
- Vendors List
- Employees List

To view QBO Lists, select the lists from the Navigation Bar as follows.

1. Select **Accounting** to display the Chart of Accounts. (If necessary, select See your Chart of Accounts.)

2. Select **Sales > Customers** to display the Customers List. Select **Sales > Products** and Services to view the Product and Services List.

3. Select **Expenses > Vendors** to display the Vendors List

4. Select **Employees** to view the Employees List

Chart of Accounts is a list of all the accounts a company uses when recording transactions. Accounts (such as the Checking account or Inventory account) permit us to sort and track accounting information.

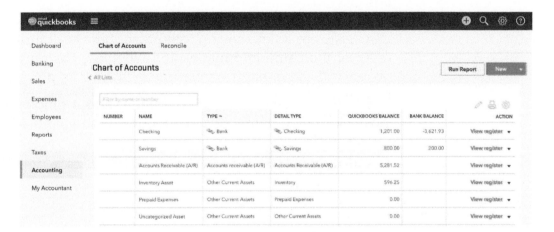

Customers List, also called the Clients List, collects information about customers, such as customer name, customer number, address, and contact information.

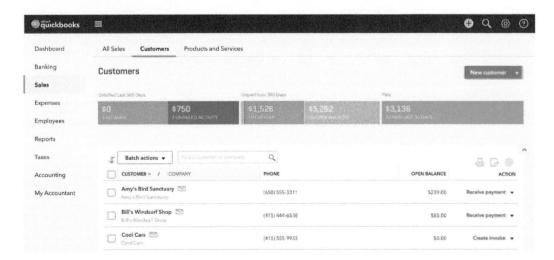

Vendors List collects information about vendors, such as vendor name, vendor number, and contact information.

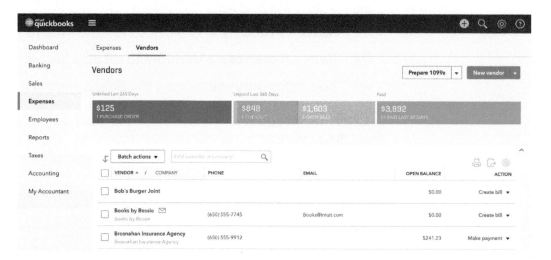

Employees List collects information about employees for payroll purposes including name, Social Security number, and address.

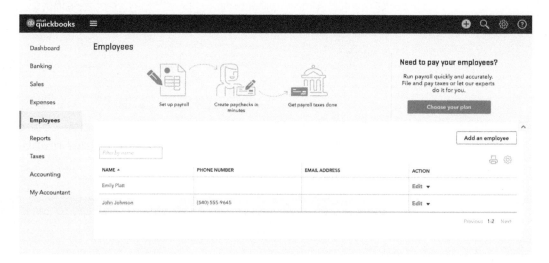

Products and Services List collects information about the products and services *sold to customers,* such as hours worked and types of products or services.

The Products and Services List is found under the Gear icon shown as follows.

① Select **Gear** icon

② Under Lists select **Product and Services**

The Product and Services List can also be viewed from the Navigation Bar, select Sales > Products and Services.

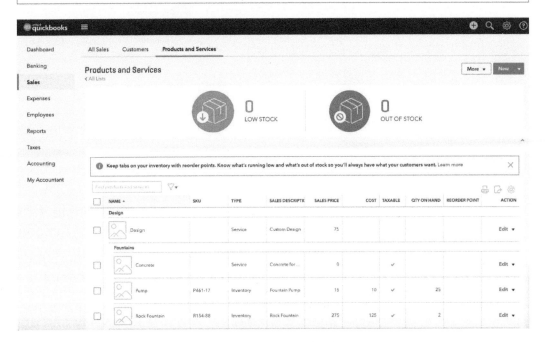

The Sample Company Products and Services List contains information about products and services that Craig's Design and Landscaping Service buys and sells.

Note: **If items in the Products and Services List appear in a different order than shown here, click the Name tab in the column header to resort the Products and Services List.**

HOW DO WE UPDATE QBO LISTS?

There are basically two ways that we can update QBO Lists.

1. *Before* entering transactions
2. *While* entering transactions

1. *Before* entering transactions, we can update lists from the QBO Navigation Bar as follows.

① Select **Accounting** to display and update the Chart of Accounts. (If necessary, select See your Chart of Accounts.)

② Select **Sales > Customers** to display and update the Customers List. Select **Sales > Products and Services** to view and update the Product and Services List.

③ Select **Expenses > Vendors** to display and update the Vendors List

④ Select **Employees** to view and update the Employees List

2. *While* entering transactions, we can update lists on the fly from the screen where we enter the transaction. If a customer, for example, has not been entered in the list and is needed for a sales transaction, we can add the customer as follows from an onscreen Invoice form.

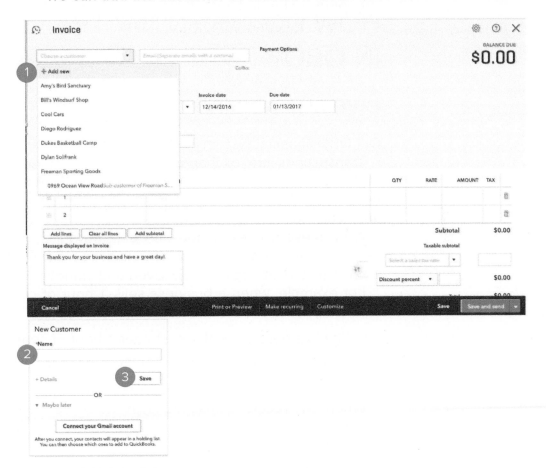

① For example, to view an onscreen form such as an Invoice, select **Create (+)** icon **> Invoice.** Then select **Choose a customer drop-down arrow > + Add new.**

② For example, then we would enter **new customer information**

③ Normally, we would then select **Save** to save the new customer information. Then we would complete and save the Invoice. In this case, select **Cancel** to leave the Invoice window.

Section 3.4

HOW DO WE ENTER TRANSACTIONS IN QBO?

GIVE AND RECEIVE

Our QBO financial system needs to collect information about transactions.

Transactions are exchanges. A business enters into transactions or exchanges between the business and other parties, such as customers, vendors, and employers. The business gives and receives something in an exchange.

A business can exchange services, products, cash, or a promise to pay later (Accounts Payable). A transaction must have two parts to the exchange: something must be given and something must be received.

For example, when a business sells 1 hour of consulting services to a customer, the two parts to the transaction are:

1. The business gives the customer 1 hour of consulting services.

2. In exchange, the business receives cash (or a promise to pay later) from the customer.

When we record transactions in QBO we need to record what is exchanged, what is given, and what is received.

ONSCREEN FORM OR ONSCREEN JOURNAL

QBO offers us two different ways to enter transaction information:

1. Onscreen Journal

2. Onscreen forms

Onscreen Journal. We can make debit and credit entries to enter transactions using an onscreen Journal.

> The onscreen Journal **using debits and credits to enter transactions is accessed from the Create (+) icon > Other > Journal Entry.**

An onscreen Journal is often used to make adjusting entries at year end to bring accounts up to date before preparing financial statements.

Instead of using the onscreen Journal, we can use onscreen forms to enter transaction information in QBO.

Onscreen forms. We can enter information about transactions using onscreen forms such as the following onscreen credit card form. After using the business credit card to make a charge for a car wash, we would use the QBO onscreen form for recording the expense and the credit card charge.

When we enter information into an onscreen form, behind the screen QBO automatically converts that information into a journal entry with debits and credits. QBO maintains a list of journal entries for all the transactions entered—whether entered using the onscreen Journal or onscreen forms.

For example, to view the journal entry that QBO created behind the screen for the transaction entered and saved using the previous onscreen form, complete the following steps.

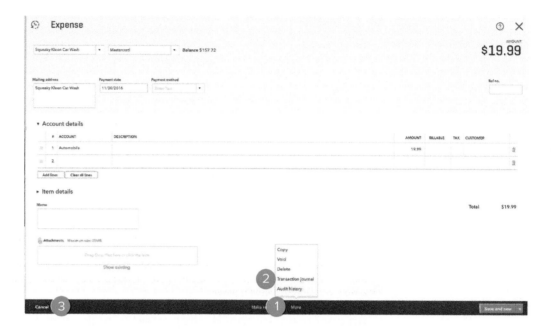

1   For example, to view an onscreen form such as an Expense, go to the **Navigation Bar > Expenses.** From the Expense Transactions screen, click on an Expense transaction, such as a Credit Card Expense like the one for Squeaky Kleen Car Wash shown here. From the Expense window, select **More** at the bottom of the Expense window.

2   Select **Transaction journal.** Behind the screen, QBO automatically converted the information in the onscreen form into the following journal entry with debits and credits.

3   Normally, we would then select Save. In this case, select **Cancel** to leave the window.

THREE WAYS TO ENTER TRANSACTIONS IN QBO

QBO offers us three different options for accessing how to enter transactions by using the:

1. Navigation Bar
2. Create (+) icon or
3. Recurring transactions feature that permits us to save transactions that we expect to reuse in the future

> **Notice that QBO organizes transactions** somewhat differently in the Navigation Bar versus the Create (+) icon. In the Navigation Bar, Banking, Sales and Expenses are the main transactions. In the Create (+) icon, banking transactions, such as bank deposit and transfer and shown under the heading Other. In addition, the Create (+) icon labels the transactions by parties to the transactions such as Customers, Vendors, and Employees.

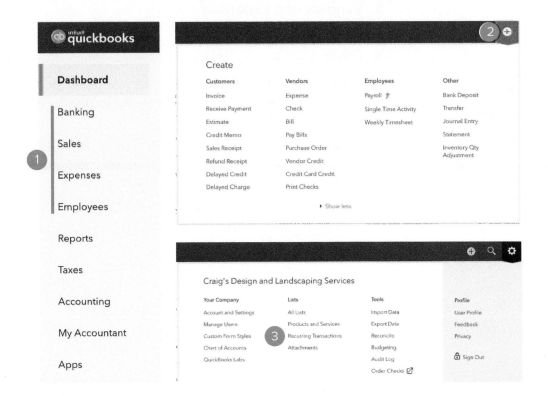

1. Navigation Bar
2. Create (+) icon
3. Gear icon > Recurring transactions

Section 3.5

WHAT ARE THE DIFFERENT TYPES OF TRANSACTIONS?

A transaction is simply an exchange between our QBO business and another party, such as a customer, vendor, or employee. Although there are many different types of transactions, generally we can group transactions into the following different types based upon the other party to the transaction:

1. Banking and Credit Card
2. Customers and Sales
3. Vendors and Expenses
4. Employees and Payroll
5. Other

QBO organizes how we enter transactions according to the type of transaction and onscreen form we need to use to enter the transaction.

Section 3.6

BANKING AND CREDIT CARD TRANSACTIONS

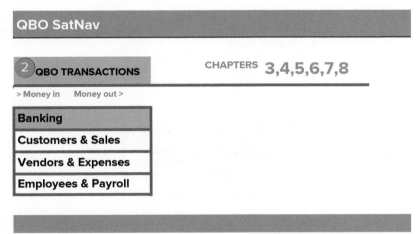

Transactions that involve depositing or transferring funds with our bank can be entered using the Create (+) icon.

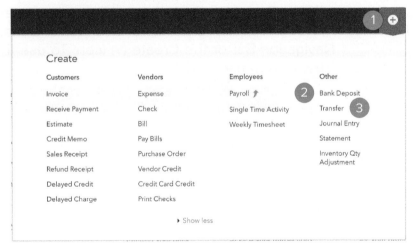

1. Select **Create (+)** icon
2. Select **Bank Deposit** to record a bank deposit
3. Select **Transfer** to record a transfer between our company's bank accounts

Additional banking activities are covered in the next chapter.

Section 3.7

CUSTOMER AND SALES TRANSACTIONS

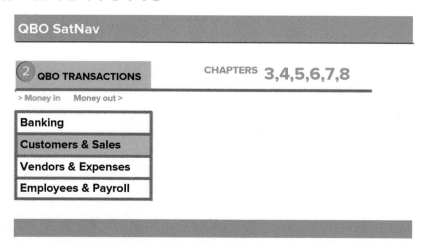

Customers transactions are exchanges between our company and customers of our company. Typically, these exchanges focus on sales transactions. Customers include parties to whom we sell products or services.

We can enter customers and sales transactions using either the Navigation Bar or the Create (+) icon. To use the Create (+) icon to enter Customer transactions:

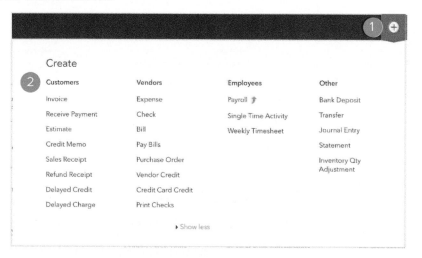

① Select **Create (+)** icon

② From the **Customers** column select the appropriate task

Customers transactions can include:

1. Entering invoices
2. Receiving customer payments
3. Entering estimates
4. Entering credit memos for reductions to customers accounts
5. Entering sales receipts
6. Entering refund receipts

Section 3.8

VENDOR AND EXPENSE TRANSACTIONS

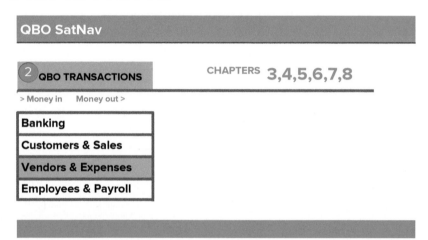

Vendors transactions are exchanges between our company and vendors of our company. Typically, these exchanges focus on expense transactions. Vendors include suppliers who sell products and professionals who provide services to our company.

We can enter vendors and expenses transactions using either the Navigation Bar or the Create (+) icon. To use the Create (+) icon to enter Vendors transactions:

1 Select **Create (+)** icon

2 From the **Vendors** column select the appropriate task

Vendors transactions can include:

1. Entering expenses
2. Entering checks
3. Entering bills
4. Paying bills
5. Entering purchase orders
6. Entering vendor credits
7. Entering credit card credits

Section 3.9

EMPLOYEE AND PAYROLL TRANSACTIONS

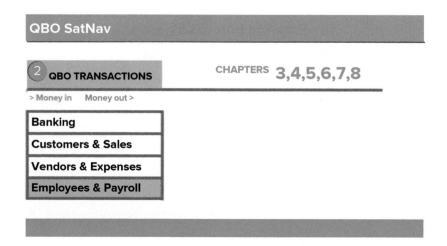

Employee transactions are exchanges between our company and the employees of our company. Typically, these exchanges focus on payroll transactions, including tracking employee time and paying employees for their services to the company.

We can enter employees and payroll transactions using either the Navigation Bar or the Create (+) icon. To use the Create (+) icon to access Employees transactions:

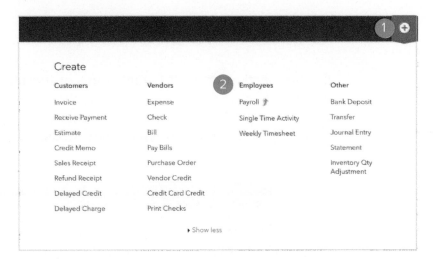

1 Select **Create (+)** icon

2 From the **Employees** column select the appropriate task

Notice that QBO can be used to track employees time using Single Time Activity or Weekly Timesheet.

Section 3.10

OTHER TRANSACTIONS

If a transaction doesn't fall into one of the above categories, then it can be classified as Other. Other transactions might include adjusting entries that are required to bring our accounts up to date at year end before preparing financial reports. We make adjusting entries using the onscreen Journal accessed as follows.

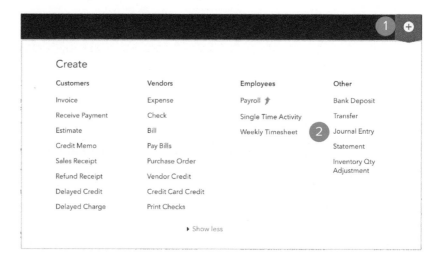

①   Select **Create (+)** icon

②   Select **Journal Entry**

Section 3.11

RECURRING TRANSACTIONS

To save time entering transactions, QBO offers a feature that permits us to save a transaction that will be recurring. One way we reduce errors and save time when entering transactions is to save frequently used transactions as recurring transactions.

To access the Recurring Transactions List, complete the following steps.

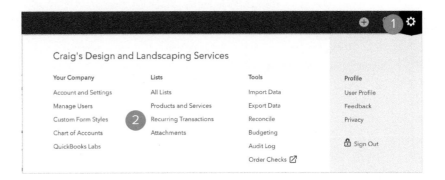

1   Select **Gear** icon

2   Select **Recurring Transactions**

3   Select **New** to add a new recurring transaction

4   Select **Edit** to update the recurring transaction previously entered

5   Select **Use** to use the recurring transaction to enter a new transaction

Recurring transactions can be classified as one of three types:

1. Scheduled
2. Unscheduled
3. Reminder

Notice in the Type column shown that the two recurring transactions are Scheduled. This indicates that the recurring transaction is scheduled for QBO to automatically enter the transaction on a date we specified. Unscheduled transactions will appear in the Recurring Transaction List but QBO will not automatically enter the transaction. Instead, we must go to the Recurring Transaction List and select Use. Recurring transactions with a Reminder Type will alert us with a reminder when we should use a recurring transaction to enter a new transaction.

Section 3.12

ACCOUNTING ESSENTIALS

Double-Entry Accounting

Accounting Essentials summarize important foundational accounting knowledge you may find useful when using QBO

What is double-entry accounting?

- Double-entry accounting is used with a journal to record what is exchanged in a transaction:
  1. The amount received, such as equipment purchased, is recorded with a debit
  2. The amount given, such as cash or a promise to pay later, is recorded with a credit
- Each journal entry must balance; debits must equal credits. This is true whether it is a manual accounting system or a cloud-based accounting system, such as QBO.

In double-entry accounting, how do we know if a debit is an increase or a decrease to an account? How do we know if a credit is an increase or a decrease to an account?

- Whether a debit or credit increases or decreases an account depends upon the type of account.

Account Type	Debit	Credit
Assets	Increase	Decrease
Liabilities	Decrease	Increase
Equity	Decrease	Increase
Revenues (Income)	Decrease	Increase
Expenses	Increase	Decrease

What are the different types of accounts and the effect of debits and credits on the accounts?

- Five different types of accounts are listed as follows along with the normal balance of the account that increases the account balance.

Account Type	Debit/Credit	Effect on Balance
Asset	Debit	Increase
Liabilities	Credit	Increase
Equity	Credit	Increase
Revenues (Income)	Credit	Increase
Expenses	Debit	Increase

- For example, if the transaction is the owner invests $100,000 in the business, the journal entry with debits and credits would be as follows.

Account	Account Type	Debit/Credit	Effect on Balance	Amount
Checking	Asset	Debit	Increase	$100,000
Capital Stock	Equity	Credit	Increase	$100,000

PRACTICE QUIZ 3

Q3.1

In QuickBooks Online, information about transactions can be entered in onscreen forms, such as:

a. Check

b. Invoice

c. Purchase Order

d. All of the above

Q3.2

Which of the following transactions are displayed in the QBO Navigation Bar?

a. Sales

b. Adjusting Entries

c. Banking

d. Products and Services

Q3.3

Which of the following two transactions are considered Customer and Sales transactions?

a. Invoice

b. Receive Payment

c. Pay Bills

d. Check

Q3.4

Which of the following two transactions are considered Vendor and Expense transactions?

a. Invoice

b. Receive Payment

c. Pay Bills

d. Check

Q3.5

To enter transactions in QBO:

a. From the Navigation Bar select Reports

b. From the Create (+) icon select transaction to enter

c. From the Gear icon select transaction to enter

d. From the Navigation Bar select Home

Q3.6

QBO Lists include:

a. Chart of Accounts

b. Customers List

c. Vendors List

d. Employees List

e. All of the above are QBO Lists

Q3.7

The Products and Services List can be accessed from the:

a. Navigation Bar > Expenses

b. Gear icon

c. Create (+) icon

d. None of the above

Q3.8

Match the following transactions with the type of transaction.

Transaction Types

1. **Banking**
2. **Customers and Sales**
3. **Vendors and Expenses**
4. **Employees and Payroll**

   a. Estimate

   b. Deposit

   c. Print Checks

   d. Single-Time Activity

Q3.9

Two ways to update QBO Lists are:

   a. Before entering transactions

   b. While entering transactions

   c. After entering transactions

Q3.10

Two different ways to enter transaction information into QBO are:

   a. Onscreen forms

   b. Chart of Accounts

   c. Onscreen Journal

   d. QBO Lists

Q3.11

Which of the following QBO features can be used to save a transaction that will be re-used in the future?

   a. Saved transactions

   b. Create (+) icon

   c. Recurring transactions

   d. None of the above

Q3.12

Access the Recurring Transactions List from the:

   a. Navigation Bar

   b. Gear icon

   c. Create (+) icon

   d. None of the above

Q3.13

Recurring transactions can be classified as which of the following types?

   a. Scheduled

   b. Unscheduled

   c. Reminder

   d. All of the above

Q3.14

Which of the following two are correct when double-entry accounting using a journal is used to record what is exchanged in a transaction?

   a. The amount received is recorded with a credit

   b. The amount received is recorded with a debit

   c. The amount given is recorded with a debit

   d. The amount given is recorded with a credit

EXERCISES 3

We use the QBO Sample Company, Craig's Design and Landscaping Services **for practice throughout the exercises. The Sample Company will reset each time it is reopened. So make certain to allow enough time to complete exercises before closing the Sample Company. Otherwise, you will lose the work you have entered when you reopen the Sample Company.**

To access the QBO Sample Company, complete the following steps.

1. Open a web browser. (Note: Intuit recommends using Google Chrome.)
2. Go to https://qbo.intuit.com/redir/testdrive
3. Follow onscreen instructions for security verification.

Craig's Design and Landscaping Services should appear on your screen.

E3.1 Transaction Types

What is the Transaction Type for the following transactions?

Transaction Types

- **Banking**
- **Customers and Sales**
- **Vendors and Expenses**
- **Employees and Payroll**

Transaction Type

1. Transfers
2. Weekly Timesheet
3. Credit Card Credit
4. Purchase Order
5. Estimate
6. Bill
7. Invoice
8. Pay Bills
9. Receive Payment
10. Deposit
11. Sales Receipt
12. Credit Memo

E3.2 QBO Lists

Which QBO List would be used with the following transactions?

QBO Lists

- **Customers List**
- **Vendors List**
- **Employees List**
- **Recurring Transactions List**

QBO List

1. Weekly Payroll

2. Expense

3. Credit Card Credit

4. Invoice

5. Estimate

6. Bill

7. Purchase Order

8. Pay Bills

9. Receive Payment

10. Saved Deposit Transaction

11. Sales Receipt

12. Check

E3.3 Invoice and Transaction Journal

Using the QBO Sample Company, Craig's Design and Landscaping Company, complete the following.

1. Complete an Invoice.

    a. Select **Create (+) icon > Invoice**

    b. Select Customer: **Bill's Windsurf Shop**

    c. Select PRODUCT/SERVICE: **Design**

    d. Select QTY: **2**

    e. Select RATE: **75.00**

    f. The balance due for the invoice is $ _____

    g. Select **Save and Close**

2. View the Transaction Journal for the Invoice.

   a. From the Navigation Bar select **Sales**

   b. From the Sales Transactions List select the **Bill's Windsurf Shop Invoice** just entered.

   c. From the bottom of the Bill's Windsurf Shop Invoice select **More > Transaction Journal**

   d. What Account and Amount is Debited?

   e. What Account and Amount is Credited?

E3.4 Expense and Transaction Journal

Using the QBO Sample Company, Craig's Design and Landscaping Company, complete the following.

1. Complete an Expense.

   a. Select **Create (+) icon > Expense**

   b. Select Choose a payee: **Books by Bessie**

   c. Select Choose an account: **Visa**

   d. Select Payment method: **Visa**

   e. Enter AMOUNT: **50.00**

   f. What is the Total Amount for the Expense?

   g. Select **Save and Close**

2. View the Transaction Journal for the Expense.

   a. From the Navigation Bar select **Expenses**

   b. From the Expense Transactions List select the **Books by Bessie Expense** just entered

   c. From the bottom of the Books by Bessie Expense select **More > Transaction Journal**

   d. What Account and Amount is Debited?

   e. What Account and Amount is Credited?

E3.5 Check and Transaction Journal

Using the QBO Sample Company, Craig's Design and Landscaping Company, complete the following.

1. Complete an Check.

   a. Select **Create (+) icon > Check**

   b. Select Choose a payee: **Ellis Equipment Rental**

   c. Select Choose an account: **Checking**

   d. Select ACCOUNT: **Rent or Lease**

   e. Enter AMOUNT: **200.00**

   f. What is the Total for the Check?

   g. Select **Save and Close**

2. View the Transaction Journal for the Check.

   a. From the Navigation Bar select **Expenses**

   b. From the Expense Transactions List select the **Ellis Equipment Rental Check** just entered.

   c. From the bottom of the Ellis Equipment Rental Check select **More > Transaction Journal**

   d. What Account and Amount is Debited?

   e. What Account and Amount is Credited?

E3.6 Recurring Transactions

Using the QBO Sample Company, Craig's Design and Landscaping Company, complete the following.

1. Edit a Recurring Transaction.

   a. Select **Gear icon > Recurring Transactions**

   b. Select from the Recurring Transaction List **Telephone Bill > Edit**

   c. What is the amount for the Recurring Bill?

   d. Update the amount to **81.00**

   e. Select **Save Template**

2. Use a Recurring Transaction.

   a. From the Recurring Transaction List select **Monthly Building Lease Edit drop-down arrow > Use**

   b. Select **Save**

   c. From the bottom of the Hall Properties Building Lease Bill select **More > Transaction Journal**

d. What Account and Amount is Debited?

e. What Account and Amount is Credited?

E3.7 Debits and Credits

Complete the following statements.

- **Debits**
- **Credits**

1. Assets are increased by _____
2. Liabilities are increased by _____
3. Equity is increased by _____
4. Revenue (Income) is increased by _____
5. Expenses are increased by _____
6. Assets are decreased by _____
7. Liabilities are decreased by _____
8. Equity is decreased by _____
9. Revenue (Income) is decreased by _____
10. Expenses are decreased by _____

E3.8 Debits and Credits

The following accounts are from Craig's Design and Landscaping Services Chart of Accounts. For each account indicate:

- If the account is increased by a:
  - **Debit**
  - **Credit**
- Type of account as:
  - **Asset**
  - **Liability**
  - **Equity**
  - **Revenue (Income)**
  - **Expense**

		Debit/Credit	**Account Type**
1.	Design Income		
2.	Savings		
3.	Accounts Receivable (A/R)		
4.	Rent or Lease		
5.	Prepaid Expenses		
6.	Notes Payable		
7.	Inventory Asset		
8.	Opening Balance Equity		
9.	Utilities		
10.	Undeposited Funds		
11.	Accounts Payable (A/P)		
12.	MasterCard		
13.	Visa		
14.	Loan Payable		
15.	Sales of Product Income		
16.	Legal and Professional Fees		
17.	Advertising		
18.	Meals and Entertainment		
19.	Retained Earnings		
20.	Checking		
21.	Landscaping Services		
22.	Pest Control Services		
23.	Cost of Goods Sold		
24.	Automobile: Fuel		
25.	Bank Charges		
26.	Interest Earned		

PROJECT 3.1

Project 3.1 is a continuation of Project 2.1. You will use the QBO client company you created for Project 1.1 and updated in Project 2.1. Keep in mind the QBO company for Project 3.1 does not reset and carries your data forward, including any errors. So it is important to check and crosscheck your work to verify it is correct before clicking the Save button.

BACKSTORY

Mookie The Beagle™ Concierge, a concierge pet care service, provides convenient, high-quality pet care. CK, the founder of Mookie The Beagle Concierge, has requested for us to assist in identifying how QBO can be used to save time recording transactions for Mookie The Beagle Concierge.

Complete the following for Mookie The Beagle Concierge.

QBO SatNav

Project 3.1 focuses on the QBO Transactions, including Banking, Sales, and Expenses transactions shown in the following partial QBO SatNav.

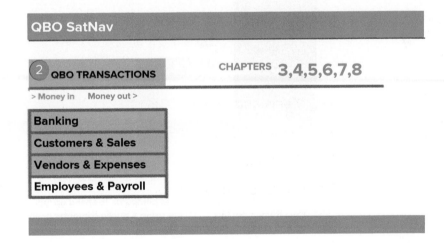

How to LOG into QBO+

To log into QBO, complete the following steps.

1. Using a web browser go to qbo.intuit.com
2. Enter **User ID** (the email address you used to set up your QBO Account)
3. Enter **Password** (the password you used to set up your QBO Account)
4. Select **Sign in**

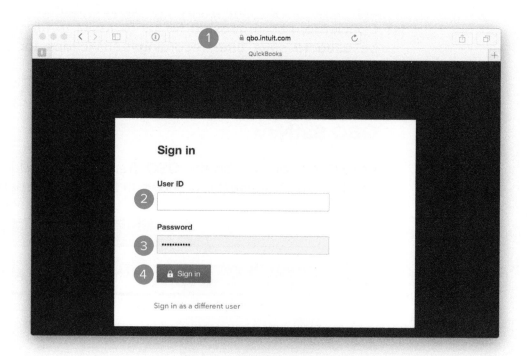

If you are <u>not</u> using a public or shared computer, **to speed up login, you can save your login to your desktop and select Remember Me. If you are using a public computer or shared computer, do not save to your desktop and unselect Remember Me.**

The new QBO company **we created in Project 1.1 will carry all work forward into future chapters. So it is important to check and crosscheck your work to verify it is correct before clicking the Save button. Any errors entered are carried forward in the QBO company you create for text projects.**

P3.1.1 QBO Lists

Since Mookie The Beagle Concierge does not have a complete list of customers and vendors to enter into a Customers List and Vendors List before we begin entering transactions, we will enter customer and vendor information while we enter transactions.

CK has information about the services Mookie The Beagle Concierge will be providing customers, so we can enter the following services into the QBO Products and Services List. None of the services are subject to sales tax.

To access the Products and Services List to enter the following, select **Gear** icon > **Products and Services List** > **New** > **Service.** Use the Income account: 4001 Sales.

Enter the following information.

CATEGORY	NAME	TYPE	SALES DESCRIPTION	SALES PRICE
Pet Care	Transport	Service	Pick up and drop off pet at various locations, such as pick up at doggie day care and take home if owner has to work late, 1 hour minimum	$30
Pet Care	Errand	Service	Pet Personal Shopper, 1 hour minimum	$20
Pet Care	Short Visit	Service	Pet Check to check on status of pet, let pet out, and short walk, 1 hour minimum	$20
Pet Care	Medium Visit	Service	2–4 hours	$15
Pet Care	Extended Visit	Service	4–8 hours	$20
Pet Care	Intensive	Service	Assume responsibility for pet care while owner is OOT or gone for extended period	$25
Pet Health Care	Vet Visit	Service	Take pet to vet	$60
Pet Health Care	Medium Visit	Service	1–4 hours with administration of medication, home cooked food, wound dressing changes and other pet healthcare services	$30
Pet Health Care	Extended	Service	4–8 hours providing pet healthcare services	$25
Pet Health Care	Intensive	Service	Assume responsibility for pet healthcare while owner is OOT or intensive healthcare responsibilities	$35

1. Export the Products and Services List to PDF.

P3.1.2 Deposit Transaction

To launch Mookie The Beagle Concierge, CK invests $5,000 of his personal savings. Record the transactions as follows.

1. Complete a Deposit.

    a. Select **Create (+) icon > Bank Deposit**

    b. Select **Checking**

    c. Select Date **01/01/2018**

    d. In Add New Deposits ACCOUNT select **Owner Contributions**

    e. Select PAYMENT METHOD **Check**

    f. Enter REF NO **5001**

    g. Enter AMOUNT **5000.00**

    h. What type of account is Owner Contributions?

    i. Select **Save and Close**

2. View the Transaction Journal for the Deposit.

    a. From the Navigation Bar select **Accounting**

    b. From the Chart of Accounts select **Checking > View Register > Deposit > Edit**

    c. From the bottom of the screen select **More > Transaction Journal**

    d. What Account and Amount is Debited?

    e. What Account and Amount is Credited?

P3.1.3 Expense Transaction Check

Mookie The Beagle Concierge hired Carole Design Media to promote the Mookie The Beagle Concierge launch using social media marketing. Mookie The Beagle Concierge paid the bill in full when received with its Visa credit card. The bill was for 20 hours of service at $50 per hour.

Enter the Expense Transaction as follows.

1. Complete an Expense.

   a. Select **Create (+) icon > Expense**

   b. Select +Add New Payee: **Carole Design Media > Vendor Type > Save**

   c. Select Date **01/05/2018**

   d. Select **Checking**

   e. Select Payment Method **Check**

   f. Enter ACCOUNT: **Advertising**

   g. Enter AMOUNT for **20 hours @ $50 per hour**

   h. What is the total amount paid to Carole Design Media?

   i. Select **Save and Close**

2. View the Transaction Journal for the Expense.

   a. From the Navigation Bar select **Expenses**

   b. From the Expenses Transactions List select the **Carole Design Media** just entered.

   c. From the bottom of the Carole Design Media Group Expense select **More > Transaction Journal**

   d. What Account and Amount is Debited?

   e. What Account and Amount is Credited?

P3.1.4 Expense Transaction Credit Card

Mookie The Beagle Concierge obtained liability insurance from Cyprus Insurance for $300 for 3 months of insurance coverage to protect Mookie The Beagle Concierge from the risk of legal liability for injury or damages of its business operations in providing pet care and pet health care.

1. Complete an Expense.

   a. Select **Create (+) icon > Expense**

   b. Add new payee: **Cyprus Insurance**

   c. Select Date **01/07/2018**

   d. Select: **VISA Credit Card**

   e. Select Payment Method **Credit Card**

    f. Enter ACCOUNT: **Insurance: Liability**

    g. Enter AMOUNT: **300.00**

    h. What is the total amount paid to Cyprus Insurance?

    i. Select **Save and Close**

2. View the Transaction Journal for the Expense.

    a. From the Navigation Bar select **Expenses**

    b. From the Expenses Transactions List select the **Cyprus Insurance** transaction just entered.

    c. From the bottom of the Cyprus Insurance Expense select **More > Transaction Journal**

    d. What Account and Amount is Debited?

    e. What Account and Amount is Credited?

P3.1.5 Invoice Transaction

Mookie The Beagle Concierge negotiated an agreement with the local veterinary program for student interns to work as subcontractors to provide Mookie The Beagle Concierge services as needed.

Mookie The Beagle Concierge's first customer, Mimi, used the Mookie The Beagle Concierge app to schedule care for her pet French Bulldog puppy, Bebe, whose paw was injured at doggie day care. Mimi was unable to leave work so she was relieved to be able to use the Mookie The Beagle Concierge app to schedule pet healthcare services.

    Pet Care: Transport 1 hour (pickup at doggie day care)

    Pet Healthcare: Vet Visit 2 hours

    Pet Healthcare: Intensive 6 hours

    Pet Care: Errand 1 hour to obtain pet supplies

    In order to avoid confusion in customer names, the customer name will be the pet name followed by the pet parent name.

1. Complete an Invoice.

    a. Select **Create (+) icon > Invoice**

    b. Add New Customer: **Bebe Mimi**

    c. Select Date **01/02/2018**

    d. Select PRODUCT/SERVICE: **Pet Care: Transport**

e. Select QTY: **1**

f. RATE and AMOUNT should autofill

g. Select PRODUCT/SERVICE: **Pet Healthcare: Vet Visit**

h. Select QTY: **2**

i. RATE and AMOUNT should autofill

j. Select PRODUCT/SERVICE: **Pet Healthcare: Intensive**

k. Select QTY: **6**

l. RATE and AMOUNT should autofill

m. Select PRODUCT/SERVICE: **Pet Care: Errand**

n. Select QTY: **1**

o. RATE and AMOUNT should autofill

p. What is the balance due for the invoice?

q. Select **Save and Close**

2. View the Transaction Journal for the Invoice.

a. From the Navigation Bar select **Sales**

b. From the Sales Transactions List select the **Bebe Invoice** just entered.

c. From the bottom of the Bebe Invoice select **More > Transaction Journal**

d. What Account and Amount is Debited?

e. What Accounts and Amounts are Credited?

P3.1.6 Invoice Transaction

Using the Mookie The Beagle Concierge app, Graziella requests pet care services for Bella, her pet Italian Greyhound, during an unexpected 2-day out of town business trip.

Services provided by Mookie The Beagle Concierge were as follows.
   Pet Care: Intensive (48 hours total)

1. Complete an Invoice.

a. Select **Create (+) icon > Invoice**

b. Add New Customer: **Bella Graziella**

c. Select Date **01/04/2018**

    d. Select PRODUCT/SERVICE: **Pet Care: Intensive**

    e. Select QTY: **48**

    f. RATE and AMOUNT should autofill

    g. What is the balance due for the invoice?

    h. Select **Save and Close**

2. View the Transaction Journal for the Invoice.

    a. From the Navigation Bar select **Sales**

    b. From the Sales Transactions List select the **Bella Invoice** just entered

    c. From the bottom of the Bella Invoice select **More > Transaction Journal**

    d. What Account and Amount is Debited?

    e. What Account and Amount is Credited?

P3.1.7 Recurring Transactions

Mookie The Beagle Concierge will have a recurring Subcontractor Expense to pay the vet program students who provide the pet care services. CK asks us to save it as a QBO Recurring Transaction for ease of future use.

Mary Dolan was the subcontractor who provided the pet care services for both Bebe and Bella. Mookie The Beagle Concierge will pay Mary Dolan $10 per hour for those services.

1. Create a Recurring Transaction.

    a. Select **Gear icon > Recurring Transactions > New**

    b. Select Transaction Type **Expense**

    c. Enter Template Name **Subcontractor Expense**

    d. Select Type **Unscheduled**

    e. Add New Payee Choose a Vendor **Mary Dolan**

    f. Select Account **Checking**

    g. Select ACCOUNT **Subcontractors Expense**

    h. Enter AMOUNT **based upon the number of hours Mary Dolan provided for Bebe and Bella**

    i. What is the amount for the Recurring Expense?

    j. Select **Save Template**

2. Use a Recurring Transaction.

    a. From the Recurring Transaction List select **Subcontractor Expense > Use**

    b. Select Payment Date **01/10/2018**

    c. Select Payment Method **Check**

    d. Select **Save**

    e. From the bottom of the Subcontractor Expense select **More > Transaction Journal**

    f. What Account and Amount is Debited?

    g. What Account and Amount is Credited?

P3.1.8 COA Debits and Credits

The following accounts are from Mookie The Beagle Concierge Chart of Accounts. For each account indicate:

- If the account is increased by a:
  - **Debit**
  - **Credit**
- Which type of account:
  - **Asset**
  - **Liability**
  - **Equity**
  - **Revenue (Income)**
  - **Expense**

Debit/Credit   **Account Type**

1. Checking

2. Accounts Receivable (A/R)

3. Inventory

4. Prepaid Expenses

5. Prepaid Expenses: Supplies

6. Prepaid Expenses: Insurance

7. Uncategorized Asset

Debit/Credit   Account Type

8. Undeposited Funds

9. Accounts Payable (A/P)

10. VISA Credit Card

11. Owner Contributions

12. Owner Distributions

13. Retained Earnings

14. Sales

15. Subcontractors

16. Supplies & Materials - COGS

17. Advertising

18. Bank Charges

19. Insurance: Liability

20. Interest Expense

21. Legal & Professional Fees

22. Meals and Entertainment

23. Office Expenses

24. Other General and Admin Expenses

25. Rent or Lease

26. Subcontractors

27. Supplies

28. Utilities

29. Interest Earned

30. Other Ordinary Income

www.my-quickbooksonline.com

Go to www.My-QuickBooksOnline.com for additional resources for you including QBO Help, QBO Videos and more.

Chapter 4

Banking

The QBO Banking function encompasses Checking accounts and Credit Cards. Adequate cash flows determine whether a company can pay its bills on time. So a business needs to track cash going into and cash going out of its bank accounts. QBO provides several banking features to make tracking cash flows easier for businesses.

Section 4.1

QBO SatNav

QBO SatNav is your satellite navigation for QuickBooks Online, assisting you in navigating QBO

Chapter 4 focuses on QBO banking, shown in the following QBO SatNav.

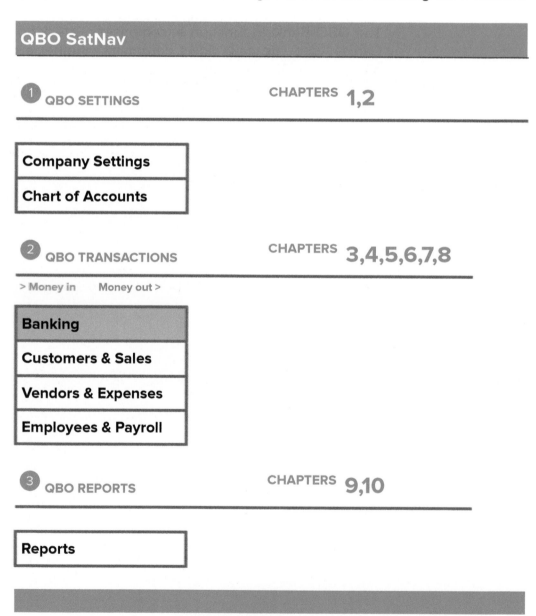

QBO SatNav

1 **QBO SETTINGS**   CHAPTERS **1,2**

| Company Settings |
| Chart of Accounts |

2 **QBO TRANSACTIONS**   CHAPTERS **3,4,5,6,7,8**

> Money in   Money out >

| **Banking** |
| Customers & Sales |
| Vendors & Expenses |
| Employees & Payroll |

3 **QBO REPORTS**   CHAPTERS **9,10**

| Reports |

Section 4.2

QBO LOGIN TO SAMPLE COMPANY

To log into the QBO Sample Company:

1. Open a web browser. (Note: Intuit recommends using Google Chrome.)

2. Go to https://qbo.intuit.com/redir/testdrive

3. Follow onscreen instructions for security verification.

Craig's Design and Landscaping Services should appear on your screen.

We use the Sample Company for practice throughout the chapter and exercises. The Sample Company will reset each time it is reopened. So make certain to allow enough time to complete all chapter activities before closing the Sample Company. Otherwise, you will lose the work you have entered when you reopen the Sample Company.

Section 4.3

CHECK REGISTER

The Check Register keeps track of all banking activities. Typically banking activities involve money going into and out of our company's bank accounts. Some of the banking activities that we can use QBO to record include the following:

- Bank deposits (money into bank accounts)
- Bank transfers (money into and out of bank accounts)
- Bank checks (money out of bank accounts)
- Enter and pay credit card charges (money out of bank accounts)

VIEW CHECK REGISTER

To view the Check Register:

1. From the Navigation Bar select **Accounting**
2. From the Chart of Accounts window select **View Register** for the Checking account
3. **Date** column lists the date of the transaction

④ **REF NO. TYPE** column lists the type of transaction

⑤ **PAYEE ACCOUNT** column lists the payee and the account used to record the transaction

⑥ **PAYMENT** column lists the amount of money out of the Checking account

⑦ **DEPOSIT** column lists the amount of money into the Checking account

⑧ ✓ column indicates whether the bank transaction is C (Cleared) R (Reconciled) or blank (uncleared, unreconciled)

⑨ **BALANCE** column displays the running balance for the Checking account, updating the balance with each new transaction in the account

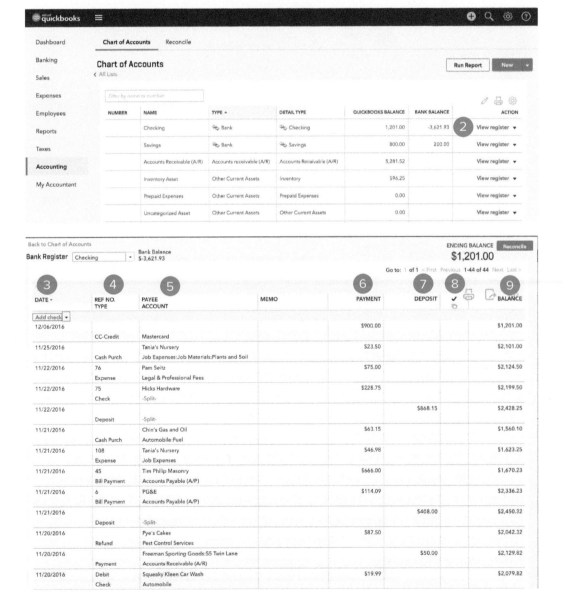

CHECK REGISTER DRILL DOWN

QBO offers a drill-down feature from its registers. For example, from the Check Register, we can double click on a transaction to drill down to the source document for that transaction.

To drill down on a transaction in the Check Register:

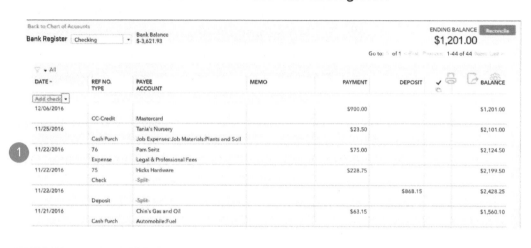

1. **Double-click** on a **transaction** appearing in the Check Register, such as the expense No 76 to Pam Seitz. (Note that the date on your screen for this transaction may differ from the date shown here.)

2. Select **Edit** to view the source document onscreen form used to enter Expense #76.

3. Notice that Checking is selected on the form, which is why the transaction appears in the Checking account Register.

4. If we wanted to make changes to the transaction we could make the changes and select Save. In this case select **Cancel.**

ADD NEW TRANSACTIONS FROM CHECK REGISTER

To add new transactions from the Check Register window:

1. Select the **drop-down arrow** by Add Check in the Check Register window

2. Select the new type of transaction to enter, such as **Deposit**

3. Enter the new transaction in the Check Register

4. Normally we would select Save, but in this case select **Cancel.** We will enter new transactions in the exercises at the end of the chapter.

Section 4.4

MONEY IN

Money coming into the business must be recorded in QBO so there is a record and paper trail. Three main ways to use QBO to record money coming in:

1. Customer Sales using Sales Receipts
2. Customer Sales using Invoices > Receive Payments
3. Bank Deposit

When using QBO, customer sales can be recorded using Sales Receipts or Invoices. These customer sales tasks, options 1 and 2 above, are covered in the next chapter. The current chapter focuses on other bank deposits besides customer sales recorded using the Bank Deposit onscreen form.

MONEY IN: BANK DEPOSITS NOT RELATED TO CUSTOMER SALES

If money coming in is not related to customer sales, then we can use a Bank Deposit form to record the money coming in. Examples of money coming in that is not a customer sales include:

- Investments from company owners
- Cash received from loans
- Interest earned
- Other income, such as rental income when our primary business is not a rental business

The above items can be recorded using the Bank Deposit form.

> Customer sales **should be only recorded using Sales Receipts or Invoices. The Bank Deposit form that is discussed next only should be used for bank deposits not related to customer sales. Recording customer sales is covered in the next chapter.**

MONEY IN: RECORDING BANK DEPOSITS

To record a bank deposit not related to a customer sale:

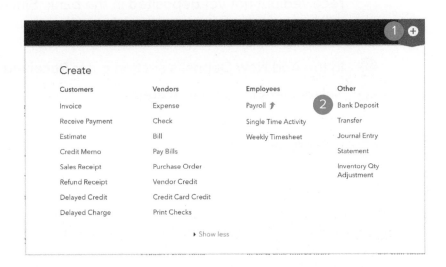

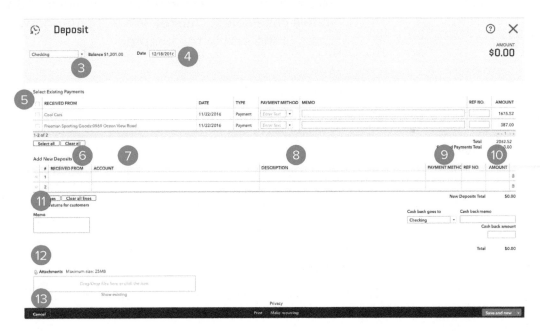

1   Select **Create (+)** icon

2   Under Other select **Bank Deposit**

3   Select **Bank** account

4   Enter **Date** of deposit

⑤ The Select Existing Payments section lists payments received from customers but not deposited yet. These customer payments listed are undeposited funds that have been recorded as received but not yet deposited in the bank. Since these amounts will be deposited at a later time, leave these customer payments **unchecked.** Customer payments are covered in the next chapter.

⑥ In the Add New Deposits section enter **Received From**

⑦ Select the appropriate **Account**

⑧ Enter a **Description** of the deposit

⑨ Enter **Payment Method**

⑩ Enter **Amount**

⑪ Enter **Memo**

⑫ Select **Attachments** to add a file or photo of any accompanying document

⑬ Normally we would select Save and New or Save and Close, but in this case select **Cancel.** We will enter new deposits in the exercises at the end of the chapter.

Section 4.5

MONEY OUT

A business needs to track all money out, including all cash paid out of the company's checking account. Examples of payments include purchases of inventory, office supplies, employee salaries, rent payments, and insurance payments.

Supporting documents (source documents) for payments include canceled checks, receipts, and paid invoices. These source documents provide proof that the transaction occurred; therefore, source documents should be kept on file for tax purposes. QBO permits us to add source documents as attachments.

Four main ways to use QBO to record money out include:

1. Expense
2. Check
3. Bill > Pay Bills
4. Purchase Order > Bill > Pay Bills

Recording money out using options 3 and 4 above are covered in Chapter 6. The current chapter focuses on using an Expense or Check onscreen form to record money out.

MONEY OUT: CHECK OR EXPENSE FORM

If money going out is paid at the time the product or service is received (instead of later) it can be recorded using the Expense or Check onscreen form. Examples of money going out that could be recorded using the Expense or Check onscreen form include:

- Rent expense
- Utilities expense
- Insurance expense
- Office supplies expense
- Services expense, such as accounting or legal services

If we are paying a bill immediately using cash, check or credit card, then we can use the Expenses onscreen form.

If we are paying a bill immediately with a check, then use the Check onscreen form to record the check.

Examples of money going out that should not be recorded using a Check or Expense onscreen form include:

- Paychecks to employees for wages and salaries
- Payroll taxes and liabilities
- Sales taxes
- Bills already entered using the Bills onscreen form

MONEY OUT: RECORDING EXPENSES

To record a bill payment that is made immediately, use the Expense form as follows:

1. Select **Create (+)** icon
2. Under Vendors select **Expense**
3. Select **Payee**
4. Select **Bank** or **Credit Card** account
5. Enter **Date**
6. Select **Payment method** from the drop-down list
7. Select the appropriate **Account**
8. Enter a **Description** of the transaction
9. Enter **Amount**
10. If the payment was billable to a specific customer, select **Billable**
11. Select **Tax** if applicable
12. If the payment was billable to a specific customer, select that customer in the **Customer** column from the Customer drop-down list
13. Enter **Ref no.** such as Check no. if applicable
14. Enter **Memo**
15. Select **Attachments** to add a file or photo of any accompanying source document, such as a bill
16. Normally we would select Save and New or Save and Close, but in this case select **Cancel.** We will enter new transactions in the exercises at the end of the chapter.

MONEY OUT: RECORDING CHECKS

To record a bill payment that is made immediately with a check:

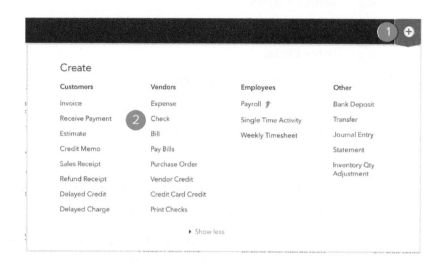

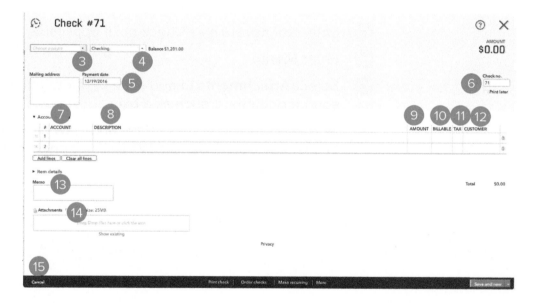

(1) Select **Create (+)** icon

(2) Under Vendors select **Check**

(3) Select **Payee**

(4) Select **Bank** account

(5) Enter **Date**

(6) Verify **Check no.** is correct

(7) Select the appropriate **Account**

(8) Enter a **Description** of the transaction

(9) Enter **Amount**

(10) If the payment was billable to a specific customer, select **Billable**

(11) Select **Tax** if applicable

(12) If the payment was billable to a specific customer, select that customer in the **Customer** column from the Customer drop-down list

(13) Enter **Memo**

(14) Select **Attachments** to add a file or photo of any accompanying source document, such as a bill

(15) Normally we would select Save and New or Save and Close, but in this case select **Cancel.** We will enter new checks in the exercises at the end of the chapter.

Section 4.6

CONNECTING BANK AND CREDIT CARDS WITH QBO

We can connect our bank accounts and our credit card accounts with QBO. This results in the expenses automatically being downloaded from the bank or credit card company into QBO. Then we can Add or Match the downloaded bank and credit card transactions with our QBO entries.

ADD BANK AND CREDIT CARD ACCOUNTS FOR AUTOMATIC DOWNLOADS

To connect a bank or credit card account to QBO for automatic downloads:

1   Select **Accounting** to add the bank or credit card account to the Chart of Accounts

2   Select **Banking** from the Navigation Bar

3   From the Bank and Credit Cards window select **Add Account.** Follow the onscreen instructions to complete adding the account.

After bank and credit card accounts are connected to QBO, then the transactions download automatically as shown above in the Bank and Credit Cards window. Each connected account appears in a card at the top of the Bank and Credit Cards window, showing the bank balance and your QBO balance. The number of unmatched transactions appears on the card. For example, there are 7 unmatched transactions in the MasterCard account.

ADD BANK AND CREDIT CARD TRANSACTIONS

To add a bank or credit card downloaded transaction that we have not entered in QBO yet:

1 Select **Update** to update the downloaded transactions

2 Select the appropriate **bank** or **credit card account** to display the downloaded transactions

3 Select **For Review** to view new downloaded transactions that have not been added or matched yet

4 Select the **transaction** to display the drop-down window

5 Select the appropriate **account** from the drop-down menu

6 Select **Add**

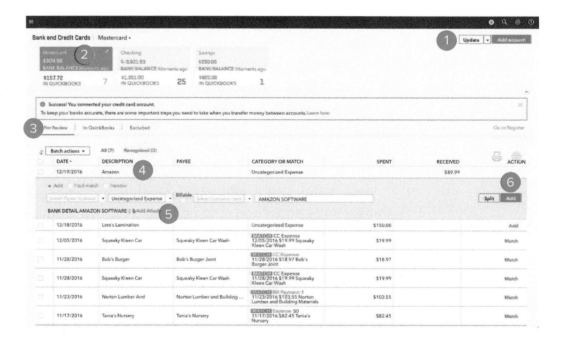

The transaction will disappear from our screen and be moved to the In QuickBooks tab on the Bank and Credit Cards window.

MATCH BANK AND CREDIT CARD TRANSACTIONS

To match a bank or credit card downloaded transaction to a transaction we have already entered in QBO:

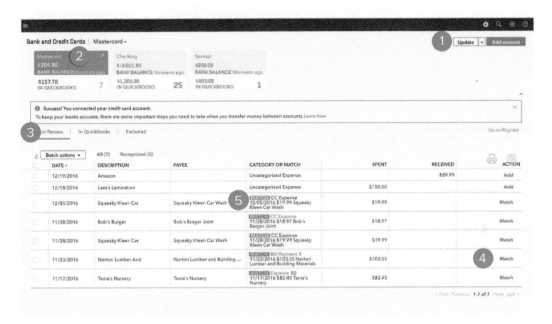

   1   Select **Update** to update the downloaded transactions

   2   Select the appropriate **bank** or **credit card account** to display the downloaded transactions

   3   Select **For Review** to view new downloaded transactions that have not been added or matched yet

   4   For the appropriate transaction displaying a green MATCH, select **Match** in the Action column

   5   If the transaction displays a gray MATCH, select the **transaction** to display the drop-down window and make the appropriate selections. Then select **Match.**

> Note that Matched downloaded bank and credit card transactions were entered into QBO before the transaction was downloaded from the bank or credit card company.

Section 4.7

ACCOUNTING ESSENTIALS

Banking for Business

Accounting Essentials summarize important foundational accounting knowledge you may find useful when using QBO

How many Checking accounts does a business need?

- A business needs at least one business checking account in the business name. A business should establish a business checking account completely separate from the owner's personal checking account.

- The company's business checking account should be used only for business transactions, such as business insurance and mortgage payments for the company's office building. An owner should maintain a completely separate checking account for personal transactions, such as mortgage payments for the owner's home.

- In addition, a business may need more than one business checking account with one business checking account for operations and a separate business checking account for payroll, for example.

What is a bank reconciliation?

- Typically once a month, the bank sends you a Checking account bank statement. The bank statement lists each deposit, check, and withdrawal from the account during the month. A bank reconciliation is the process of comparing, or reconciling, the bank statement with your accounting records for the Checking account.

What are the objectives of a bank reconciliation?

- The bank reconciliation has two objectives: (1) to detect errors and (2) to update your accounting records for unrecorded items listed on the bank statement (such as service charges). Reconciling bank statements is part of good internal controls that involve comparing the actual asset (what the bank says you have) with your accounting records (QBO Checking account).

Why are there differences between the bank statement and my accounting records?

- Differences between the balance the bank reports on the bank statement and the balance the business shows in its accounting records usually arise for two reasons:

    1. **Errors** (either the bank's errors or the company's errors).

    2. **Timing differences.** This occurs when the company records an amount before the bank does or the bank records an amount before the company does. For example, the company may record a deposit in its accounting records, but the bank does not record the deposit before the company's bank statement is prepared.

- Timing differences include:

    - Items the bank has not recorded yet, such as:

        o **Deposits in transit.** Deposits the company has recorded but the bank has not.

        o **Outstanding checks.** Checks the company has written and recorded but the bank has not recorded yet.

    - Items the company has not recorded yet, such as:

        o **Unrecorded charges.** Charges that the bank has recorded on the bank statement but the company has not recorded in its accounting records yet. Unrecorded charges include service charges, loan payments, automatic withdrawals, and ATM withdrawals.

        o **Interest earned on the account.** Interest the bank has recorded as earned but the company has not recorded yet.

PRACTICE QUIZ 4

Q4.1

The Checking Register:

   a. Tracks company purchase orders and vendors

   b. Tracks company invoices and customers

   c. Records all transactions affecting the Checking account

   d. Lists all accounts and their account numbers

Q4.2

In the Check Register, the term "split" indicates the payment is split between two or more:

   a. Purchase orders

   b. Invoices

   c. Checks

   d. Accounts

Q4.3

Deposits other than customer payments are entered using:

   a. Receive Payments

   b. Pay Bills

   c. Bank Deposit

   d. All of the above

Q4.4

If we are paying a bill immediately when we receive products or services we can use the Expenses onscreen form when we pay with:

   a. Cash

   b. Check

   c. Credit Card

   d. All of the above

Q4.5

Examples of money going out that can be recorded using the Expense or Check onscreen forms include all of the following except:

a. Rent expense

b. Payroll expense

c. Insurance expense

d. Legal Services expense

Q4.6

Examples of money going out that should not be recorded using a Check or Expense onscreen form include:

a. Paychecks to employees

b. Payroll taxes

c. Sales taxes

d. Bills already entered using the Bills onscreen form

e. All of the above

Q4.7

Ways to record money out using QBO include:

a. Enter Bill > Pay Bills

b. Check

c. Expense

d. Purchase Order > Bill > Pay Bills

e. All of the above

Q4.8

Ways to record money coming into QBO include:

a. Customer Sales using Sales Receipts

b. Customer Sales using Invoices and Receive Payments

c. Bank Deposit

d. All of the above

Q4.9

To record a bill payment that is made immediately with a credit card when the product or service is received, use the following onscreen form:

a. Bill

b. Check

c. Pay Bills

d. Expense

Q4.10

Identify the order in which the following steps should be completed in order to connect a bank or credit card account to QBO for automatic downloads.

a. Select Banking from the Navigation Bar

b. Select Add Account from the Bank and Credit Cards window.

c. Select Accounting to add the bank or credit card account to the Chart of Accounts

Q4.11

A company should always use the same checking account for business transactions and for the owner's personal transactions to streamline recording transactions.

a. True

b. False

Q4.12

Differences between the balance the bank reports on the bank statement and the balance the business shows in its accounting records usually arise for which of the following two reasons:

a. Adjusting entries have been made twice

b. Errors (bank errors or company errors)

c. Timing differences between when the bank records and when the company records an item

d. Closing entries have been made

Q4.13

One of the objectives of bank reconciliation is:

a. To update the bank's records

b. Update accounting records with unrecorded items

c. To record monthly adjusting entries

d. To update the Chart of Accounts

Q4.14

When reconciling a bank account, which of the following is not considered a timing difference (difference between the bank balance and the book balance)?

a. Interest earned

b. Deposits in transit

c. Errors

d. Unrecorded charges

EXERCISES 4

We use the QBO Sample Company, Craig's Design and Landscaping Services for practice throughout the exercises. The Sample Company will reset each time it is reopened. So make certain to allow enough time to complete exercises before closing the Sample Company. Otherwise, you will lose the work you have entered when you reopen the Sample Company.

To access the QBO Sample Company, complete the following steps.

1. Open a web browser. (Note: Intuit recommends using Google Chrome.)

2. Go to https://qbo.intuit.com/redir/testdrive

3. Follow onscreen instructions for security verification.

Craig's Design and Landscaping Services should appear on your screen.

E4.1 Check Register

Go to the QBO Sample Company, Craig's Design and Landscaping Services. Match the following items identified in the Check Register with the description of Check Register items.

Check Register Item Descriptions

a. Deposit column listing the amount of money going into the Checking account

b. ✓ column indicating whether the bank transaction is Cleared, Reconciled, or blank (uncleared and unreconciled)

c. Date column listing the date of the transaction

d. Ref No. and Type lists the type of transaction

e. Balance column displaying the running balance for the Checking account

f. Payee Account column listing the payee and the account used to record the transaction

g. Payment column listing the amount of money going out of the Checking account

Check Register Item

1. _____

2. _____

3. _____

4. _____

5. _____

6. _____

7. _____

E4.2 Check

Using the QBO Sample Company, Craig's Design and Landscaping Company, complete the following.

1. Complete a Check.

    a. Select **Create (+) icon > Check**

    b. Select Choose a payee: **Kookies by Kathy**

    c. Select Choose an account: **Checking**

    d. Select ACCOUNT: **Office Expense**

    e. Enter DESCRIPTION: **Office party**

    f. Enter AMOUNT: **33.00**

    g. What is the Total for the Check?

    h. Select **Save and Close**

2. View the Transaction Journal for the Check.

    a. From the Navigation Bar select **Expenses**

    b. From the Expense Transactions List select the **Kookies by Kathy Check** just entered.

    c. From the bottom of the Cookies by Kathy Check select **More > Transaction Journal.** Note: with some browsers you will need to scroll to view and select More to display the More menu.

    d. What Account and Amount is Debited?

    e. What Account and Amount is Credited?

E4.3 Check

Using the QBO Sample Company, Craig's Design and Landscaping Company, complete the following.

1. Complete a Check.

    a. Select **Create (+) icon > Check**

    b. Select Choose a payee: **Pye's Cakes**

    c. Select Choose an account: **Checking**

    d. Select ACCOUNT: **Office Expense**

    e. Enter DESCRIPTION: **Office party**

    f. Enter AMOUNT: **42.00**

g. What is the Total for the Check?

h. Select **Save and Close**

2. View the Transaction Journal for the Check.

a. From the Navigation Bar select **Expenses**

b. From the Expense Transactions List select the **Pye's Cakes Check** just entered.

c. From the bottom of the Cookies by Kathy Check select **More > Transaction Journal**

d. What Account and Amount is Debited?

e. What Account and Amount is Credited?

E4.4 Check

Using the QBO Sample Company, Craig's Design and Landscaping Company, complete the following.

1. Complete a Check.

a. Select **Create (+) icon > Check**

b. Select Choose a payee: **Computers by Jenni**

c. Select Choose an account: **Checking**

d. Select ACCOUNT: **Supplies**

e. Enter DESCRIPTION: **Computer cable replacement**

f. Enter AMOUNT: **12.00**

g. What is the Total for the Check?

h. Select **Save and Close**

2. View the Transaction Journal for the Check.

a. From the Navigation Bar select **Expenses**

b. From the Expense Transactions List select the **Computers by Jenni Check** just entered

c. From the bottom of the Cookies by Kathy Check select **More > Transaction Journal**

d. What Account and Amount is Debited?

e. What Account and Amount is Credited?

E4.5 Expense

Using the QBO Sample Company, Craig's Design and Landscaping Company, complete the following.

1. Complete an Expense.
   a. Select **Create (+) icon > Expense**
   b. Select Choose a payee: **Cal Telephone**
   c. Select Choose an account: **Mastercard**
   d. Select ACCOUNT: **Utilities: Telephone**
   e. Enter AMOUNT: **22.00**
   f. What is the Total for the Expense?
   g. Select **Save**
2. View the Transaction Journal for the Expense.
   a. From the bottom of the Cal Telephone Expense select **More > Transaction Journal**
   b. What Account and Amount is Debited?
   c. What Account and Amount is Credited?

E4.6 Expense

Using the QBO Sample Company, Craig's Design and Landscaping Company, complete the following.

1. Complete an Expense.
   a. Select **Create (+) icon > Expense**
   b. Select Choose a payee: **Lee Advertising**
   c. Select Choose an account: **Visa**
   d. Select ACCOUNT: **Advertising**
   e. Enter AMOUNT: **54.00**
   f. What is the Total for the Expense?
   g. Select **Save**

2. View the Transaction Journal for the Expense.

   a. From the bottom of the Lee Advertising Expense select **More > Transaction Journal**

   b. What Account and Amount is Debited?

   c. What Account and Amount is Credited?

E4.7 Bank Transfer

Using the QBO Sample Company, Craig's Design and Landscaping Company, complete the following.

1. Complete a Transfer.

   a. Select **Create (+) icon > Transfer**

   b. Select Transfer Funds From: **Savings**

   c. Select Transfer Funds To: **Checking**

   d. What is the Balance in the Savings Account?

   e. Enter Transfer Amount: **100.00**

   f. Select **Save and Close**

   g. What is the balance in the Savings account after transfer?

2. View the Transaction Journal for the Savings Account transfer.

   a. From the Navigation Bar select **Banking**

   b. Select the Savings card at the top of the Bank and Credit Cards screen

   c. Select **Go to Register**

   d. Select the entry in the Savings Account Register for the **$100 Transfer to Checking > Edit**

   e. From the bottom of the Transfer form select **More > Transaction Journal**

   f. What Account and Amount is Debited?

   g. What Account and Amount is Credited?

E4.8 Banking Update Add

Using the QBO Sample Company, Craig's Design and Landscaping Company, complete the following.

1. Complete a Bank Add.

   a. From the Navigation Bar select **Banking**

   b. Select the **Mastercard** card at the top of the Bank and Credit Cards screen

   c. Select Lara's Lamination to display a drop-down menu

   d. Change Uncategorized Expense to **Office Expenses**

   e. Select **Add**

   f. How many unmatched items appear on the Mastercard card at the top of the screen after selecting Add?

E4.9 Banking Update Match

This assignment is a continuation of E4.8

  Using the QBO Sample Company, Craig's Design and Landscaping Company, complete the following.

1. Complete a Bank Match.

   a. From the Navigation Bar select **Banking**

   b. Select the **Checking** card at the top of the Bank and Credit Cards screen

   c. For Hicks Hardware for $228.75 select **Match**

   d. How many open items appear on the Checking card at the top of the screen after selecting Match?

2. Complete a Bank Match.

   a. From the Bank and Credit Cards screen select the **Mastercard** card at the top of the screen

   b. For Bob's Burger for $18.97 select **Match**

   c. How many open items appear on the Mastercard card at the top of the screen after selecting Match?

3. Complete a Bank Match.

   a. From the Bank and Credit Cards screen select the **Savings** card at the top of the screen.

   b. For the $200 deposit select **Match**

   c. What appears for open items on the Savings card at the top of the screen after selecting Match?

PROJECT 4.1

Project 4.1 is a continuation of Project 3.1. You will use the QBO client company you created for Project 1.1 and updated in subsequent Projects 2.1 and 3.1. Keep in mind the QBO company for Project 4.1 does not reset and carries your data forward, including any errors. So it is important to check and crosscheck your work to verify it is correct before clicking the Save button.

BACKSTORY

Mookie The Beagle™ Concierge provides convenient, high-quality pet care on demand. CK, the founder of Mookie The Beagle Concierge, has requested for us to assist in identifying how QBO can be used for banking transactions.

Complete the following for Mookie The Beagle Concierge.

QBO SatNav

Project 4.1 focuses on QBO Transactions, specifically Banking Transactions as shown in the following partial QBO SatNav.

QBO SatNav

2 QBO TRANSACTIONS   CHAPTERS **3,4,5,6,7,8**

> Money in   Money out >

| Banking |
| Customers & Sales |
| Vendors & Expenses |
| Employees & Payroll |

How to LOG into QBO+

To log into QBO, complete the following steps.

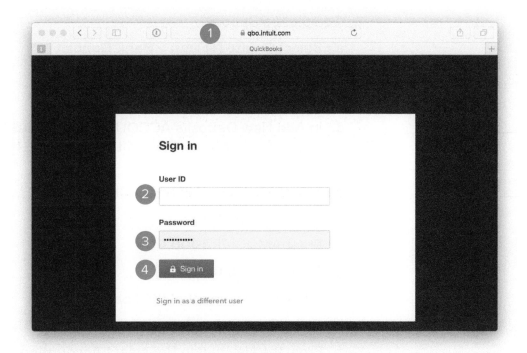

1. Using a web browser go to qbo.intuit.com
2. Enter **User ID** (the email address you used to set up your QBO Account)
3. Enter **Password** (the password you used to set up your QBO Account)
4. Select **Sign in**

If you are <u>not</u> using a public or shared computer, **to speed up login, you can save your login to your desktop and select Remember Me. If you are using a public computer or shared computer, do not save to your desktop and unselect Remember Me.**

The new QBO company **we created in Project 1 will carry all work forward into future chapters. So it is important to check and crosscheck your work to verify it is correct before clicking the Save button. Any errors entered are carried forward in the QBO company you create for text projects.**

P4.1.1 Bank Deposit

CK loans Mookie The Beagle Concierge $1,000 at 6% annual interest. Record the transaction as a loan payable as follows.

1. Complete a Deposit.

    a. Select **Create (+) icon > Bank Deposit**

    b. Select **Checking**

    c. Select Date **01/12/2018**

    d. In Add New Deposits ACCOUNT select **+ Add New > Loan Payable > Category Type: Other Current Liability > Detail Type: Loan Payable**

    e. Select PAYMENT METHOD **Check**

    f. Enter REF NO **5002**

    g. Enter AMOUNT **1000.00**

    h. Select **Save and Close**

    i. What is the amount of the Loan Payable?

2. View the Transaction Journal for the Deposit.

    a. From the Navigation Bar select **Accounting**

    b. From the Chart of Accounts select the **Loan Payable > View Register**

    c. From the Register, select the transaction just recorded

    d. From the bottom of the Loan Payable transaction select **More > Transaction Journal**

    e. What Account and Amount is Debited?

    f. What Account and Amount is Credited?

P4.1.2 Expense Credit Card

Complete the following to record Internet services that Mookie The Beagle Concierge incurred.

1. Complete an Expense paid with Credit Card.

    a. Select **Create (+) icon > Expense**

    b. Add New Payee: **Luminesse Link**

    c. Select Date **01/13/2018**

   d. Select Credit Card: **VISA Credit Card**

   e. Select Payment Method **Credit Card**

   f. Enter ACCOUNT: **Utilities**

   g. Enter DESCRIPTION: **Internet Service**

   h. Enter AMOUNT: **100.00**

   i. What is the total amount paid to **Luminesse Link**?

   j. Select **Save and leave the Expense displayed**

2. View the Transaction Journal for the Expense.

   a. From the displayed Expense select **More > Transaction Journal**

   b. What Account and Amount is Debited?

   c. What Account and Amount is Credited?

P4.1.3 Expense Credit Card

Complete the following to record telephone service that Mookie The Beagle Concierge incurred and paid by credit card.

1. Complete an Expense paid with Credit Card.

   a. Select **Create (+) icon > Expense**

   b. Select Payee: **Luminesse Link**

   c. Select Date **01/14/2018**

   d. Select Credit Card: **VISA Credit Card**

   e. Select Payment Method **Credit Card**

   f. Enter ACCOUNT: **Utilities**

   g. Enter DESCRIPTION: **Telephone Service**

   h. Enter AMOUNT: **72.00**

   i. What is the total amount paid to **Luminesse Link**?

   j. Select **Save and leave the Expense displayed**

2. View the Transaction Journal for the Expense.

   a. From the displayed Expense select **More > Transaction Journal**

   b. What Account and Amount is Debited?

   c. What Account and Amount is Credited?

P4.1.4 Check

Complete the following to record office expenses that Mookie The Beagle Concierge incurred and paid by check.

1. Complete a Check.

   a. Select **Create (+) icon > Check**

   b. Add New Payee: **Bichotte Supplies**

   c. Select Date **01/13/2018**

   d. Select Choose an account: **Checking**

   e. Select ACCOUNT: **Supplies Expense**

   f. Enter DESCRIPTION: **Office Supplies**

   g. Enter AMOUNT: **42.00**

   h. What is the Total for the Check?

   i. Select **Save and Close**

2. View the Transaction Journal for the Check.

   a. From the Navigation Bar select **Expenses**

   b. From the Expense Transactions List select the **Bichotte Supplies Check** just entered

   c. From the bottom of the **Bichotte Supplies** Check select **More > Transaction Journal**

   d. What Account and Amount is Debited?

   e. What Account and Amount is Credited?

P4.1.5 Check

Complete the following to record technology accessories that Mookie The Beagle Concierge paid by check to Maria Cecilia Associates, a firm that specializes in technology supplies and consulting services.

1. Complete a Check.

   a. Select **Create (+) icon > Check**

   b. Add New Payee: **Maria Cecilia Associates**

   c. Select Date **01/15/2018**

   d. Select Choose an account: **Checking**

    e. Select ACCOUNT: **Supplies Expense**

    f. Enter DESCRIPTION: **Technology supplies**

    g. Enter AMOUNT: **58.00**

    h. What is the Total for the Check?

    i. Select **Save and Close**

2. View the Transaction Journal for the Check.

    a. From the Navigation Bar select **Expenses**

    b. From the Expense Transactions List select the **Maria Cecilia Associates Check** just entered

    c. From the bottom of the Maria Cecilia Associates Check select **More > Transaction Journal**

    d. What Account and Amount is Debited?

    e. What Account and Amount is Credited?

P4.1.6 Match Bank Transactions Checking

Mookie The Beagle Concierge has the following bank transactions for the Checking account in spreadsheet form to upload. Mookie The Beagle Concierge has asked us to upload the bank transactions into QBO and then match them to transactions already entered in QBO.

CHECKING				
Type	**Trans Date**	**Post Date**	**Description**	**Amount**
Sale	01/15/2018	01/16/2018	MARIA CECILIA ASSOCIATES	−58.00
Sale	01/13/2018	01/14/2018	BICHOTTE SUPPLIES	−42.00
Deposit	01/12/2018	01/13/2018	CK WALKER	1000.00
Sale	01/10/2018	01/11/2018	MARY DOLAN	−580.00
Sale	01/05/2018	01/06/2018	CAROLE DESIGN MEDIA	−1000.00
Deposit	01/01/2018	01/02/2018	CK WALKER	5000.00

1. Using the file P4.1.6 Checking, upload Checking account Bank Transactions to QBO.

   a. From the Navigation Bar select **Banking > Upload Transactions Manually**

   b. Select **Browse** to select the file to upload > select File **QBO 1E P4.1.6 Checking.csv > Next**

   c. Select a QuickBooks account for the bank file you want to upload: **Checking**

   d. Select **Next**

   e. Select Your Statement Fields Date: **Column 2 Trans Date mm/dd/yyyy**

   f. Select Your Statement Fields Description: **Column 4 Description**

   g. Select Your Statement Fields Amount: **Column 5: Amount**

   h. Select CSV file has amounts in: 1 column: **both positive and negative numbers**

   i. Select **Next**

   j. Select CSV transactions for import: **Select All > Next**

   k. When asked Do you want to import now? Select **Yes**

   l. How many transactions were imported?

   m. Select **Let's go!**

2. Complete a Checking Account Bank Match.

   a. From the Navigation Bar select **Banking**

   b. How many open items appear on the Checking card at the top of the screen?

   c. Select **Match** for all Matching items

   d. Now what appears for open items on the Checking card at the top of the screen?

P4.1.7 Match Bank Transactions Credit Card

Mookie The Beagle Concierge has the following transactions for its VISA Credit Card in spreadsheet form to upload. Mookie The Beagle Concierge has asked us to upload the credit card transactions into QBO and then match them to transactions entered in QBO.

VISA CREDIT CARD				
Type	**Trans Date**	**Post Date**	**Description**	**Amount**
Sale	01/14/2018	01/14/2018	LUMINESSE LINK	−72.00
Sale	01/13/2018	01/13/2018	LUMINESSE LINK	−100.00
Deposit	01/07/2018	01/08/2018	CYPRUS INSURANCE	−300.00

1. Using the spreadsheet file P4.1.6, upload Checking account Bank Transactions to QBO.

    a. From the Navigation Bar select **Banking > File upload**

    b. Select **Browse** to select the file to upload > select File **QBO 1E P4.1.6 Credit Card.csv > Next**

    c. Select a QuickBooks account for the bank file you want to upload: **VISA Credit Card**

    d. Select **Next**

    e. Select Your Statement Fields Date: **Column 2 Trans Date mm/dd/yyyy**

    f. Select Your Statement Fields Description: **Column 4 Description**

    g. Select Your Statement Fields Amount: **Column 5: Amount**

    h. Select CSV file has amounts in: 1 column: **both positive and negative numbers**

    i. Select **Next**

    j. Select CSV transactions for import: **Select All > Next**

    k. When asked Do you want to import now? Select **Yes**

    l. How many transactions were imported?

    m. Select **Let's go!**

2. Complete a Checking Account Bank Match.

    a. From the Navigation Bar select **Banking**

    b. How many open items appear on the VISA Credit Card at the top of the screen?

    c. Select **Match** for all Matching items

    d. Now what appears for open items on the VISA Credit Card at the top of the screen?

www.my-quickbooksonline.com

Go to www.My-QuickBooksOnline.com for additional resources for you including QBO Help, QBO Videos, and more.

Chapter 5

Customers and Sales

Chapter 5 covers how to use QBO to record customer transactions, including sales to customers and collection of customer payments. Chapter 5 focuses on selling services, such as consulting services, to customers. A later chapter will focus on selling products, such as landscape fountains, to customers.

Section 5.1

QBO SatNav

QBO SatNav is your satellite navigation for QuickBooks Online, assisting you in navigating QBO

Chapter 5 focuses on QuickBooks Online Customers and Sales transactions, shown in the following QBO SatNav.

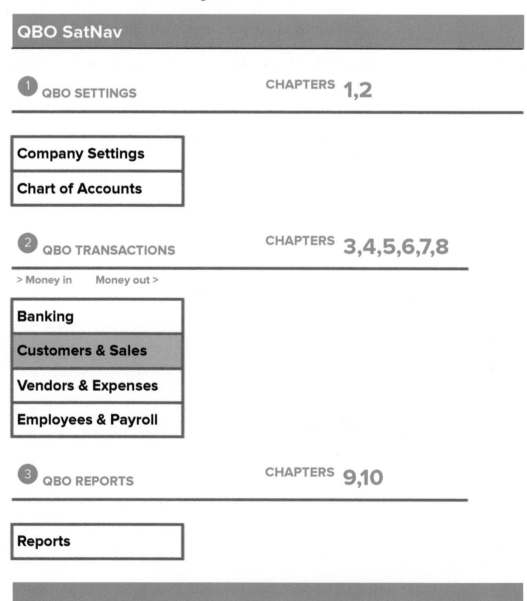

QBO SatNav	
1 QBO SETTINGS	CHAPTERS **1,2**
Company Settings	
Chart of Accounts	
2 QBO TRANSACTIONS	CHAPTERS **3,4,5,6,7,8**
> Money in Money out >	
Banking	
Customers & Sales	
Vendors & Expenses	
Employees & Payroll	
3 QBO REPORTS	CHAPTERS **9,10**
Reports	

Section 5.2

QBO LOGIN TO SAMPLE COMPANY

To log into the QBO Sample Company:

1. Open a web browser. (Note: Intuit recommends using Google Chrome.)
2. Go to https://qbo.intuit.com/redir/testdrive
3. Follow onscreen instructions for security verification.

Craig's Design and Landscaping Services should appear on your screen.

> **We use the Sample Company** for practice throughout the chapter and exercises. The Sample Company will reset each time it is reopened. So make certain to allow enough time to complete all chapter activities before closing the Sample Company. Otherwise, you will lose the work you have entered when you reopen the Sample Company.

Section 5.3

NAVIGATING SALES TRANSACTIONS

Two different ways to navigate entering sales transactions into QBO are:

1. Navigation Bar
2. Create (+) icon

NAVIGATION BAR

To use the Navigation Bar to enter sales transactions:

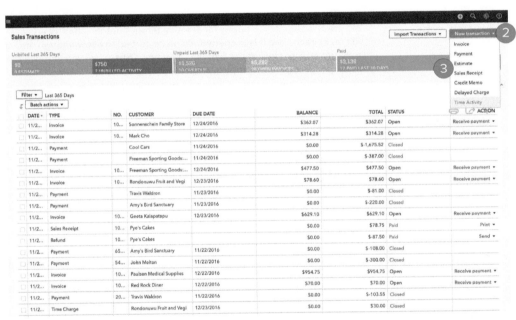

①   From the Navigation Bar select **Sales**

②   From the Sales Transactions window select the drop-down arrow for **New transaction**

③   Select the type of **new transaction** to enter and complete the onscreen form for the new transaction

CREATE (+) ICON

To use the Create (+) icon to enter sales transactions:

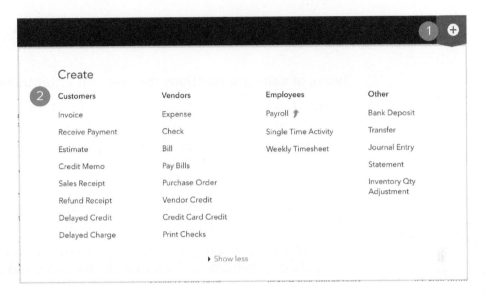

① Select **Create (+)** icon

② Select the **new transaction** from the Customers transactions shown

Section 5.4

TYPES OF SALES TRANSACTIONS

Types of sales transactions that we can enter using QBO include:

- **Invoice.** A sales transaction is recorded on an invoice when the product or service is provided to the customer, and the customer promises to pay later. These customer promises are called *accounts receivable*—amounts that we expect to *receive* in the future.
- **Receive Payment.** The Receive Payment onscreen form is used to record the transaction when the customer pays its account with cash, check, credit card, or online payment.
- **Estimate.** The Estimate onscreen form is used to record estimated costs of products and services to be provided to a customer in the future.
- **Credit Memo.** A Credit Memo onscreen form is used when we need to record a credit, or reduction, in the amount the customer is charged.
- **Sales Receipt.** A Sales Receipt is used to record a sales transaction when the customer pays at the time of sale when the product or service is provided to the customer.
- **Refund Receipt.** The Refund Receipt is used when we give the customer a refund.
- **Delayed Credit.** A Delayed Credit form is used to record a pending credit to a customer that will occur at a specified future date.
- **Delayed Charge.** A Delayed Charge form is used to record a pending charge to a customer that will occur at a specified future date.

When we enter the above customer transactions, we need to use two QBO Lists:

1. Customers List
2. Products and Services List

Section 5.5

CUSTOMERS LIST

Lists permit us to collect information about the customer, such as customer name, address, and contact information, so we can reuse that information without re-entering. The Customers List is a time-saving feature so that we don't have to continually re-enter the same customer information each time we enter a new transaction for the customer.

   Two ways that we can update the Customers List are:

1. *Before* entering transactions
2. *While* entering transactions

UPDATE CUSTOMERS LIST BEFORE ENTERING TRANSACTIONS

Before entering transactions, we can update the Customers List from the QBO Navigation Bar as follows.

1 From the Navigation Bar select **Sales**

2 Select **Customers**

3 To enter new customers select **New customer**

4 To edit an existing customer click on the customer on the list, then select **Edit**

5 To enter a new transaction for the customer select **New transaction** then select the appropriate transaction

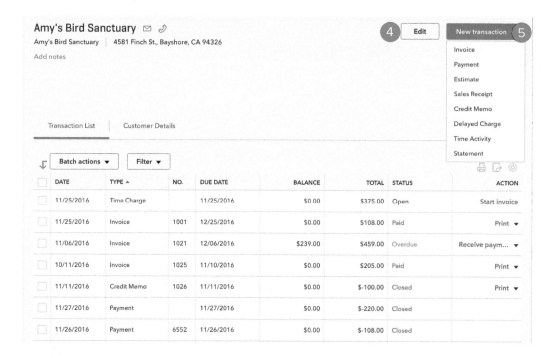

UPDATE CUSTOMERS LIST WHILE ENTERING TRANSACTIONS

While entering transactions, we can update the Customers List from the screen where we enter the transaction. If a customer has not been entered in the list and is needed for a sales transaction, we can add the customer as follows from an onscreen form.

New Customer

*Name

② [   ]

+ Details   ③ Save

———————— OR ————————

▼ Maybe later

[Connect your Gmail account   ]

After you connect, your contacts will appear in a holding list.
You can then choose which ones to add to QuickBooks.

① For example, to view an onscreen form such as an Invoice, select **Create (+)** icon > **Invoice.** Then select **Choose a customer drop-down arrow > + Add new.**

② For example, then we would enter **new customer information**

③ Normally, we would then select Save to save the new customer information. Then we would complete and save the Invoice. In this case, select **Cancel** to leave the Invoice window.

Section 5.6

PRODUCT AND SERVICES LIST

The Products and Services List collects information about the products and services sold to customers. The Products and Services List is a time-saving feature so that we don't have to continually re-enter the same products and services information each time we enter a new sales transaction.

QBO uses four types of products and services:

1. **Inventory.** Products that we sell for which we track quantities, such as fountains that we sell.

2. **Non-inventory.** Products that we sell but we do not need to track the quantity of the product. For example, bolts used in fountain installations.

3. **Service.** Services that we provide to customers, such as QBO consulting services.

4. **Bundle.** A bundle is a collection of products and services that we sell together as a bundle. For example, installation of a fountain might include hoses (products) and installation hours (services).

In this chapter we will focus on services and later we will focus on products. Two ways that we can update the Products and Services List are:

1. *Before* entering transactions
2. *While* entering transactions

UPDATE PRODUCTS AND SERVICES LIST
BEFORE ENTERING TRANSACTIONS

Before entering transactions, we can update the Products and Services List as follows.

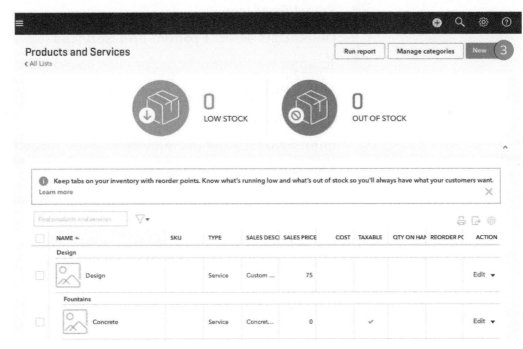

1. Select **Gear** icon

2. Under Lists select **Product and Services**

3. To enter new products or services select **New**

4. Select Product/Service Type: **Service**

5. Enter **Service Name**

6. Enter **SKU** or other product/service identification number

7. Attach a product/service **photo**

8. Select an appropriate product/service **Category**

9. Under Sales Information check **I will sell this product/service to my customers**

10. Enter **Description of the service**

11. Enter **Sales price/rate**

12. Select **Income account** for the Chart of Accounts

13. Select **Is Taxable**

14. Under Purchasing information uncheck **I purchase this product/service from a vendor**

15. Typically we would select Save and Close, but in this case select **Cancel**

UPDATE PRODUCTS AND SERVICES LIST WHILE ENTERING TRANSACTIONS

While entering transactions, we can update the Products and Service List on the go from the screen where we enter the sales transaction. If a product or service has not been entered in the list and is needed for a sales transaction, we can add the product or service as follows from an onscreen form.

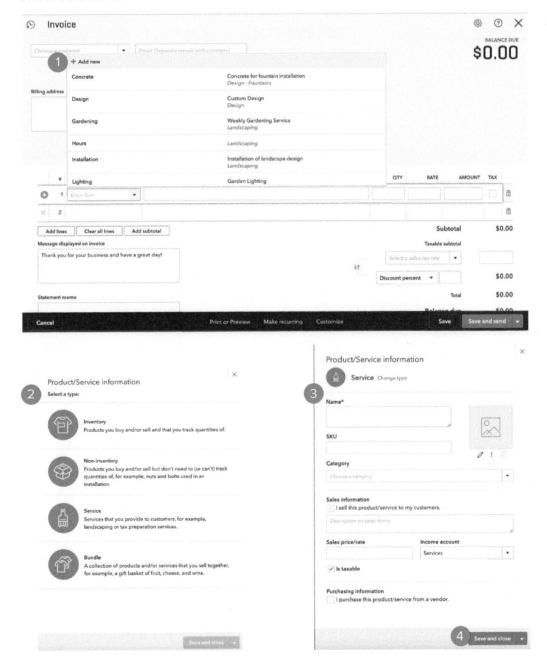

1. For example, to view an onscreen form such as an Invoice, select **Create (+)** icon > **Invoice.** Then select **Product/Service drop-down arrow > + Add new.**

2. Select **product/service type**

3. Enter **new product or service information**

4. Normally, we would then select Save and Close to save the new product/service information. Then we would complete and save the Invoice. In this case, select **Cancel** to leave the Invoice window.

Section 5.7

RECORDING SALES TRANSACTIONS

Two main ways to record customers and sales transactions using QBO are:

- Customer Sales using Sales Receipts
- Customer Sales using Invoices

If the customer pays on the spot when purchasing a product or service, then the Sales Receipt can be used to record the sale. If the customer pays later after receiving products or services, then an Invoice is used.

When using QBO, customer sales must be recorded using Sales Receipts or Invoices.

> Bank deposits other than customer sales are recorded using the Bank Deposit onscreen form. Bank deposits not related to customer sales was covered in Chapter 4.

Section 5.8

CUSTOMER SALES RECEIPTS

If the customer payment is *received at the same time* the product or service is provided, we record the customer sale using the Sales Receipt form.

The customer payment may consist of cash, check, or credit card.

When using Sales Receipts to record customer sales:

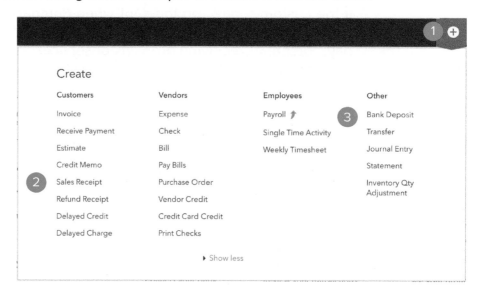

1. Select **Create (+)** icon

2. Create **Sales Receipt** to record the customer sale for product given and customer payment received in form of cash, check or credit card. If Undeposited Funds is selected on the Sales Receipt, then complete the next step.

3. Create **Bank Deposit** to move customer payment from Undeposited Funds account to the Checking account. This third step is only required if Undeposited Funds is selected on the Sales Receipt. Otherwise, this Step is not necessary.

CREATE SALES RECEIPT

To create a Sales Receipt for a customer sale:

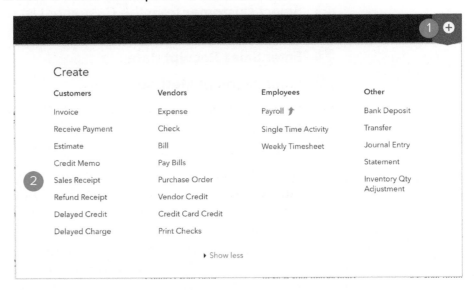

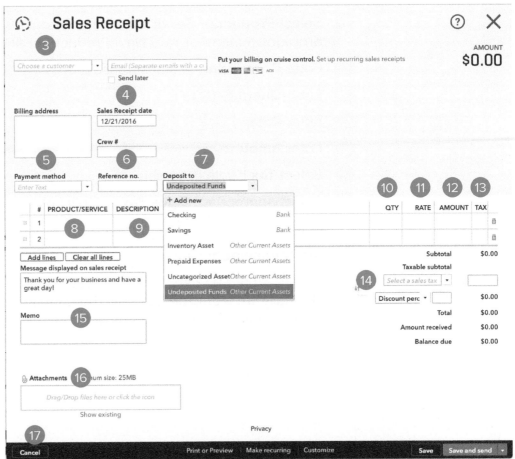

1. Select **Create (+)** icon

2. Select **Sales Receipt**

3. Select **Customer** from the Customer List drop-down menu or Add New Customer

4. Enter **Sales Receipt date**

5. Enter **Payment Method**

6. If Payment Method is Check, enter the customer check no. in **Reference no.**

7. Select **Deposit to** account from the drop-down list. If this deposit will be bundled with other deposits, then select Undeposited Funds and after completing the Sales Receipt, enter a Bank Deposit to move the funds from Undeposited Funds to the Checking account. If this deposit is not bundled with other deposits, then select the appropriate Checking account from the drop-down list. The funds are deposited directly to the Checking account selected and we do not enter a separate Bank Deposit.

8. Select **Product or Service** from the Product/Services List drop-down menu or Add New Product/Service

9. Enter **Description** of sales transaction

10. Enter **Quantity (QTY)**

11. Enter **Rate**

12. Enter **Amount**

13. Select **Tax** if sale is taxable

14. Select appropriate **Sales Tax** if applicable

15. Enter **Memo** describing the sale

16. Add **Attachments** such as source documents associated with the sales receipt

17. Normally we would select Save, but in this case select **Cancel.** We will enter new transactions in the exercises at the end of the chapter.

CREATE BANK DEPOSIT FOR UNDEPOSITED FUNDS FROM SALES RECEIPT

If Undeposited Funds was selected on the Sales Receipt, then we must create a Bank Deposit to transfer the funds from the Undeposited Funds account to the appropriate Checking account. Sometimes the Undeposited Funds is used on the Sales Receipt if the customer payment will be bundled with other customer payments when deposited. Then our totals will correspond to the bank deposit total shown by the bank.

> **If we selected Undeposited Funds on the sales receipt we *must* create a bank deposit to transfer the funds from the Undeposited Funds account to the appropriate bank account. Otherwise, the funds will remain in the Undeposited Funds account and we will not be able to use the funds to pay bills, for example.**

> **If we selected a specific bank account, such as Checking account, on the sales receipt we do *not* need to create a bank deposit. We have already deposited the customer payment in the bank account.**

To record a bank deposit related to a customer sale when Undeposited Funds was selected on the Sales Receipt:

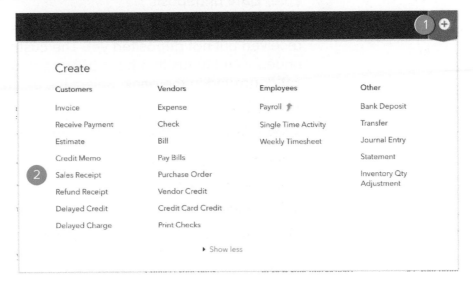

1. Select **Create (+)** icon

2. Under Other select **Bank Deposit**

3. Select **Bank** account

4. Enter **Date** of deposit

5. The Select Existing Payments section lists customer payments received but not deposited yet. The customer payments listed are undeposited funds that have been recorded as received but not yet deposited in the bank. Select the **existing customer payment** to deposit.

6. Enter appropriate **Payment Method**

7. If appropriate, enter **Memo** describing the deposit

8. Verify **Amount** is correct

9. Select **Attachments** to add a file or photo of any accompanying document

10. Normally we would select Save and New or Save and Close, but in this case select **Cancel.** We will enter new deposits in the exercises at the end of the chapter.

Section 5.9

CUSTOMER INVOICES

If products or services are given to the customer and the customer will pay later, then we use an Invoice instead of a Sales Receipt to record the sales transaction.

When using an Invoice to record customer sales:

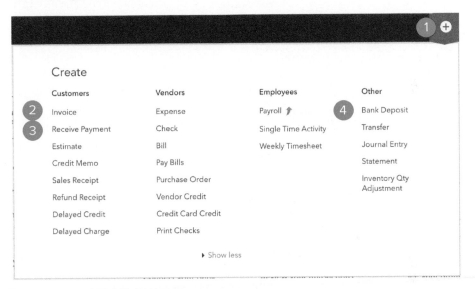

1. Select **Create (+)** icon

2. Create **Invoice** to record the customer sale for product or service given to customer

3. Create **Receive Payment** to record customer payment

4. Create **Bank Deposit** to move the customer payment from the Undeposited Funds account to the appropriate Checking account

CREATE INVOICE

An invoice is used to record sales when the customer will pay later. An invoice is a bill that contains detailed information about the products and services provided to a customer.

To create an Invoice:

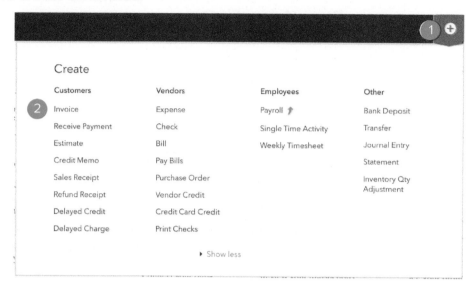

① Select **Create (+)** icon

② Select **Invoice**

③ Select **Customer** from the Customer List drop-down menu or Add New Customer

④ Enter **Terms**

⑤ Enter **Invoice Date**

⑥ Verify **Due Date**

⑦ Select **Product or Service** from the Product/Services List drop-down menu or Add New Product/Service

8　Enter **Description** of sales transaction

9　Enter Quantity **(QTY)**

10　Enter **Rate**

11　Enter **Amount**

12　Select **Tax** if sale is taxable

13　Select appropriate **Sales Tax** if applicable

14　Enter **Statement Memo** describing the sale

15　Add **Attachments** such as source documents associated with the sale

16　Normally we would select Save, but in this case select **Cancel.** We will enter new transactions in the exercises at the end of the chapter.

CREATE RECEIVE PAYMENT

Customers may pay in the following ways:

1. **Credit card,** such as Visa, MasterCard, American Express, or Diners Club over the phone, in person, or by mail. Using QuickBooks' Merchant Account Service, you can obtain online authorization and then download payments directly into QuickBooks.

2. **Online** by credit card or bank account transfer.

3. **Customer check** delivered either in person or by mail.

To record a customer's payment received to pay an outstanding invoice:

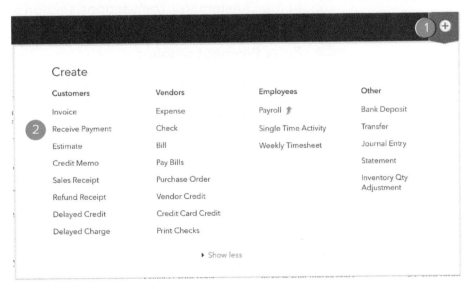

1. Select **Create (+)** icon

2. Select **Receive Payment**

3. Select **Customer** from the Customer List drop-down menu

4. Enter **Payment date**

5. Enter **Payment Method**

6. If Payment Method is Check, enter the customer check no. in **Reference no.**

7. Select **Deposit to** account from the drop-down list. If this deposit will be bundled with other deposits, then select Undeposited Funds and after completing the Invoice, enter a Bank Deposit to move the funds from Undeposited Funds to the Checking account. If this deposit is not bundled with other deposits, then select the appropriate Checking account from the drop-down list. The funds are deposited directly to the Checking account selected and we do not enter a separate Bank Deposit.

8. In the Outstanding Transactions section select the **Invoice** to which payment should be applied

9. Enter **Payment amount**

10. Normally we would select Save, but in this case select **Cancel**. We will enter new transactions in the exercises at the end of the chapter.

CREATE BANK DEPOSIT FOR UNDEPOSITED FUNDS FROM RECEIVE PAYMENT

If Undeposited Funds was selected on Receive Payment, then we must create a Bank Deposit to transfer the funds from the Undeposited Funds account to the appropriate Checking account. Sometimes Undeposited Funds is used on the Invoice if the customer payment will be bundled with other customer payments when deposited. Then our totals will correspond to the bank deposit total shown by the bank.

> If we selected Undeposited Funds on Receive Payment we *must* create a bank deposit to transfer the funds from the Undeposited Funds account to the appropriate bank account. Otherwise, the funds will remain in the Undeposited Funds account and we will not be able to use the funds to pay bills, for example.

> If we selected a specific bank account, such as Checking account, on Receive Payment we do *not* need to create a bank deposit. We have already deposited the customer payment in the bank account.

To record a bank deposit related to a customer sale when Undeposited Funds was selected on the Receive Payment:

1. Select **Create (+)** icon

2. Under Other select **Bank Deposit**

3. Select **Bank** account

4. Enter **Date** of deposit

5. The Select Existing Payments section lists customer payments received but not deposited yet. The customer payments listed are undeposited funds that have been recorded as received but not yet deposited in the bank. Select the **existing customer payment** to deposit.

6. Enter appropriate **Payment Method**

7. If appropriate, enter **Memo** describing the deposit

8. Verify **Amount** is correct

9. Select **Attachments** to add a file or photo of any accompanying document

10. Normally we would select Save and New or Save and Close, but in this case select **Cancel.** We will enter new deposits in the exercises at the end of the chapter.

Section 5.10

ACCOUNTING ESSENTIALS

Customer Sales and Accounts Receivable

Accounting Essentials summarize important foundational accounting knowledge you may find useful when using QBO

What are Accounts Receivable?

- Accounts Receivable are amounts that a customer owes our business. When our business makes a credit sale, our business provides goods and services to a customer in exchange for the customer's promise to pay later.

- When a credit sale is recorded on an invoice, QuickBooks Online records (debits) an Account Receivable—an amount to be received from the customer in the future. When the customer's payment is received, the Account Receivable account is reduced (credited).

- Sometimes the customer breaks the promise and does not pay. So a business should have a credit policy to ensure that credit is extended only to customers who are likely to keep their promise and pay their bills.

- After credit has been extended, a business needs to track accounts receivable to determine if accounts are being collected in a timely manner.

How can a business track accounts receivable to make certain customers are paying on time?

- Accounts Receivable Aging reports provide information about which customers owe our business money, how much the customer owes, and the age of the customer accounts receivable balances.

- In general, the older an account, the less likely the customer will pay the bill. So it is important to monitor the age of accounts receivable and take action to collect old accounts.

What happens if a customer does not pay the accounts receivable balance?

- When a customer does not pay the accounts receivable balance, then it is called a bad debt or uncollectible account.

- At the time a credit sale occurs, it is recorded as an increase to sales and an increase to accounts receivable.

- Occasionally a company is unable to collect a customer payment and must write off the customer's account as a bad debt or uncollectible account. When an account is uncollectible, the account receivable is written off or removed from the accounting records.

- There are two different methods that can be used to account for bad debts:

    1. **Direct write-off method.** This method records bad debt expense when it becomes apparent that the customer is not going to pay the amount due. If the direct write-off method is used, the customer's uncollectible account receivable is removed and bad debt expense is recorded at the time a specific customer's account becomes uncollectible. The direct write-off method is used for tax purposes.

    2. **Allowance method.** The allowance method estimates bad debt expense and establishes an allowance or reserve for uncollectible accounts. When using the allowance method, uncollectible accounts expense is estimated in advance of the write-off. The estimate can be calculated as a percentage of sales or as a percentage of accounts receivable. (For example, 2% of credit sales might be estimated to be uncollectible.) This method should be used if uncollectible accounts have a material effect on the company's financial statements used by investors and creditors.

- To record a bad debt, make a journal entry to remove the customer's account receivable (credit Accounts Receivable) and debit either Bad Debt Expense (direct write-off method) or the Allowance for Uncollectible Accounts (allowance method).

PRACTICE QUIZ 5

Q5.1

To enter sales transactions:

a. From the Navigation Bar select Transactions > Vendors
b. From the Navigation Bar select Sales > New Transaction
c. From the Gear icon, select Customers > New Transaction
d. From the Gear icon, select Sales Transactions

Q5.2

To enter a sales transaction with payment to be received later:

a. From the Navigation Bar select Vendors
b. From the Navigation Bar select Expenses
c. From the Create (+) icon, select Invoice
d. From the Gear icon, select Sales Transactions

Q5.3

When a customer pays cash at the time of sale, what do you record?

a. A sales receipt
b. An invoice
c. A purchase order
d. A thank you note

Q5.4

When a customer purchases products or services but does not pay at the point of sale, what do you record?

a. A sales receipt
b. An invoice
c. A purchase order
d. A reminder

Q5.5

We can update the Customers List at which of the following two points?

   a. Before entering transactions

   b. While entering transactions

   c. After entering transactions

Q5.6

Which of the following two are Customer and Sales transactions?

   a. Invoice

   b. Receive Payment

   c. Pay Bills

   d. Check

Q5.7

Types of products and services on the Products and Services List include which two of the following?

   a. Service

   b. Batch

   c. Inventory

   d. All of the above

Q5.8

Which of the following products and services types track quantities?

   a. Service items

   b. Inventory items

   c. Non-inventory items

   d. None of the above

Q5.9

When preparing a Sales Receipt, if we select Deposit to Undeposited Funds, then we must:

a. Create a Bank Deposit to move the customer payment from Undeposited Funds to the Checking account

b. No further action is required

c. Create a second Sales Receipt depositing the amount to the Checking account

d. Create a subsequent Invoice depositing the amount to the Checking account

Q5.10

When preparing a Sales Receipt, if we select Deposit to a Checking account, then we:

a. Create a Bank Deposit to move the customer payment from the Checking account to the Undeposited Funds account

b. No further action is required

c. Create a second Sales Receipt depositing the amount to the Checking account

d. Create a subsequent Invoice depositing the amount to the Checking account

Q5.11

Indicate the order in which the following onscreen customer and sales transaction forms typically should be prepared:

a. Invoice > Bank Deposit > Receive Payment

b. Invoice > Sales Receipt > Bank Deposit

c. Invoice > Receive Payment > Bank Deposit

d. None of the above

Q5.12

Which of the following reports provides information about which customers owe money to a business?

a. Profit & Loss

b. Balance Sheet

c. Statement of Cash Flows

d. Accounts Receivable Aging

Q5.13

Accounts Receivable (A/R) are:

a. Amounts totaling the net worth of a company

b. Amounts paid to owners

c. Amounts that customers owe your business

d. Amounts owed to others and are future obligations

Q5.14

When a sale is recorded on an invoice, QBO records a:

a. Debit (increase) to cash

b. Credit (increase) to owner's contribution

c. Debit (increase) to accounts receivable

d. Credit (increase) to accounts payable

EXERCISES 5

> We use the QBO Sample Company, Craig's Design and Landscaping Services **for practice throughout the exercises. The Sample Company will reset each time it is reopened. So make certain to allow enough time to complete exercises before closing the Sample Company. Otherwise, you will lose the work you have entered when you reopen the Sample Company.**

To access the QBO Sample Company, complete the following steps.

1 Open a web browser. (Note: Intuit recommends using Google Chrome.)

2 Go to the https://qbo.intuit.com/redir/testdrive

3 Follow onscreen instructions for security verification.

Craig's Design and Landscaping Services should appear on your screen.

E5.1 Customer and Sales Transactions

Match the following customer and sales transactions with the description of the transaction.

Customer and Sales Transaction Descriptions

a. The onscreen form used when we need to record a credit, or reduction, in the amount the customer is charged.

b. An onscreen form used to record a sales transaction when the customer pays at the time of sale when the product or service is provided to the customer.

c. A sales transaction recorded when the product or service is provided to the customer, and the customer promises to pay later.

d. This onscreen form is used when we give the customer a refund.

e. This onscreen form is used to record the transaction when the customer pays its account with cash, check, credit card, or online payment.

f. A form used to record a pending credit to a customer that will occur at a specified future date.

g. This onscreen form is used to record projected costs of products and services to be provided to a customer in the future.

h. An onscreen form used to record a pending charge to a customer that will occur at a specified future date.

Customer and Sales Transaction

1. Invoice

2. Receive Payment

3. Estimate

4. Credit Memo

5. Sales Receipt

6. Refund Receipt

7. Delayed Credit

8. Delayed Charge

E5.2 Customer Transaction: Create Sales Receipt

Using the QBO Sample Company, Craig's Design and Landscaping Services, complete the following.

1. Create Sales Receipt.

   a. From the Create (+) icon select **Sales Receipt**

   b. Select Choose a customer: **Sonnenschein Family Store**

   c. Select Payment method: **Check**

   d. Enter Reference no.: **2020**

   e. Select Deposit to: **Checking**

   f. Select PRODUCT/SERVICE: **Landscaping: Gardening (Weekly Gardening Service)**

   g. Enter QTY: **3**

   h. Enter RATE: **27.00**

   i. What is the Total for the Sales Receipt?

   j. Select **Save and Close**

2. View the Transaction Journal for the Sales Receipt.

   a. From the Navigation Bar select **Sales**

   b. From the Sales Transactions List select the **Sonnenschein Family Store Sales Receipt** just entered

   c. From the bottom of the Sonnenschein Family Store Sales Receipt select **More > Transaction Journal**

   d. What Account and Amount is Debited?

   e. What Account and Amount is Credited?

E5.3 Customer Transaction: Create Sales Receipt

Using the QBO Sample Company, Craig's Design and Landscaping Company, complete the following.

1. Create Sales Receipt.

   a. From the Create (+) icon select **Sales Receipt**

   b. Select Choose a customer: **Duke's Basketball Camp**

   c. Select Payment method: **Check**

   d. Enter Reference no.: **432**

   e. Select Deposit to: **Undeposited Funds**

    f. Select PRODUCT/SERVICE: **Landscaping: Maintenance & Repair**

    g. Enter QTY: **8**

    h. Enter RATE: **33.00**

    i. What is the Total for the Sales Receipt?

    j. Select **Save and Close**

2. View the Transaction Journal for the Sales Receipt.

    a. From the Navigation Bar select **Sales**

    b. From the Sales Transactions List select the **Duke's Basketball Camp Sales Receipt** just entered

    c. From the bottom of the Duke's Basketball Camp Sales Receipt select **More > Transaction Journal**

    d. What Account and Amount is Debited?

    e. What Account and Amount is Credited?

E5.4 Customer Transaction: Create Bank Deposit

This assignment is a continuation of E5.3

   Using the QBO Sample Company, Craig's Design and Landscaping Company, complete the following.

1. Create Bank Deposit.

    a. From the Create (+) icon select **Bank Deposit**

    b. Select account: **Checking**

    c. Select Existing Payments check **Duke's Basketball Camp**

    d. What is the Total for Selected Payments?

    e. Select **Save and Close**

2. View the Transaction Journal for the Deposit.

    a. From the Navigation Bar select **Accounting**

    b. From the Chart of Accounts select **View Register** for the Checking account

    c. Select **Duke's Basketball Camp deposit > Edit**

    d. From the bottom of the Duke's Basketball Camp Deposit select **More > Transaction Journal**

    e. What Account and Amount is Debited?

    f. What Account and Amount is Credited?

E5.5 Customer Transaction: Create Invoice

Using the QBO Sample Company, Craig's Design and Landscaping Company, complete the following.

1. Create Invoice.

   a. From the Create (+) icon select **Invoice**

   b. Select Choose a customer: **Sushi by Katsuyuki**

   c. Select PRODUCT/SERVICE: **Design**

   d. Enter QTY: **20**

   e. RATE should autofill

   f. What is the Total for the Invoice?

   g. Select **Save** and leave the Invoice displayed

2. View the Transaction Journal for the Invoice.

   a. From the bottom of the Sushi by Katsuyuki Invoice select **More > Transaction Journal**

   b. What Account and Amount is Debited?

   c. What Account and Amount is Credited?

E5.6 Customer Transaction: Receive Payment

This assignment is a continuation of E5.7

   Using the QBO Sample Company, Craig's Design and Landscaping Company, complete the following.

1. Create Receive Payment.

   a. From the Create (+) icon select **Receive Payment**

   b. Select Choose a customer: **Sushi by Katsuyuki**

   c. Select Payment method : **Check**

   d. Select Deposit to: **Undeposited Funds**

   e. Select Invoice just entered

   f. After selecting the Invoice what is the Amount Received displayed on the Invoice?

   g. Select **Save and Close**

2. View the Transaction Journal for Receive Payment.

   a. From the Navigation Bar select **Sales**

   b. From the Sales Transactions List select the **Sushi by Katsuyuki Receive Payment** just entered

   c. From the bottom of the Sushi by Katsuyuki Receive Payment select **More > Transaction Journal**

   d. What Account and Amount is Debited?

   e. What Account and Amount is Credited?

E5.7 Customer Transaction: Create Bank Deposit

This assignment is a continuation of E5.5 and E5.6

   Using the QBO Sample Company, Craig's Design and Landscaping Company, complete the following.

1. Create Bank Deposit.

   a. From the Create (+) icon select **Bank Deposit**

   b. Select account: **Checking**

   c. Select Existing Payments check **Sushi by Katsuyuki**

   d. What is the Total for Selected Payments?

   e. Select **Save and Close**

2. View the Transaction Journal for the Deposit.

   a. From the Navigation Bar select **Accounting**

   b. From the Chart of Accounts select **View Register** for the Checking account

   c. Select **Sushi by Katsuyuki deposit > Edit**

   d. From the bottom of the Sushi by Katsuyuki Deposit select **More > Transaction Journal**

   e. What Account and Amount is Debited?

   f. What Account and Amount is Credited?

E5.8 Customer Transaction: Create Invoice

Using the QBO Sample Company, Craig's Design and Landscaping Company, complete the following.

1. Create Invoice.

   a. From the Create (+) icon select **Invoice**

   b. Select Choose a customer: **Gevelber Photography**

   c. Select PRODUCT/SERVICE: **Design**

   d. Enter QTY: **10**

   e. RATE should autofill

   f. What is the Total for the Invoice?

   g. Select **Save** and leave the Invoice displayed

2. View the Transaction Journal for the Invoice.

   a. From the bottom of the Gevelber Photography Invoice select **More > Transaction Journal**

   b. What Account and Amount is Debited?

   c. What Account and Amount is Credited?

E5.9 Customer Transaction: Credit Memo

This assignment is a continuation of E5.8

Using the QBO Sample Company, Craig's Design and Landscaping Company, complete the following to credit Gevelber Photography for overcharging design by 2 hours.

1. Create Credit Memo.

   a. From the Create (+) icon select **Credit Memo**

   b. Select Choose a customer: **Gevelber Photography**

   c. Select PRODUCT/SERVICE: **Design**

   d. Enter QTY: **2**

   e. RATE should autofill

   f. What is the Total for the Credit Memo?

   g. Select **Save and Close**

2. View the Transaction Journal for Credit Memo.

   a. From the Navigation Bar select **Sales**

   b. From the Sales Transactions List select the **Gevelber Photography Credit Memo** just entered

   c. From the bottom of the Gevelber Photography Credit Memo select **More > Transaction Journal**

   d. What Account and Amount is Debited?

   e. What Account and Amount is Credited?

E5.10 Customer Transaction: Receive Payment

This assignment is a continuation of E5.8 and E5.9

Using the QBO Sample Company, Craig's Design and Landscaping Company, complete the following.

1. Create Receive Payment.

   a. From the Create (+) icon select **Receive Payment**

   b. Select Choose a customer: **Gevelber Photography**

   c. Select Payment method: **Visa**

   d. Select Deposit to: **Checking**

   e. Select Invoice entered

   f. What is the ORIGINAL AMOUNT of the Invoice?

   g. What is the OPEN BALANCE?

   h. After selecting the Invoice, what is the AMOUNT RECEIVED displayed on the Invoice?

   i. Select **Save and Close**

2. View the Transaction Journal for Receive Payment.

   a. From the Navigation Bar select **Sales**

   b. From the Sales Transactions List select the **Gevelber Photography Receive Payment** just entered

   c. From the bottom of the Gevelber Photography Receive Payment select **More > Transaction Journal**

   d. What Account and Amount is Debited?

   e. What Account and Amount is Credited?

PROJECT 5.1

Project 5.1 is a continuation of Project 4.1. You will use the QBO client company you created for Project 1.1 and updated in subsequent Projects 2.1 through 4.1. Keep in mind the QBO company for Project 5.1 does not reset and carries your data forward, including any errors. So it is important to check and crosscheck your work to verify it is correct before clicking the Save button.

BACKSTORY

Mookie The Beagle™ Concierge provides convenient, high-quality pet care on demand. CK processes customer and sales transactions using QBO and has asked for your assistance.

Complete the following for Mookie The Beagle Concierge.

QBO SatNav

Project 5.1 focuses on the QBO Transactions, specifically Sales Transactions as shown in the following partial QBO SatNav.

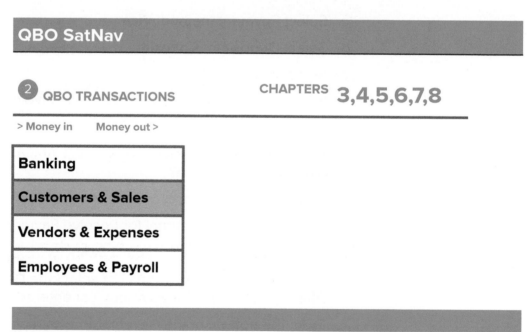

HOW TO LOG INTO QBO+

To log into QBO, complete the following steps.

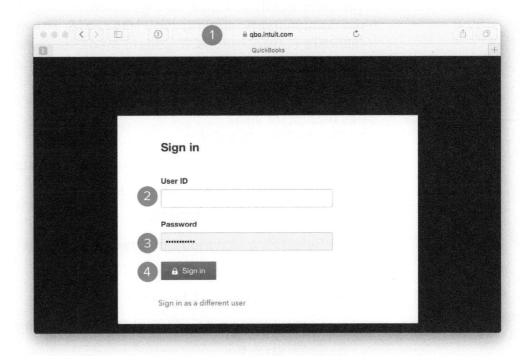

1. Using a web browser go to **qbo.intuit.com**

2. Enter **User ID** (the email address you used to set up your QBO Account)

3. Enter **Password** (the password you used to set up your QBO Account)

4. Select **Sign in**

If you are <u>not</u> using a public or shared computer, **to speed up login, you can save your login to your desktop and select Remember Me. If you are using a public computer or shared computer, do not save to your desktop and unselect Remember Me.**

The new QBO company **we created in Project 1 will carry all work forward into future chapters. So it is important to check and crosscheck your work to verify it is correct before clicking the Save button. Any errors entered are carried forward in the QBO company you create for text projects.**

P5.1.1 Sales Receipt

Julie used the Mookie The Beagle Concierge app to schedule pet care for Honey, her pet yellow Labrador Retriever. Each Friday from 1 pm until 9 pm Julie needs pet care for Honey when both Julie and her husband have commitments, starting on 01/12/2018. Honey's age requires extra healthcare considerations, including medications, so the nine hours each week will be billed at the Pet Health Care: Extended rate. Julie paid in advance by check for 8 weeks of pet care services.

Complete the following for Mookie The Beagle Concierge to record a sales receipt for Julie.

1. Create Sales Receipt.

    a. From the Create (+) icon select **Sales Receipt**

    b. Add New Customer: **Honey Julie**

    c. Select Date **01/12/2018**

    d. Select Payment method: **Check**

    e. Enter Reference no.: **3033**

    f. Select Deposit to: **Checking**

    g. Select PRODUCT/SERVICE: **Pet Health Care: Extended**

    h. Enter QTY: **64**

    i. Enter RATE: **25.00**

    j. What is the Total for the Sales Receipt?

    k. Select **Save and leave the Sales Receipt displayed**

2. View the Transaction Journal for the Sales Receipt.

    a. From the bottom of the Honey Julie Sales Receipt select **More > Transaction Journal**

    b. What Account and Amount is Debited?

    c. What Account and Amount is Credited?

P5.1.2 Sales Receipt

Julie used the Mookie The Beagle Concierge app to schedule pet care for Honey, her pet Labrador, for the last weekend in January (01/27/2018 2 pm until 01/28/2018 11 pm) while she and her husband attend Super Bowl celebrations. Honey requires extra health care considerations so the service will be billed at Pet Health Care: Intensive rates.

1. Create Sales Receipt.

   a. From the Create (+) icon select **Sales Receipt**

   b. Select Choose a customer: **Honey Julie**

   c. Select Date **01/27/2018**

   d. Select Payment method: **Check**

   e. Enter Reference no.: **3042**

   f. Select Deposit to: **Checking**

   g. Select PRODUCT/SERVICE: **Pet Health Care: Intensive**

   h. Enter QTY: **33**

   i. Enter RATE: **35.00**

   j. What is the Total for the Sales Receipt?

   k. Select **Save** and leave the Sales Receipt displayed

2. View the Transaction Journal for the Sales Receipt.

   a. From the bottom of the Honey Julie Sales Receipt select **More > Transaction Journal**

   b. What Account and Amount is Debited?

   c. What Account and Amount is Credited?

P5.1.3 Invoice

Asher has to work late to meet ridiculous deadlines on a major project, much later than the time that doggie day care closes for his pet Tibetan Spaniel puppy, Venus. So Asher uses the Mookie The Beagle Concierge app to schedule a pickup from doggie day care to take Venus home and pick up puppy food which Asher hasn't had time to buy because of his demanding work schedule.

So when Asher had to work late he was pleased to have the Mookie The Beagle Concierge app to schedule the following pet care services.

Pet Care: Transport 1 hour (pickup at doggie day care)

Pet Care: Errand 1 hour (minimum) to obtain puppy food

Pet Care: Medium 4 hours

Complete the following to record the invoice for services provided.

1. Complete an Invoice.

    a. Select **Create (+) icon > Invoice**

    b. Add New Customer: **Venus Asher**

    c. Select Date **01/18/2018**

    d. Select PRODUCT/SERVICE: **Pet Care: Transport**

    e. Select QTY: **1**

    f. RATE and AMOUNT should autofill.

    g. Select PRODUCT/SERVICE: **Pet Care: Errand**

    h. Select QTY: **1**

    i. RATE and AMOUNT should autofill.

    j. Select PRODUCT/SERVICE: **Pet Care: Medium**

    k. Select QTY: **4**

    l. RATE and AMOUNT should autofill.

    m. What is the balance due for the invoice?

    n. Select **Save** and leave the Invoice displayed

2. View the Transaction Journal for the Invoice.

    a. From the bottom of the Venus Asher Invoice select **More > Transaction Journal**

    b. What Account and Amount is Debited?

    c. What Accounts and Amounts are Credited?

P5.1.4 Invoice

Asher learns that he has to work late the next two nights, once again much later than the time that doggie day care closes for his pet Tibetan Spaniel, Venus. So Asher uses the Mookie The Beagle Concierge app to schedule a pickup from doggie day care to take Venus home and provide pet care services.

Asher uses the Mookie The Beagle Concierge app to schedule the following pet care services for the next two nights.

Pet Care: Transport 1 hour (pickup at doggie day care)

Pet Care: Medium 4 hours

Pet Care: Transport 1 hour (pickup at doggie day care)

Pet Care: Extended 5 hours

Complete the following to record the invoice for services provided.

1. Complete an Invoice.

    a. Select **Create (+) icon > Invoice**

    b. Select Customer: **Venus Asher**

    c. Select Date **01/19/2018**

    d. Select PRODUCT/SERVICE: **Pet Care: Transport**

    e. Select QTY: **1**

    f. RATE and AMOUNT should autofill.

    g. Select PRODUCT/SERVICE: **Pet Care: Medium**

    h. Select QTY: **4**

    i. RATE and AMOUNT should autofill.

    j. Select PRODUCT/SERVICE: **Pet Care: Transport**

    k. Select QTY: **1**

    l. RATE and AMOUNT should autofill.

    m. Select PRODUCT/SERVICE: **Pet Care: Extended**

    n. Select QTY: **5**

    o. RATE and AMOUNT should autofill.

    p. What is the balance due for the invoice?

    q. Select **Save** and leave the Invoice displayed

2. View the Transaction Journal for the Invoice.

    a. From the bottom of the Venus Asher Invoice select **More > Transaction Journal**

    b. What Account and Amount is Debited?

    c. What Account and Amount is Credited?

P5.1.5 Receive Payment

Record the payment that Mookie The Beagle Concierge receives from Mimi in payment for the prior invoice for services provided Bebe.

1. Create Receive Payment.

    a. From the Create (+) icon select **Receive Payment**

    b. Select Choose a customer: **Bebe Mimi**

    c. Select Date **01/13/2018**

    d. Select Payment method : **Check**

    e. Select Deposit to: **Checking**

    f. Select Invoice previously entered

    g. After selecting the Invoice what is the Amount Received displayed on the Invoice?

    h. Select **Save and Close**

2. View the Transaction Journal for Receive Payment.

    a. From the Navigation Bar select **Sales**

    b. From the Sales Transactions List select the **Bebe Mimi Receive Payment** just entered

    c. From the bottom of the Bebe Mimi Receive Payment select **More > Transaction Journal**

    d. What Account and Amount is Debited?

    e. What Account and Amount is Credited?

P5.1.6 Receive Payment

Record the payment that Mookie The Beagle Concierge receives from Graziella in payment for the prior invoice for services provided Bella.

1. Create Receive Payment.

    a. From the Create (+) icon select **Receive Payment**

    b. Select Choose a customer: **Bella Graziella**

    c. Select Date **01/13/2018**

    d. Select Payment method: **Check**

    e. Select Deposit to: **Checking**

    f. Select Invoice previously entered

    g. After selecting the Invoice what is the Amount Received displayed on the Invoice?

    h. Select **Save and Close**

2. View the Transaction Journal for Receive Payment.

    a. From the Navigation Bar select **Sales**

    b. From the Sales Transactions List select the **Bella Graziella Receive Payment** just entered

    c. From the bottom of the Bella Graziella Receive Payment select **More > Transaction Journal**

d. What Account and Amount is Debited?

e. What Account and Amount is Credited?

P5.1.7 Receive payment

Record the payment that Mookie The Beagle Concierge receives from Asher in payment for the invoice for the first services provided Venus.

1. Create Receive Payment.

    a. From the Create (+) icon select **Receive Payment**

    b. Select Choose a customer: **Venus Asher**

    c. Select Date **01/20/2018**

    d. Select Payment method : **Credit Card**

    e. Select Deposit to: **Undeposited Funds**

    f. Select Invoice dated 01/18/2018

    g. After selecting the Invoice what is the Amount Received displayed?

    h. Select **Save and Close**

2. View the Transaction Journal for Receive Payment.

    a. From the Navigation Bar select **Sales**

    b. From the Sales Transactions List select the **Venus Asher Receive Payment** just entered

    c. From the bottom of the Venus Asher Receive Payment select **More > Transaction Journal**

    d. What Account and Amount is Debited?

    e. What Account and Amount is Credited?

P5.1.8 Bank Deposit

Record the bank deposit for Mookie The Beagle Concierge related to the Asher payment for the first services provided Venus.

1. Create Bank Deposit.

    a. From the Create (+) icon select **Bank Deposit**

    b. Select account: **Checking**

    c. Select Date **01/22/2018**

    d. Select Existing Payments check **Venus Asher**

e. What is the Total for Selected Payments?

f. Select **Save and Close**

2. View the Transaction Journal for the Deposit

a. From the Navigation Bar select **Accounting**

b. From the Chart of Accounts select **View Register** for the Checking account

c. Select **Venus Asher deposit > Edit**

d. From the bottom of the Venus Asher Deposit select **More > Transaction Journal**

e. What Account and Amount is Debited?

f. What Account and Amount is Credited?

www.my-quickbooksonline.com

Go to www.My-QuickBooksOnline.com for additional resources for you including QBO Help, QBO Videos, and more.

Chapter 6

Vendors and Expenses

Chapter 6 covers on how we use QBO to record vendor transactions, such as purchasing from vendors, recording expenses, and paying bills.

Chapter 6 focuses on expenses and the purchasing of services, such as consulting services, from vendors. A later chapter will focus on purchasing products that are inventory for resale to customers, such as landscape fountains.

Section 6.1

QBO SatNav

QBO SatNav is your satellite navigation for QuickBooks Online, assisting you in navigating QBO

Chapter 6 focuses on QuickBooks Online Vendors and Expenses transactions, shown in the following QBO SatNav.

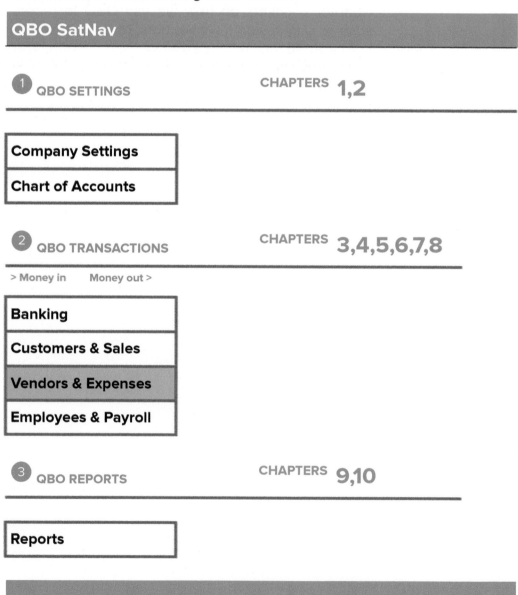

QBO SatNav

1 QBO SETTINGS   CHAPTERS **1,2**

| Company Settings |
| Chart of Accounts |

2 QBO TRANSACTIONS   CHAPTERS **3,4,5,6,7,8**

> Money in   Money out >

| Banking |
| Customers & Sales |
| **Vendors & Expenses** |
| Employees & Payroll |

3 QBO REPORTS   CHAPTERS **9,10**

| Reports |

Section 6.2

QBO LOGIN TO SAMPLE COMPANY

To log into the QBO Sample Company:

1. Open a web browser. (Note: Intuit recommends using Google Chrome.)
2. Go to the https://qbo.intuit.com/redir/testdrive
3. Follow onscreen instructions for security verification.

Craig's Design and Landscaping Services should appear on the screen.

> We use the Sample Company for practice throughout the chapter and exercises. The Sample Company will reset each time it is reopened. So make certain to allow enough time to complete all chapter activities before closing the Sample Company. Otherwise, you will lose the work you have entered when you reopen the Sample Company.

Section 6.3

NAVIGATING VENDOR AND EXPENSE TRANSACTIONS

Two different ways to navigate entering vendor and expense transactions into QBO are:

1. Navigation Bar
2. Create (+) icon

NAVIGATION BAR

To use the Navigation Bar to enter expense transactions:

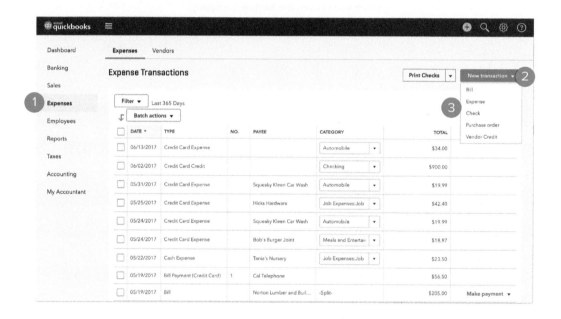

① From the Navigation Bar select **Expenses**

② From the Expense Transactions window select the drop-down arrow for **New transaction**

③ Select the type of **new transaction** to enter and complete the onscreen form for the new transaction

CREATE (+) ICON

To use the Create (+) icon to enter expense transactions:

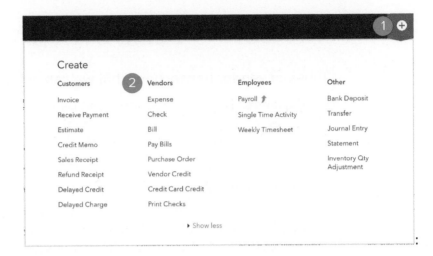

1. Select **Create (+)** icon
2. Select the **new transaction** from the Vendors transactions shown

Section 6.4

TYPES OF VENDOR TRANSACTIONS

Types of vendor transactions that we can enter using QBO include:

- **Expense.** The Expense form can be used to record expenses that we pay for at the time we receive the product or service. We can pay using cash, credit card, or check.
- **Check.** The Check form is used when we write a check. Using the Check form was covered in Chapter 4, Banking.
- **Bill.** The Bill onscreen form is used to record services, such as utilities or accounting services. We use the Bill forms to record bills we received and our obligation to pay the vendor later (accounts payable).
- **Pay Bills.** The Pay Bills form is used to select bills we want to pay.
- **Purchase Order.** A Purchase Order is used to track products ordered from vendors.
- **Vendor Credit.** The Vendor Credit form is used when a vendor gives us a refund or reduction in our bill in what we owe the vendor.
- **Credit Card Credit.** A Credit Card Credit form is used to record a credit, or reduction in charges by the vendor, to our credit card.

Section 6.5

VENDORS LIST

When we enter vendor transactions, we typically need to use the Vendors Lists. The Vendors List permits us to store information about the vendor, such as vendor name, address, and contact information, so we can reuse that information without re-entering. Vendor information is entered in the Vendor List and then QBO automatically transfers the vendor information to the appropriate forms, such as checks. This feature enables us to enter vendor information only once in QBO instead of entering the vendor information each time a form is prepared.

QBO considers a vendor to be any individual or organization that provides products or services to our company. QBO considers all of the following to be vendors:

- Suppliers from whom we buy inventory or supplies
- Service companies that provide services to our company, such as cleaning services or landscaping services
- Financial institutions, such as banks, that provide financial services including checking accounts and loans
- Tax agencies such as the IRS (the IRS is considered a vendor because we pay taxes to the IRS)
- Utility and telephone companies

Two ways that we can update the Vendors List are:

1. *Before* entering transactions
2. *While* entering transactions

UPDATE VENDORS LIST BEFORE ENTERING TRANSACTIONS

Before entering transactions, we can update the Vendors List from the QBO Navigation Bar as follows.

1. From the Navigation Bar select **Expenses**
2. Select **Vendors**
3. To enter new vendors select **New vendor**

④ To edit an existing vendor click on the vendor on the list, then select **Edit**

⑤ To enter a new transaction for the vendor select **New transaction** then select the appropriate transaction

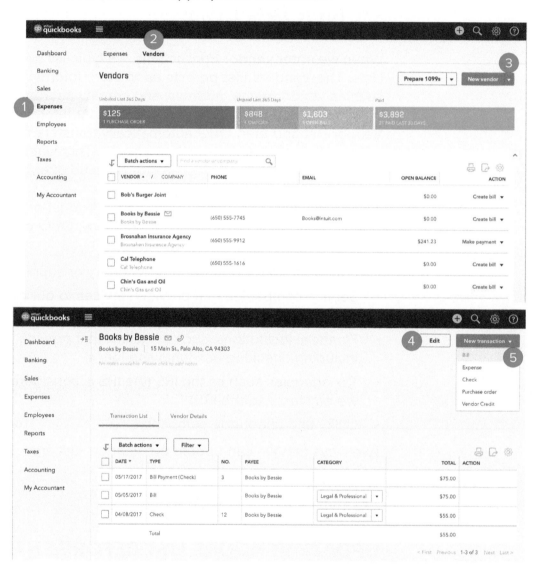

UPDATE VENDORS LIST WHILE ENTERING TRANSACTIONS

While entering transactions, we can update the Vendors List from the screen where we enter the transaction. If a vendor has not been entered in the list and is needed for a vendor transaction, we can add the vendor as follows from an onscreen form.

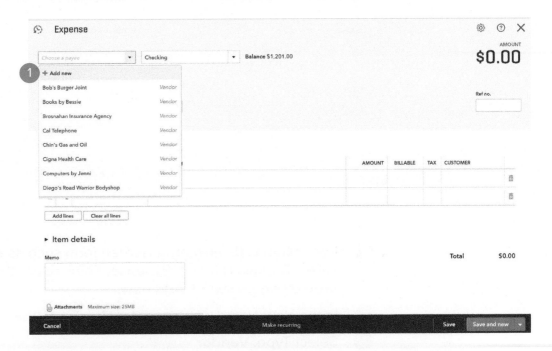

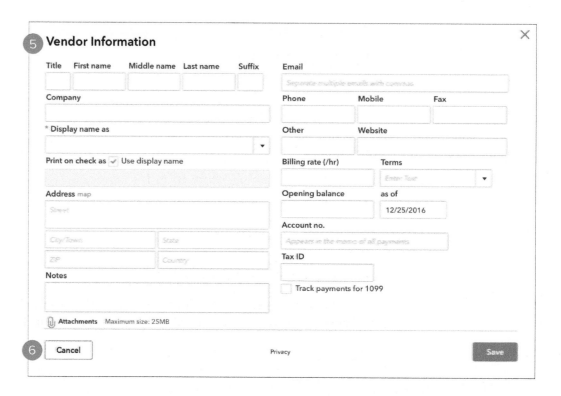

1. For example, to view an onscreen form such as an Expense, select **Create (+)** icon > **Expense.** Then select **Choose a payee drop-down arrow > + Add new.**

2. In the New Name window enter **Vendor Name**

3. Select Type: **Vendor**

4. Select **Details**

5. Enter **Vendor Information**

6. Normally we would select Save, but in this case select **Cancel.** We will enter new transactions in the exercises at the end of the chapter.

Section 6.6

RECORDING VENDOR TRANSACTIONS

Ways to record vendors and expenses transactions using QBO include using the following QBO onscreen forms in the following sequences:

- Expense
- Check
- Bill > Pay Bills
- Purchase Order > Bill > Pay Bills

This chapter focuses on the first three listed above. Purchase Orders followed by entering bills and paying bills is covered in the next chapter.

Section 6.7

EXPENSE

If our payment is *made at the same time* we make a purchase, then we can record the purchase using the Expense form.

Our payment may consist of cash, check, or credit card.

> If our purchase is paid by check at the same time as the purchase **then we can use the Expense form or the Check form to record the transaction.**

When using the Expense form to record a vendor transaction:

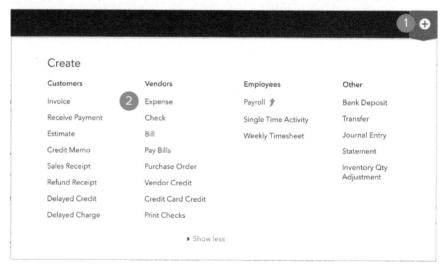

1. Select **Create (+)** icon

2. Create **Expense** to record the vendor transaction when we make payment at the same time the expense is incurred and we use cash, check or credit card.

3. Select **Vendor** from the Choose a payee drop-down menu or Add New

4. Using the drop-down menu by Checking, select the **Payment Account**

5. Enter **Payment Date**

6. Enter **Payment Method** by selecting from the drop-down menu either Cash, Check, or appropriate Credit Card

7. If Payment Method is Check, enter the check no. in **Reference no.**

8. In the Account Information section select appropriate **Account** from the drop-down menu of accounts

9. Enter **Description** of the transaction

10. Enter **Amount** of the expense

11. Select **Billable** if the expense is billable to a specific customer

12. Select **Tax** if purchase is taxable

13. If billable, select appropriate **Customer** associated with the expense

14. An expense transaction can be entered using **Item details** instead of Account details, which is covered in Chapter 7

15. Enter **Memo** describing the transaction

16. Add **Attachments** such as source documents associated with the transaction

17. Normally we would select Save, but in this case select **Cancel.** We will enter new transactions in the exercises at the end of the chapter.

Section 6.8

CHECK

If our payment is *made by check at the same time* we make a purchase, then we can record the purchase using the Check form.

When using a Check form to record the vendor transaction:

1   Select **Create (+)** icon

2   Select **Check**

3. Select **Vendor** from the Choose a payee drop-down menu or Add New

4. Select appropriate **Bank** account such as **Checking**

5. **Mailing address** should autofill when the vendor is selected

6. Enter **Payment Date**

7. If Payment Method is Check, enter the check no. in **Reference no.**

8. In the Account Information section select appropriate **Account** from the drop-down menu of accounts

9. Enter **Description** of the transaction

10. Enter **Amount** of the expense

11. Select **Billable** if the expense is billable to a specific customer

12. Select **Tax** if taxable

13. If billable, select appropriate **Customer** associated with the expense

14. A vendor transaction can be entered using **Item details** instead of Account details, which is covered in Chapter 7

15. Enter **Memo** describing the transaction

16. Add **Attachments** such as source documents associated with the transaction

17. If a printed check is required, select **Print check** and complete the onscreen instructions

18. Normally we would select Save, but in this case select **Cancel.** We will enter new transactions in the exercises at the end of the chapter.

Section 6.9

BILL > PAY BILLS

If we receive a bill and plan to pay the bill later, then we use the Bill form to enter the bill and the Pay Bills form when paying the bill at a later time. When using the Bill and Pay Bills forms to record the vendor transactions:

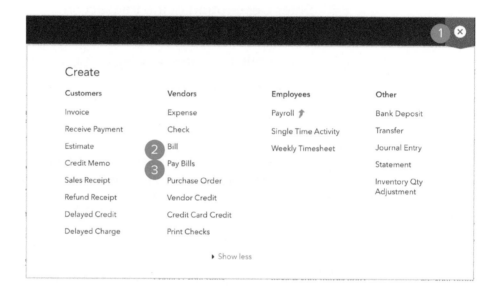

① Select **Create (+)** icon

② Select **Bill** to enter a bill when received

③ Select **Pay Bills** to select bills when we are ready to pay

CREATE BILL

When we receive a bill from a vendor, we use the Bill form to create the bill in QBO. The Bill form is used to record vendor transactions that we will pay later. Examples of bills include rent, utilities expense, insurance expense, and accounting and professional services. QBO will record an obligation (accounts payable liability) to pay the bill later.

> If we are paying the bill at the time we receive the product or service, **then we can use the Expense form to record the transaction.**

To record a bill received that we will pay later:

1. Select **Create (+)** icon

2. Select **Bill**

3. Select **Vendor** from the Vendor List drop-down menu

4. **Mailing address** should auto-fill when vendor is selected

5. Select **Terms** if this does not auto-fill correctly when vendor is selected

6. Select **Bill date**

7. Select **Due date** if different than the due date automatically displayed

8. Enter **Bill no.**

9. Select **Account** from the drop-down list for the Chart of Accounts

10. Enter **Description** of the transaction

⑪ Enter **Amount** of the transaction

⑫ Select **Billable** if the item is billable to a specific customer

⑬ Select **Tax** if taxable

⑭ If billable, select appropriate **Customer** associated with the item

⑮ A vendor transaction can be entered using **Item details** instead of Account details, which is covered in Chapter 7

⑯ Enter **Memo** describing the transaction

⑰ Add **Attachments** such as source documents associated with the transaction

⑱ Normally we would select Save, but in this case select **Cancel.** We will enter new transactions in the exercises at the end of the chapter.

CREATE PAY BILLS

Use Pay Bills to select the bills that are due and we are ready to pay. If the bill has been entered using the Bill form, then the bill will automatically appear in the Pay Bills List.

> **Use Pay Bills only for bills that have been entered using the Bill forms.**

> **If the Expense form or the Check form** was used to enter the vendor transaction, we do not use the Pay Bills form for that item, since it has already been paid at the time the Expense or Check was entered into QBO.

To use Pay Bills to select bills to pay:

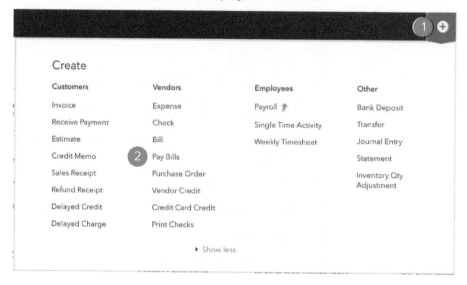

1. Select **Create (+)** icon

2. Select **Pay Bills**

3. Select **Payment account** drop-down menu

4. From the Payment account drop-down menu select the **Payment account**

5. Enter **Payment Date**

6. Select **bills to pay**

7. Enter **Payment**

8. Normally we would select Save and New or Save and Close, but in this case select **Cancel.** We will enter new transactions in the exercises at the end of the chapter.

Section 6.10

ACCOUNTING ESSENTIALS

Vendors Transactions, Accounts Payable, and 1099s

Accounting Essentials summarize important foundational accounting knowledge you may find useful when using QBO

What are Accounts Payable?

- Accounts payable consists of amounts that our business is obligated to pay in the future. When our business makes purchases on credit, our business is promising to pay that amount in the future.

- When a purchase is made and recorded as a bill, accounts payable is increased by a credit. When the bill is paid, the accounts payable is decreased by a debit.

How can a business track accounts payables to make certain it's paying on time?

- Accounts Payable reports provide information to track amounts we owe vendors. An Accounts Payable Aging report summarizes accounts payable balances by the age of the account. This report helps us to track how much we owe vendors and when amounts are due, including the age of past due bills.

What is a 1099 and when does my company need to prepare 1099s?

- IRS Form 1099 must be completed for sole proprietorships and partnerships to which we paid $600 or more for services in a year. The vendor's Tax ID No. is required to complete the 1099. QBO can assist in tracking amounts and preparing 1099s for appropriate vendors. To learn more about preparing 1099s, see www.irs.gov.

PRACTICE QUIZ 6

Q6.1

To enter Vendor and Expense transactions:

   a. From the Navigation Bar select Customers

   b. From the Navigation Bar select Expenses > New Transaction

   c. From the Gear icon, select Vendors

   d. From the Gear icon, select Expense Transactions

Q6.2

To enter an Expense transaction:

   a. From the Navigation Bar select Customers

   b. From the Navigation Bar select Sales

   c. From the Create (+) icon, select Expense

   d. From the Gear icon, select Vendor transactions

Q6.3

QuickBooks considers all of the following to be vendors except:

   a. Utility companies

   b. Suppliers of inventory and supplies

   c. Tax agencies such as the IRS

   d. Customers purchasing products

Q6.4

Which of the following is not a vendor transaction?

   a. Order products

   b. Pay bills

   c. Make deposits

   d. Receive bills

Q6.5

We can update the Vendors List at which of the following two points?

   a. Before entering transactions

   b. While entering transactions

   c. After entering transactions

Q6.6

Which of the following two are Vendor and Expense transactions?

   a. Invoice

   b. Receive Payment

   c. Pay Bills

   d. Check

Q6.7

The Bills form is used to record which one of the following transactions?

   a. Owners investment

   b. Services received but not yet paid

   c. Products sold to customers

   d. Cash purchases of supplies

Q6.8

Which of the following activities, and the QBO form used to record it, is incorrect?

   a. Receive products, Customers List

   b. Order products, Purchase Order

   c. Record inventory information, Products and Services List

   d. Sell products and bill customers, Invoice

Q6.9

Indicate the order in which the following onscreen vendor and expense transaction forms typically should be prepared.

a. Expense > Pay Bills

b. Check > Pay Bills

c. Bill > Pay Bills

d. Invoice > Pay Bills

Q6.10

Which of the following reports tracks past due bills and bills that are due shortly?

a. Profit & Loss

b. Statement of Cash Flows

c. Accounts Payable Aging

d. Accounts Receivable Aging

Q6.11

Accounts Payable (A/P) are:

a. Amounts totaling the net worth of a company

b. Amounts paid to owners

c. Amounts that customers owe your business

d. Amounts owed to others and are future obligations

Q6.12

When a purchase is made recorded as a bill, QBO records a:

a. Debit (increase) to cash

b. Credit (increase) to owner's contribution

c. Debit (increase) to accounts receivable

d. Credit (increase) to accounts payable

EXERCISES 6

We use the QBO Sample Company, Craig's Design and Landscaping Services for practice throughout the exercises. The Sample Company will reset each time it is reopened. So make certain to allow enough time to complete exercises before closing the Sample Company. Otherwise, you will lose the work you have entered when you reopen the Sample Company.

To access the QBO Sample Company, complete the following steps.

1. Open a web browser. (Note: Intuit recommends using Google Chrome.)
2. Go to the https://qbo.intuit.com/redir/testdrive
3. Follow onscreen instructions for security verification.

Craig's Design and Landscaping Services should appear on your screen.

E6.1 Vendor and Expense Transactions

Match the following vendor and expense transactions with the description of the transaction.

Vendor and Expense Transaction Descriptions

  a. The form used to select bills we want to pay.

  b. The form used to order and track products from vendors.

  c. The onscreen form used to record products and services that we pay for at the time we receive the product or service with cash, credit card, or check.

  d. The form used when a vendor gives us a refund or reduction in our bill in what we owe the vendor.

  e. This form can be used when we pay for products and services at the time of purchase, but cannot be used when we pay with cash or credit card.

  f. A form used to record a reduction in charges by the vendor to our credit card.

  g. The onscreen form used to record bills we received and our obligation to pay the vendor later (accounts payable).

Vendor and Expense Transaction

1. Expense
2. Check

3. Bill

4. Pay Bills

5. Purchase Order

6. Vendor Credit

7. Credit Card Credit

E6.2 Vendor Transaction: Expense Credit Card

Using the QBO Sample Company, Craig's Design and Landscaping Services, complete the following.

1. Create Expense paid with Credit Card.

   a. From the Create (+) icon select **Expense**

   b. Select Choose a vendor: **Squeaky Kleen Car Wash**

   c. Select Choose an account: **Mastercard**

   d. Select Payment method.: **Mastercard**

   e. Select Account Details: ACCOUNT: **Automobile**

   f. Enter AMOUNT: **19.99**

   g. What is the Total for the Expense?

   h. Select **Save** and leave the Expense displayed on your screen

2. View the Transaction Journal for the Expense.

   a. From the bottom of the Squeaky Kleen Car Wash Expense select **More > Transaction Journal**

   b. What Account and Amount is Debited?

   c. What Account and Amount is Credited?

E6.3 Vendor Transaction: Expense Credit Card

Using the QBO Sample Company, Craig's Design and Landscaping Company, complete the following.

1. Create Expense paid with Credit Card.

   a. From the Create (+) icon select **Expense**

   b. Select Choose a payee: **Chin's Gas and Oil**

   c. Select Choose an account: **Visa**

   d. Select Payment method: **Visa**

   e. Select Account Details: ACCOUNT: **Automobile: Fuel**

    f. Enter AMOUNT: **116.00**

    g. What is the Total for the Expense?

    h. Select **Save** and leave the Expense displayed on the screen

2. View the Transaction Journal for the Expense.

    a. From the bottom of the Chin's Gas and Oil Expense select **More > Transaction Journal**

    b. What Account and Amount is Debited?

    c. What Account and Amount is Credited?

E6.4 Vendor Transaction: Credit Card Credit

This assignment is a continuation of E6.3

    Go to the QBO Sample Company, Craig's Design and Landscaping Company. Craig's was overcharged by Chin's Gas and Oil. Complete the following to record the Credit Card Credit when Chin's reversed the overcharge.

1. Create Credit Card Credit.

    a. From the Create (+) icon select **Credit Card Credit**

    b. Select Choose a payee: **Chin's Gas and Oil**

    c. Select Choose an account: **Visa**

    d. Select Account Details: ACCOUNT: **Automobile: Fuel**

    e. Enter AMOUNT: **58.00**

    f. What is the Total for the Credit Card Credit?

    g. Select **Save and Close**

2. View the Transaction Journal for the Credit Card Credit.

    a. From the Navigation Bar select **Expenses**

    b. From the Expense Transactions List select **Chin's Gas and Oil Credit Card Credit**

    c. From the bottom of the Chin's Gas and Oil Credit Card Credit select **More > Transaction Journal**

    d. What Account and Amount is Debited?

    e. What Account and Amount is Credited?

E6.5 Vendor Transaction: Expense Checking

Using the QBO Sample Company, Craig's Design and Landscaping Company, complete the following to record an Expense paid from the Checking account.

1. Create Expense paid from the Checking account.

    a. From the Create (+) icon select **Expense**

    b. Select Choose a payee: **Tania's Nursery**

    c. Select Choose an account: **Checking**

    d. Select Payment method: **Check**

    e. Enter Reference no.: **77**

    f. Select Account Details Line 1: ACCOUNT: **Job Expenses**

    g. Enter AMOUNT: **42.00**

    h. Select Account Details Line 2: ACCOUNT: **Supplies**

    i. Enter AMOUNT: **33.00**

    j. What is the Total for the Expense?

    k. Select **Save** and leave the Expense displayed

2. View the Transaction Journal for the Expense.

    a. From the bottom of the Tania's Nursery Expense select **More > Transaction Journal**

    b. What Account and Amount is Debited?

    c. What Account and Amount is Debited?

    d. What Account and Amount is Credited?

E6.6 Vendor Transaction: Check and Debit Card

Using the QBO Sample Company, Craig's Design and Landscaping Company, complete the following to record a payment using Craig's Checking account Debit Card.

1. Create Check with Debit Card.

    a. From the Create (+) icon select **Check**

    b. Select Choose a payee: **Bob's Burger Joint**

    c. Select Choose an account: **Checking**

    d. Select Payment method: **Check**

    e. Enter Reference no.: **Debit**

    f. Select Account Details: ACCOUNT: **Meals and Entertainment**

    g. Enter AMOUNT: **10.00**

    h. What is the Total for the Check?

    i. Select **Save and Close**

2. View the Transaction Journal for the Check.

    a. From the Navigation Bar select **Accounting**

    b. From the Chart of Accounts select **View Register** for the Checking account

    c. Select **Bob's Burger Joint Check > Edit**

    d. From the bottom of the Bob's Burger Joint Check select **More > Transaction Journal**

    e. What Account and Amount is Debited?

    f. What Account and Amount is Credited?

E6.7 Vendor Transaction: Check

Using the QBO Sample Company, Craig's Design and Landscaping Company, complete the following.

1. Create Check.

    a. From the Create (+) icon select **Check**

    b. Select Choose a payee: **Mahoney Mugs**

    c. Select Choose an account: **Checking**

    d. Select Payment method: **Check**

    e. Enter Reference no.: **78**

    f. Select Account Details: ACCOUNT: **Office Expenses**

    g. Enter DESCRIPTION: **Office Supplies**

    h. Enter AMOUNT: **13.00**

    i. What is the Total for the Check?

    j. Select **Save and Close**

2. View the Transaction Journal for the Deposit.

    a. From the Navigation Bar select **Accounting**

    b. From the Chart of Accounts select **View Register** for the Checking account

    c. Select **Mahoney's Mugs Check > Edit**

    d. From the bottom of the Mahoney's Mugs Check select **More > Transaction Journal**

   e. What Account and Amount is Debited?

   f. What Account and Amount is Credited?

E6.8 Vendor Transaction: Bill

Using the QBO Sample Company, Craig's Design and Landscaping Company, complete the following to enter a bill for legal fees.

   1. Create Bill.

   a. From the Create (+) icon select **Bill**

   b. Select Choose a payee: **Tony Rondonuwu**

   c. Select Account Details: ACCOUNT: **Legal & Professional Fees: Lawyer**

   d. Enter AMOUNT: **300.00**

   e. What is the Total for the Bill?

   f. Select **Save** and leave the Bill displayed

   2. View the Transaction Journal for the Bill.

   a. From the bottom of the Tony Rondonuwu Bill select **More > Transaction Journal**

   b. What Account and Amount is Debited?

   c. What Account and Amount is Credited?

E6.9 Vendor Transaction: Bill

Using the QBO Sample Company, Craig's Design and Landscaping Company, complete the following.

   1. Create Bill.

   a. From the Create (+) icon select **Bill**

   b. Select Choose a payee: **Pam Seitz**

   c. Select Account Details: ACCOUNT: **Legal & Professional Fees: Accounting**

   d. Enter AMOUNT: **150.00**

   e. What is the Total for the Bill?

   f. Select **Save** and leave the Bill displayed

2. View the Transaction Journal for the Bill.

    a. From the bottom of the Pam Seitz Bill select **More > Transaction Journal**

    b. What Account and Amount is Debited?

    c. What Account and Amount is Credited?

E6.10 Vendor Transaction: Pay Bills

This assignment is a continuation of E6.8 and E6.9

  Using the QBO Sample Company, Craig's Design and Landscaping Company, complete the following.

1. Pay Bills.

    a. From the Create (+) icon select **Pay Bills**

    b. Select Payment account: **Checking**

    c. Select Starting Check no.: **79**

    d. Select PAYEE: **Pam Seitz**

    e. Select PAYEE: **Tony Rondonuwu**

    f. What is the TOTAL PAYMENT AMOUNT?

    g. Select **Save and Close**

2. View the Transaction Journal for Paid Bills.

    a. From the Navigation Bar select **Accounting**

    b. From the Chart of Accounts select **View Register** for the Checking account

    c. Select **Check 79 > Edit**

    d. From the bottom of Check 79 select **More > Transaction Journal**

    e. What Account and Amount is Debited?

    f. What Account and Amount is Credited?

    g. From the Chart of Accounts select **View Register** for the Checking account

    h. Select **Check 80 > Edit**

    i. From the bottom of Check 80 select **More > Transaction Journal**

    j. What Account and Amount is Debited?

    k. What Account and Amount is Credited?

PROJECT 6.1

Project 6.1 is a continuation of Project 5.1. You will use the QBO client company you created for Project 1.1 and updated in subsequent Projects 2.1 through 5.1. Keep in mind the QBO company for Project 5.1 does not reset and carries your data forward, including any errors. So it is important to check and crosscheck your work to verify it is correct before clicking the Save button.

BACKSTORY

Mookie The Beagle™ Concierge provides convenient, high-quality pet care on demand. CK processes vendor and expense transactions using QBO and has asked for your assistance.

Complete the following for Mookie The Beagle Concierge.

QBO SatNav

Project 6.1 focuses on the QBO Transactions, specifically QBO Expense Transactions shown in the following partial QBO SatNav.

QBO SatNav

② QBO TRANSACTIONS	CHAPTERS 3,4,5,6,7,8

> Money in   Money out >

Banking
Customers & Sales
Vendors & Expenses
Employees & Payroll

HOW TO LOG INTO QBO+

To log into QBO, complete the following steps.

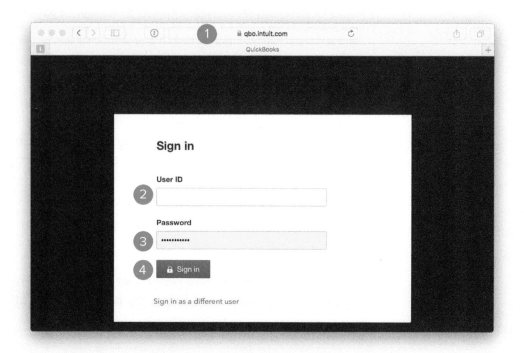

1. Using a web browser go to qbo.intuit.com

2. Enter **User ID** (the email address you used to set up your QBO Account)

3. Enter **Password** (the password you used to set up your QBO Account)

4. Select **Sign in**

If you are not using a public or shared computer, **to speed up login, you can save your login to your desktop and select Remember Me. If you are using a public computer or shared computer, do not save to your desktop and unselect Remember Me.**

The new QBO company **we created in Project 1 will carry all work forward into future chapters. So it is important to check and crosscheck your work to verify it is correct before clicking the Save button. Any errors entered are carried forward in the QBO company you create for text projects.**

P6.1.1 Expense Credit Card

Complete the following to record supplies purchased by Mookie The Beagle Concierge from Bichotte Supplies with a credit card.

1. Create Expense paid with Credit Card.

   a. From the Create (+) icon select **Expense**

   b. Select Choose a vendor: **Bichotte Supplies**

   c. Select Choose an account: **VISA Credit Card**

   d. Select Date: **01/22/2018**

   e. Select Payment method.: **Credit Card**

   f. Select Account Details: ACCOUNT: **Supplies Expense**

   g. Enter AMOUNT: **120.00**

   h. What is the Total for the Expense?

   i. Select **Save** and leave the Expense displayed

2. View the Transaction Journal for the Expense.

   a. From the bottom of the Bichotte Supplies Expense select **More > Transaction Journal**

   b. What Account and Amount is Debited?

   c. What Account and Amount is Credited?

P6.1.2 Vendor Transaction: Credit Card Credit

Bichotte Supplies mistakenly overcharged Mookie The Beagle Concierge by $20 on the supplies purchases made on 01/22/2018. Complete the following to record the Credit Card Credit when Bichotte Supplies reversed the overcharge.

1. Create Credit Card Credit.

   a. From the Create (+) icon select **Credit Card Credit**

   b. Select Choose a payee: **Bichotte Supplies**

   c. Select Choose an account: **VISA Credit Card**

   d. Select Date **01/23/2018**

   e. Select Account Details: ACCOUNT: **Supplies Expense**

   f. Enter AMOUNT: **20.00**

   g. What is the Total for the Credit Card Credit?

   h. Select **Save and Close**

2. View the Transaction Journal for the Credit Card Credit.

   a. From the Navigation Bar select **Expenses**

   b. From the Expense Transactions List select **Bichotte Supplies Credit Card Credit**

   c. From the bottom of the Bichotte Supplies Credit Card Credit select **More > Transaction Journal**

   d. What Account and Amount is Debited?

   e. What Account and Amount is Credited?

P6.1.3 Vendor Transaction: Expense Checking

Complete the following to record supplies purchased by Mookie The Beagle Concierge from Maria Cecilia Associates with a credit card.

1. Create Expense paid with Credit Card.

   a. From the Create (+) icon select **Expense**

   b. Select Choose a payee: **Maria Cecilia Associates**

   c. Select Choose an account: **VISA Credit Card**

   d. Select Date: **01/24/2018**

   e. Select Payment method.: **Credit Card**

   f. Select Account Details: ACCOUNT: **Supplies Expense**

   g. Enter AMOUNT: **216.00**

   h. What is the Total for the Expense?

   i. Select **Save** and leave the Expense displayed on your screen

2. View the Transaction Journal for the Expense.

   a. From the bottom of the Maria Cecilia Associates Expense select **More > Transaction Journal**

   b. What Account and Amount is Debited?

   c. What Account and Amount is Credited?

P6.1.4 Vendor Transaction: Checking Debit Card

Complete the following to record a payment using Mookie The Beagle Concierge's account Debit Card.

1. Create Check with Debit Card.

   a. From the Create (+) icon select **Check**

   b. Select Choose a payee: **Bichotte Supplies**

   c. Select Choose an account: **Checking**

   d. Enter Check no.: **Debit**

   e. Select Date **01/25/2018**

   f. Select Account Details: ACCOUNT: **Supplies Expense**

   g. Enter AMOUNT: **10.00**

   h. What is the Total for the Check?

   i. Select **Save and Close**

2. View the Transaction Journal for the Check.

   a. From the Navigation Bar select **Accounting**

   b. From the Chart of Accounts select **View Register** for the Checking account

   c. Select **Bichotte Supplies Debit Check > Edit**

   d. From the bottom of the Bichotte Supplies Check select **More > Transaction Journal**

   e. What Account and Amount is Debited?

   f. What Account and Amount is Credited?

P6.1.5 Vendor Transaction: Recurring Transaction Expense

Use a Recurring Transaction to record paying Mary Dolan as a subcontractor who provided the pet care services for Honey over the Super Bowl weekend. Mookie The Beagle Concierge pays Mary Dolan $10 per hour for those services.

1. Use a Recurring Transaction.

   a. From the Recurring Transaction List select **Subcontractor Expense > Use**

   b. Update Date **01/30/2018**

   c. Select Payee **Mary Dolan**

   d. Verify **Checking**

    e. Verify ACCOUNT **Subcontractors Expense**

    f. Enter AMOUNT **based upon 33 hours Mary provided service to Venus over the Super Bowl weekend.**

    g. What is the amount for the Expense?

    h. Select **Save** and leave the Expense displayed

2. View the Transaction Journal for the Expense.

    a. From the bottom of the Subcontractor Expense select **More > Transaction Journal**

    b. What Account and Amount is Debited?

    c. What Account and Amount is Credited?

P6.1.6 Vendor Transaction: Bill

Andre LaFortune, a vet student, provided pet care services as a subcontractor for Venus for a total of 17 hours summarized as follows:

- **6** hours on 01/18/2018
- **5** hours on 01/19/2018
- **6** hours on 01/20/2018

Mookie The Beagle Concierge pays Andre the same rate as Mary Dolan, $10 per hour. Complete the following to enter the bill on 01/30/2018. Mookie The Beagle Concierge will pay the subcontractor bill on 01/31/2018 (see P6.1.7).

1. Create Bill.

    a. From the Create (+) icon select **Bill**

    b. Add New Payee: **Andre LaFortune**

    c. Select Date **01/30/2018**

    d. Select Account Details: ACCOUNT: **Subcontractors Expense**

    e. Enter AMOUNT for number of hours Andre provided pet care services for Venus

    f. What is the Total for the Bill?

    g. Select **Save** and leave the Bill displayed

2. View the Transaction Journal for the Bill.

   a. From the bottom of the Andre LaFortune Bill select **More > Transaction Journal**

   b. What Account and Amount is Debited?

   c. What Account and Amount is Credited?

P6.1.7 Vendor Transaction: Pay Bills

Complete the following to pay the subcontractor bill for Andre LaFortune.

1. Pay Bills.

   a. From the Create (+) icon select **Pay Bills**

   b. Select Payment account: **Checking**

   c. Select Starting Check no.: **3**

   d. Select Payment Date **01/31/2018**

   e. Select PAYEE: **Andre LaFortune**

   f. Select BILL dated 01/30/2018

   g. What is the TOTAL PAYMENT AMOUNT?

   h. Select **Save and Close**

2. View the Transaction Journal for Paid Bills.

   a. From the Navigation Bar select **Accounting**

   b. From the Chart of Accounts select **View Register** for the Checking account

   c. Select **Check 3 for Andre LaFortune > Edit**

   d. From the bottom of the Bill Payment select **More > Transaction Journal**

   e. What Account and Amount is Debited?

   f. What Account and Amount is Credited?

www.my-quickbooksonline.com

Go to www.My-QuickBooksOnline.com for additional resources for you including QBO Help, QBO Videos, and more.

Chapter 7

Inventory

Chapter 7 focuses on how we use QBO to record the purchase and sale of product inventory. For example, Craig's Design and Landscaping purchases landscape fountains for resale to customers. QBO has the ability to track both the purchase of the fountains and the subsequent resale to customers.

Section 7.1

QBO SatNav

QBO SatNav is your satellite navigation for QuickBooks Online, assisting you in navigating QBO

Chapter 7 focuses on QuickBooks Online Vendor and Customer transactions for inventory, shown in the following QBO SatNav.

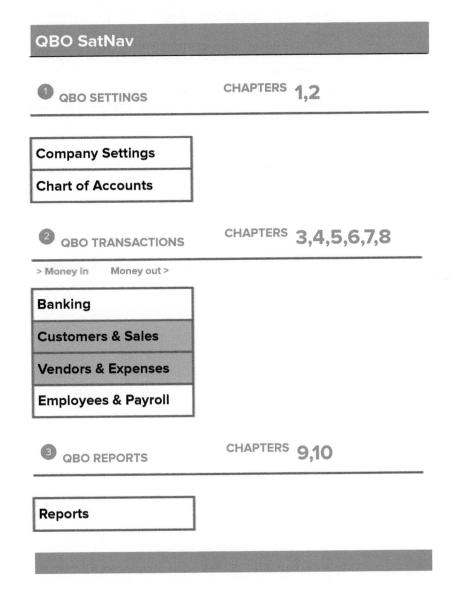

Section 7.2

QBO LOGIN TO SAMPLE COMPANY

To log into the QBO Sample Company:

1. Open a web browser. (Note: Intuit recommends using Google Chrome.)

2. Go to the https://qbo.intuit.com/redir/testdrive

3. Follow onscreen instructions for security verification.

Craig's Design and Landscaping Services should appear on your screen.

> **We use the Sample Company** for practice throughout the chapter and exercises. The Sample Company will reset each time it is reopened. So make certain to allow enough time to complete all chapter activities before closing the Sample Company. Otherwise, you will lose the work you have entered when you reopen the Sample Company.

Section 7.3

NAVIGATING INVENTORY

If we buy and resell products, then we must maintain inventory records to account for the products we purchase from vendors and resell to customers.

We can use QBO for inventory to record:

1. **Vendor transactions,** including placing product orders, receiving products, and paying bills

2. **Customer transactions,** including recording sale of product on invoices and receiving customer payments

We can view the order of the QBO tasks we need to complete for inventory from the Create (+) screen:

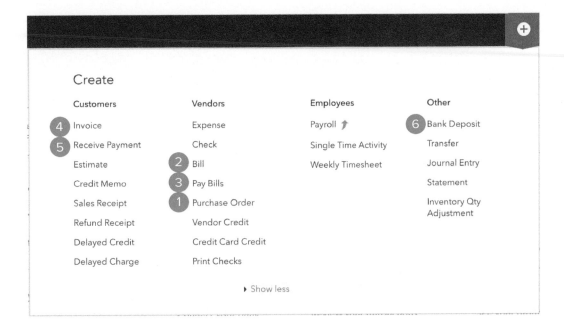

① **VENDORS: Purchase Order** to record our order of products from vendors. The purchase order is a record of the products and quantities we ordered.

② **VENDORS: Bill** to record our obligation to pay the vendor for the products (Accounts Payable). Match vendor's bill with our purchase order to verify quantities and amounts are correct.

③ **VENDORS: Pay Bills** to pay vendor bills for products received.

④ **CUSTOMERS: Invoice** to record resale of product to customer and the customer's promise to pay later (Accounts Receivable).

⑤ **CUSTOMERS: Receive Payment** to record collection of the customer's payment.

⑥ **CUSTOMERS: Bank Deposit** to record customer's payment in the bank account. (Bank Deposit is used only if Undeposited Funds is selected on the Receive Payment form.)

Section 7.4

PRODUCT AND SERVICES LIST

When we enter the inventory transactions, we will need to use the following QBO Lists:

1. Vendors List
2. Customers List
3. Products and Services List

The Products and Services List collects information about the products purchased from vendors *and* sold to customers. Notice that the Products and Services List is used for products *both* purchased and sold. The Products and Services List is a time-saving feature so that we don't have continually to re-enter the same products and services information each time we enter a new transaction. In addition, we can enter one set of product information that can be used for both purchasing and sales of the product.

  QBO uses four types of products and services:

1. **Inventory.** Products that we buy for which we track quantities, such as fountains that we buy to resell. Inventory items are products that a business purchases, holds as inventory, and then resells to customers. QBO traces the quantity and cost of inventory items in stock. For consistency, the same inventory item is used when recording sales and purchases. QBO has the capability to track both the cost and the sales price for inventory items. When the product is recorded on a sales invoice, QBO automatically updates our inventory records by reducing the quantity of doors on hand. If we purchased the product, then we would record the product on the purchase order using the same inventory item number that we use on an invoice, except the purchase order uses the product's cost while the invoice uses the product's *selling price*.

2. **Non-inventory.** Products that we buy but we don't need to track the quantity of the product. For example, pens used for office supplies.

3. **Service.** Services that we buy from vendors, such as legal services.

4. **Bundle.** A bundle is a collection of products and services that we sell together as a bundle. For example, installation of a fountain might include hoses (products) and installation hours (services). Notice that

we may buy the products separately, but then bundle the items for resale to customers.

Two ways that we can update the Products and Services List are:

1. *Before* entering transactions
2. *While* entering transactions

UPDATE PRODUCTS AND SERVICES LIST BEFORE ENTERING TRANSACTIONS

Before entering transactions, we can update the Products and Services List as follows.

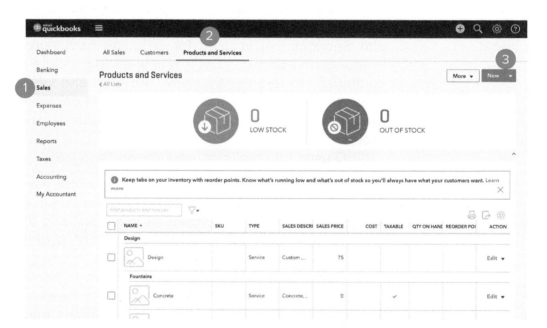

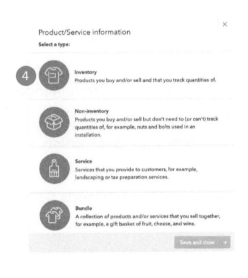

1. From the Navigation Bar, select **Sales**

2. Select **Product and Services**

3. To enter new products or services select **New**

4. Select Product/Service Type: **Inventory**

5. Enter **Name**

6. Enter **SKU** or other product identification number

7. Attach a product/service **photo**

8. Select an appropriate product/service **Category**

9. Enter **Initial quantity on hand.** This amount can be entered as -0- and adjusted later.

10. Enter **As of date**

11. Enter **Reorder point** when a new order should be placed to replenish product stock

12 Select Inventory asset account: **Inventory Asset**

13 Enter **Sales information description**

14 Enter **Sales price/rate**

15 Select Income account: **Sales of Product Income**

16 Check **Is taxable**

17 Enter **Purchasing information description**

18 Enter **Cost** of product

19 Select Expense account: **Cost of Goods Sold**

20 Typically we would select Save and Close, but in this case select **Cancel (X)**

Notice that the Products and Services List links the product item to accounts in the Chart of Accounts for Inventory (Asset account), Sales of Product Income (Income account) and Cost of Goods Sold (Expense account). When we select this product on a QBO form, then the linked accounts are automatically updated also.

UPDATE PRODUCTS AND SERVICES LIST WHILE ENTERING TRANSACTIONS

While entering transactions, we can update the Products and Services List from the screen where we enter the transaction. If a product or service has not been entered in the list and is needed for a transaction, we can add the product or service as follows from an onscreen form.

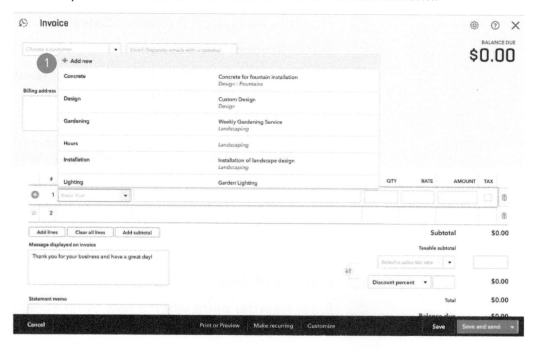

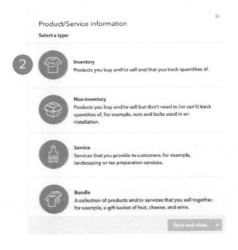

1. For example, to view an onscreen form such as an Invoice, select **Create (+)** icon > **Invoice.** Then select the **drop-down arrow** in the Product/Service field > **+ Add new.**

2. Select **Product/Service type**

3. Enter **new product or service information**

4. Typically, we would select Save and Close, but in this case select the **X** in the upper right corner of the window to Cancel

Section 7.5

PURCHASE ORDER

A purchase order is a record of an order to purchase products from a vendor. To create a purchase order:

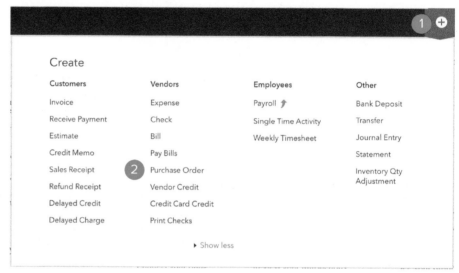

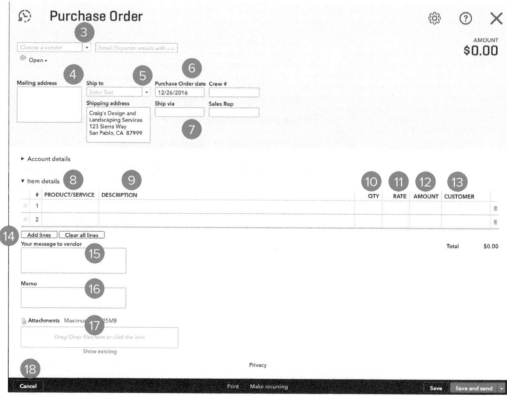

① Select **Create (+)** icon

② Select **Purchase Order**

③ Select **Vendor** from the Vendor List drop-down menu

④ **Mailing address** and email should auto-fill when vendor is selected. If not, enter mailing address and email.

⑤ Enter **Ship to** customer address if the product is to be shipped directly to a customer

⑥ Select **Purchase Order date**

⑦ Select **Ship via** as appropriate

⑧ In the Item details section, select product to order from the **Product/Service** drop-down list or Add New. The product or service selected is linked to an account in the Chart of Accounts, so when we select the product, the linked account is automatically updated.

⑨ Enter **Description**

⑩ Enter **QTY** to order

⑪ Enter **Rate** per item

⑫ Verify **Amount** is calculated correctly

⑬ If associated with a specific customer, select appropriate **Customer**

⑭ To add lines for additional products, select **Add lines**

⑮ Enter **Your Message to vendor** with additional instructions

⑯ Enter **Memo**

⑰ Add **Attachments** such as source documents associated with the transaction

⑱ Normally we would select Save, but in this case select **Cancel.** We will enter new transactions in the exercises at the end of the chapter.

Section 7.6

BILL

When a purchase order has been fulfilled and we've received the products from the vendor, we receive a bill from the vendor. If we are going to pay the bill later, we use the Bill form to record the vendor's bill in QBO.

> If we are paying the bill at the time we receive the product or service, then we can use the Expense form to record the transaction.

To record a bill received that we will pay later:

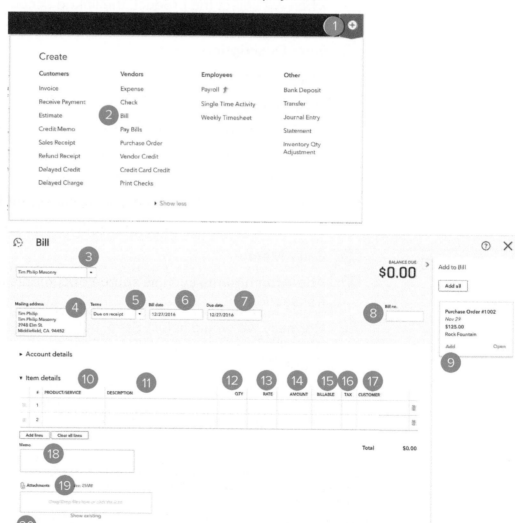

1. Select **Create (+)** icon

2. Select **Bill**

3. Select **Vendor** from the Vendor List drop-down menu

4. **Mailing address** should auto-fill when vendor is selected

5. Select **Terms** if this does not auto-fill correctly when vendor is selected

6. Select **Bill date**

7. Select **Due date** if different than the due date automatically displayed

8. Enter **Bill no.** if provided on bill

9. When a vendor is selected, open Purchase Orders appear. Select **Add** to add the related open purchase order to the bill. If we were paying the bill at the same time, we could use the Expense form instead of the Bill form and attach the PO to the Expense in the same manner.

10. The information on the purchase order is added to a **Product/Service** line in the Item Detail section of the Bill form.

11. Enter or update **Description**

12. Enter or verify automatically entered **QTY**

13. Enter or verify automatically entered **Rate**

14. Enter or verify automatically entered **Amount**

15. Select **Billable** if the item is billable to a specific customer

16. Select **Tax** if taxable

17. If billable, select appropriate **Customer** associated with the item

18. Enter **Memo** describing the transaction

19. Add **Attachments** such as source documents associated with the transaction

20. Normally we would select Save, but in this case select **Cancel.** We will enter new transactions in the exercises at the end of the chapter.

Notice that the vendor transaction is entered using Item Details instead of Account Details, which was covered in Chapter 6. When we use Item Details for Products/Services, we have already linked these products/services to Accounts in the Chart of Accounts when we entered the product/service in the Product/Service List.

Section 7.7

PAY BILLS

Use Pay Bills to select the bills that are due and we are ready to pay. If the bill has been entered using the Bill form, then the bill will automatically appear in the Pay Bills List.

> Use Pay Bills only **for bills that have been entered using the Bill form.**

> **If the Expense form or the Check form** was used to enter the vendor transaction, we do not use the **Pay Bills form for that item, since it has already been paid at the time the Expense or Check was entered into QBO.**

To use Pay Bills to select bills to pay:

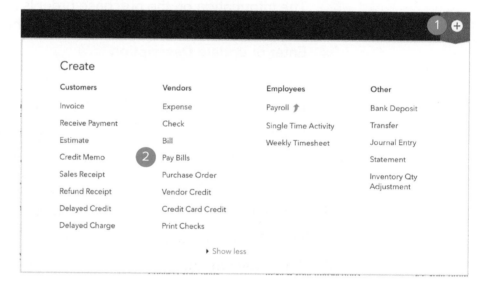

1. Select **Create (+)** icon

2. Select **Pay Bills**

3. Select **Payment account** drop-down menu

4. From the Payment account drop-down menu select the **Payment account**

5. Enter **Payment Date**

6. Select **bills to pay**

7. Enter **Payment**

8. Normally we would select Save and New or Save and Close, but in this case select **Cancel.** We will enter new deposits in the exercises at the end of the chapter.

Section 7.8

INVOICE

An invoice is used to record sales when the customer will pay later. An invoice contains detailed information about the products and services provided to a customer.

To create an Invoice:

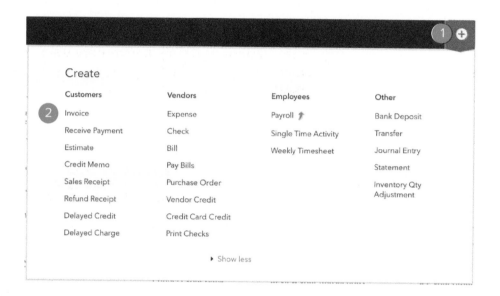

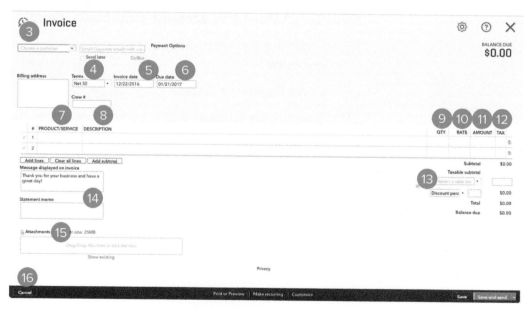

1. Select **Create (+)** icon

2. Select **Invoice**

3. Select **Customer** from the Customer List drop-down menu or Add New Customer

4. Enter **Terms**

5. Enter **Invoice Date**

6. Verify **Due Date**

7. Select **Product or Service** from the Product/Services List drop-down menu or Add New Product/Service

8. Enter **Description** of sales transaction

9. Enter **Quantity (QTY).** If inventory tracking is turned on for this item, hover over QTY to see quantity of the inventory item on hand.

10. Enter **Rate**

11. Enter **Amount**

12. Select **Tax** if sale is taxable

13. Select appropriate **Sales Tax** if applicable

14. Enter **Statement Memo** describing the sale

15. Add **Attachments** such as source documents associated with the sale

16. Normally we would select Save, but in this case select **Cancel.** We will enter new transactions in the exercises at the end of the chapter.

Section 7.9

RECEIVE PAYMENT

Customers may pay in the following ways:

1. **Credit card,** such as Visa, MasterCard, American Express, or Diners Club over the phone, in person, or by mail. Using QuickBooks Merchant Account Service, you can obtain online authorization and then download payments directly into QuickBooks.

2. **Online** by credit card or bank account transfer.

3. **Customer check** delivered either in person or by mail.

To record a customer's payment received to pay an outstanding invoice:

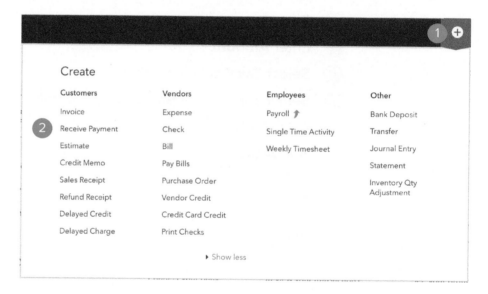

1. Select **Create (+)** icon

2. Select **Receive Payment**

3. Select **Customer** from the Customer List drop-down menu

4. Enter **Payment date**

5. Enter **Payment Method**

6. If Payment Method is Check, enter the customer check no. in **Reference no.**

7. Select **Deposit to** account from the drop-down list. If this deposit will be bundled with other deposits, then select Undeposited Funds and after completing the Invoice, enter a Bank Deposit to move the funds from Undeposited Funds to the Checking account. If this deposit is not bundled with other deposits, then select the appropriate Checking account from the drop-down list. The funds are deposited directly to the Checking account selected and we do not enter a separate Bank Deposit.

8. In the Outstanding Transactions section select the **Invoice** to which payment should be applied

9. Enter or verify automatically entered **Payment amount**

10. Normally we would select Save, but in this case select **Cancel.** We will enter new transactions in the exercises at the end of the chapter.

Section 7.10

BANK DEPOSIT FOR UNDEPOSITED FUNDS

If Undeposited Funds was selected on Receive Payment, then we must create a Bank Deposit to transfer the funds from the Undeposited Funds account to the appropriate Checking account. Sometimes Undeposited Funds is used on the Invoice if the customer payment will be bundled with other customer payments when deposited. Then our totals will correspond to the bank deposit total shown by the bank.

> If we selected Undeposited Funds on Receive Payment we *must* create a bank deposit to transfer the funds from the Undeposited Funds account to the appropriate bank account. Otherwise, the funds will remain in the Undeposited Funds account and we will not be able to use the funds to pay bills, for example.

> If we selected a specific bank account, such as Checking account, on Receive Payment we do *not* need to create a bank deposit. We have already deposited the customer payment in the bank account.

To record a bank deposit related to a customer sale when Undeposited Funds was selected on the Receive Payment:

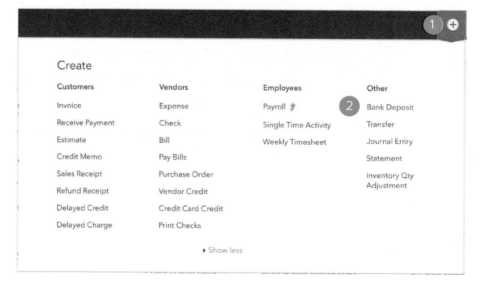

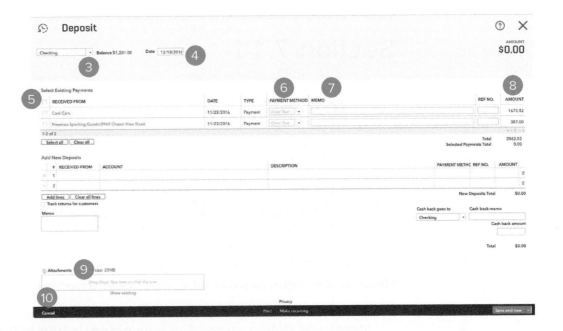

1. Select **Create (+)** icon

2. Under Other select **Bank Deposit**

3. Select **Bank** account

4. Enter **Date** of deposit

5. The Select Existing Payments section lists customer payments received but not deposited yet. The customer payments listed are undeposited funds that have been recorded as received but not yet deposited in the bank. Select the **existing customer payment** to deposit.

6. Enter appropriate **Payment Method**

7. If appropriate, enter **Memo** describing the deposit

8. Verify **Amount** is correct

9. Select **Attachments** to add a file or photo of any accompanying document

10. Normally we would select Save and New or Save and Close, but in this case select **Cancel.** We will enter new deposits in the exercises at the end of the chapter.

Section 7.11

ACCOUNTING ESSENTIALS

Inventory and Internal Control

Accounting Essentials summarize important foundational accounting knowledge you may find useful when using QBO

How do we improve internal control over inventory?

- Internal control is a set of processes and procedures to safeguard assets and detect errors. Since inventory is one of the main targets of fraud and theft, we want to have a good system of internal control to safeguard inventory.

- One principle of internal control is periodically to compare and reconcile the actual asset with the accounting records to identify and track any discrepancies. So at least once a year, businesses typically reconcile:

  1. inventory on hand confirmed by a physical count of the asset on hand with
  2. inventory recorded in the accounting records

What is a 3-way match?

- Another principle of internal control is to use a 3-way match when ordering, receiving, and paying for inventory.

- 3-way match is another internal control procedure by cross checking amounts across three different documents.

- 3-way match compares:
  1. What was *ordered*?
  2. What was *received*?
  3. What was *billed*?

- Basically, we want to compare what we *ordered* with what we *received*, and what we were *billed*. These three amounts should agree so that we are not paying for more than what we ordered or received.

PRACTICE QUIZ 7

Q7.1

To enter Customer and Sales transactions,

   a. From the Navigation Bar select Transactions > Customers

   b. From the Navigation Bar select Transactions > Expenses > New Transaction

   c. From the Create (+) icon, select the appropriate customer transaction

   d. From the Gear icon, select Expense Transactions

Q7.2

To enter Vendor and Expense transactions,

   a. From the Navigation Bar select Transactions > Customers

   b. From the Navigation Bar select Transactions > Sales

   c. From the Create (+) icon, select the appropriate vendor transaction

   d. From the Gear icon, select Vendor transactions

Q7.3

QuickBooks considers all of the following to be vendors except:

   a. Utility companies

   b. Suppliers of inventory and supplies

   c. Tax agencies such as the IRS

   d. Customers purchasing products

Q7.4

Which of the following is a vendor transaction?

   a. Purchase Order

   b. Invoice

   c. Make Deposit

   d. Receive Payment

Q7.5

We can update the Products and Services List at which of the following two points?

   a. Before entering transactions

   b. While entering transactions

   c. After entering transactions

Q7.6

Which of the following is a customer transaction?

   a. Invoice

   b. Purchase Order

   c. Pay Bills

   d. Bill

Q7.7

Types of products and services on the Products and Services List include:

   a. Service

   b. Non-inventory

   c. Inventory

   d. All of the above

Q7.8

Which of the following types of products and services track quantities?

   a. Service items

   b. Inventory items

   c. Non-inventory items

   d. None of the above

Q7.9

The Purchase Order form is used to record which one of the following transactions?

a. Owners investment

b. Services received but not yet paid

c. Products sold to customers

d. Products ordered from vendors

Q7.10

Which of the following activities, and the QBO form used to record it, is incorrect?

a. Receive customer payment, Pay Bills

b. Order products, Purchase Order

c. Receive bill to be paid later, Bill

d. Sell products and bill customers, Invoice

Q7.11

Indicate two of the following that show the order in which the following onscreen vendor transaction forms typically should be prepared.

a. Expense > Pay Bills

b. Purchase Order > Bill > Pay Bills

c. Bill > Pay Bills

d. Invoice > Pay Bills

Q7.12

Recording a purchase of products using QBO involves all of the following steps except:

a. Create invoice to bill vendors for purchases

b. Create purchase order to order items from vendors

c. Receive bill and record obligation to pay vendor later

d. Pay bill entered previously

Q7.13

To record a bill received that we will pay later, we use which of the following QBO forms?

a. Purchase Order

b. Pay Bills

c. Expense

d. Bill

Q7.14

Use the Pay Bills form only for:

a. Bills that have been entered using the Bill form

b. Bills that have been entered using the Expense form

c. Bills that have been entered using the Check form

d. Bills that have never been entered in QBO

EXERCISES 7

We use the QBO Sample Company, Craig's Design and Landscaping Services for practice throughout the exercises. The Sample Company will reset each time it is reopened. So make certain to allow enough time to complete exercises before closing the Sample Company. Otherwise, you will lose the work you have entered when you reopen the Sample Company.

To access the QBO Sample Company, complete the following steps.

1. Open a web browser. (Note: Intuit recommends using Google Chrome.)

2. Go to the https://qbo.intuit.com/redir/testdrive

3. Follow onscreen instructions for security verification.

Craig's Design and Landscaping Services should appear on your screen.

E7.1 Vendor and Expense Transactions

Match the following vendor and expense transactions with the description of the transaction.

Vendor and Expense Transaction Descriptions

a. The form used to select bills we want to pay.

b. The form used to order and track products from vendors.

c. The onscreen form used to record products and services that we pay for at the time we receive the product or service with cash, credit card, or check.

d. The form used when a vendor gives us a refund or reduction in our bill in what we owe the vendor.

e. This form can be used when we pay for products and services at the time of purchase, but cannot be used when we pay with cash or credit card.

f. A form used to record a reduction in charges by the vendor to our credit card.

g. The onscreen form used to record bills we received and our obligation to pay the vendor later (accounts payable).

Vendor and Expense Transaction

1. Expense

2. Check

3. Bill

4. Pay Bills

5. Purchase Order

6. Vendor Credit

7. Credit Card Credit

E7.2 Inventory Flow

Match the following items with the appropriate diagram number.

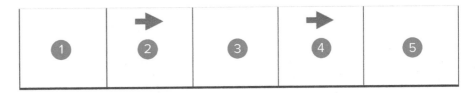

a. Sell Products to Customers

b. Purchase Products from Vendors

c. Customers

d. Vendors

e. Our Company

Item

1. _____

2. _____

3. _____

4. _____

5. _____

E7.3 Inventory and Transactions

Match the following transaction descriptions with the order in which the transactions should be recorded.

Transaction Descriptions

a. Records our order of products from vendors.

b. Records our obligation to pay the vendor for the products (Accounts Payable).

c. Records resale of product to customer and the customer's promise to pay later (Accounts Receivable).

d. Records customer's payment in the bank account, used only if Undeposited Funds is selected on the Receive Payment form.

e. Records collection of the customer's payment.

f. Pays vendors for products received.

Transaction Order

1. _____

2. _____

3. _____

4. _____

5. _____

6. _____

E7.4 Vendor Transaction: Purchase Order

Using the QBO Sample Company, Craig's Design and Landscaping Company, complete the following.

1. Create Purchase Order.

   a. From the Create (+) icon select **Purchase Order**

   b. Select Choose a vendor: **Hicks Hardware**

   c. Select Item Details Line 1: PRODUCT/SERVICE: **Design: Fountains: Rock Fountain**

   d. Enter QTY: **2**

   e. Enter RATE: **125**

   f. AMOUNT should autofill

   g. Select CUSTOMER: **Red Rock Diner**

   h. Select Item Details Line 2: PRODUCT/SERVICE: **Design: Fountains: Pump**

   i. Enter QTY: **6**

   j. Enter RATE: **10**

   k. AMOUNT should autofill

   l. Select CUSTOMER: **Red Rock Diner**

   m. What is the Total for the Purchase Order?

   n. Select **Save and New**

2. Create Purchase Order.

   a. From the Create (+) icon select **Purchase Order**

   b. Select Choose a vendor: **Hicks Hardware**

   c. Select Item Details Line 1: PRODUCT/SERVICE: **Design: Fountains: Rock Fountain**

   d. Enter QTY: **1**

   e. Enter RATE: **125**

   f. AMOUNT should autofill

   g. Select CUSTOMER: **Cool Cars**

   h. Select Item Details Line 2: PRODUCT/SERVICE: **Design: Fountains: Pump**

   i. Enter QTY: **3**

    j. Enter RATE: **10**

    k. AMOUNT should autofill

    l. Select CUSTOMER: **Cool Cars**

    m. What is the Total for the Purchase Order?

    n. Select **Save and Close**

E7.5 Vendor Transaction: Bill

This assignment is a continuation of E7.4

    Using the QBO Sample Company, Craig's Design and Landscaping Company, complete the following to record a bill received for products ordered.

1. Create Bill.

    a. From the Create (+) icon select **Bill**

    b. Select Choose a payee: **Hick's Hardware**

    c. The two Purchase Orders entered in the previous exercise should appear on the Right side of the screen. Select **Add All** to add both POs to the bill. Item Details should now show the items from the POs.

    d. What is the Total for the Bill?

    e. Select **Save**

2. View the Transaction Journal for the Bill.

    a. From the bottom of the Hick's Hardware Bill select **More > Transaction Journal**

    b. What are the Accounts and Amounts Debited?

    c. What Account and Amount is Credited?

E7.6 Vendor Transaction: Pay Bills

This assignment is a continuation of E7.4 and E7.5

    Using the QBO Sample Company, Craig's Design and Landscaping Company, complete the following.

1. Pay Bills.

    a. From the Create (+) icon select **Pay Bills**

    b. Select Payment account: **Checking**

c. Select Payee: **Hicks Hardware**

d. What is the Total Payment Amount?

e. Select **Save and Close**

2. View the Transaction Journal for Pay Bills.

a. From the Navigation Bar select **Expenses**

b. From the Expense Transactions List select **Bill Payment to Hick's Hardware**

c. From the bottom of Hick's Hardware Bill Payment select **More > Transaction Journal**

d. What Account and Amount is Debited?

e. What Account and Amount is Credited?

E7.7 Customer Transaction: Invoice

This assignment is a continuation of E7.4 to E7.6

Using the QBO Sample Company, Craig's Design and Landscaping Company, complete the following.

1. Create Invoice.

a. From the Create (+) icon select **Invoice**

b. Select Choose a customer: **Red Rock Diner**

c. Select Item Details Line 1: PRODUCT/SERVICE: **Design: Fountains: Rock Fountain**

d. Enter QTY: **2**

e. Enter RATE: **275**

f. AMOUNT should autofill

g. **Check** TAX

h. Select Item Details Line 2: PRODUCT/SERVICE: **Design: Fountains: Pump**

i. Enter QTY: **6**

j. Enter RATE: **15**

k. AMOUNT should autofill

l. **Check** TAX

m. Select a Sales Tax Rate: **California (8%)**

n. What is the Subtotal for the Invoice?

o. What is the Total for the Invoice?

p. Select **Save** and leave the Invoice displayed

2. View the Transaction Journal for the Invoice.

a. From the bottom of the Red Rock Diner Invoice select **More > Transaction Journal**

b. What are the Accounts and Amounts Debited?

c. What are the Accounts and Amounts Credited?

E7.8 Customer Transaction: Receive Payment

This assignment is a continuation of E7.4 to E7.7

Using the QBO Sample Company, Craig's Design and Landscaping Company, complete the following.

1. Create Receive Payment.

a. From the Create (+) icon select **Receive Payment**

b. Select Choose a customer: **Red Rock Diner**

c. Select Payment Amount: **Visa**

d. Select Deposit to: **Checking**

e. Select the Invoice just entered for Red Rock Diner

f. What is the Amount Received?

g. Select **Save and Close**

2. View the Transaction Journal for Receive Payments.

a. From the Navigation Bar select **Sales**

b. From the Sales Transactions List select **Red Rock Diner Payment** just entered

c. From the bottom of Red Rock Diner Receive Payment select **More > Transaction Journal**

d. What Account and Amount is Debited?

e. What Account and Amount is Credited?

E7.9 Customer Transaction: Invoice

This assignment is a continuation of E7.4 and E7.5

Using the QBO Sample Company, Craig's Design and Landscaping Company, complete the following.

1. Create Invoice.

   a. From the Create (+) icon select **Invoice**

   b. Select Choose a customer: **Cool Cars**

   c. Select Item Details Line 1: PRODUCT/SERVICE: **Design: Fountains: Rock Fountain**

   d. Enter QTY: **1**

   e. Enter RATE: **275**

   f. AMOUNT should autofill

   g. **Check** TAX

   h. Select Item Details Line 2: PRODUCT/SERVICE: **Design: Fountains: Pump**

   i. Enter QTY: **3**

   j. Enter RATE: **15**

   k. AMOUNT should autofill

   l. **Check** TAX

   m. Select a Sales Tax Rate: **California (8%)**

   n. What is the Subtotal for the Invoice?

   o. What is the Total for the Invoice?

   p. Select **Save** and leave the Invoice displayed

2. View the Transaction Journal for the Invoice.

   a. From the bottom of the Cool Cars Invoice select **More > Transaction Journal**

   b. What are the Accounts and Amounts Debited?

   c. What are the Accounts and Amounts Credited?

E7.10 Customer Transaction: Receive Payment

This assignment is a continuation of E7.4, E7.5, and E7.10

Using the QBO Sample Company, Craig's Design and Landscaping Company, complete the following.

1. Create Receive Payment.

   a. From the Create (+) icon select **Receive Payment**

   b. Select Choose a customer: **Cool Cars**

   c. Select Payment Amount: **Mastercard**

   d. Select Deposit to: **Checking**

   e. Select the Invoice just entered for Cool Cars

   f. What is the Amount Received?

   g. Select **Save and Close**

2. View the Transaction Journal for Receive Payments.

   a. From the Navigation Bar select **Sales**

   b. From the Sales Transactions List select **Cool Cars Payment** just entered

   c. From the bottom of Cool Cars Receive Payment select **More > Transaction Journal**

   d. What Account and Amount is Debited?

   e. What Account and Amount is Credited?

PROJECT 7.1

> Project 7.1 is a continuation of Project 6.1. You will use the QBO client company you created for Project 1.1 and updated in subsequent Projects 2.1 through 6.1. Keep in mind the QBO company for Project 7.1 does not reset and carries your data forward, including any errors. So it is important to check and crosscheck your work to verify it is correct before clicking the Save button.

BACKSTORY

Mookie The Beagle™ Concierge provides convenient, high-quality pet care on demand. Mookie The Beagle Concierge discovers that young professionals often didn't have time to go shopping for care items, so Mookie The

Beagle Concierge starts stocking some items, such as doggy hammocks, dog cones, activated charcoal for suspected poisoning, gauze wrap with adhesive tape for wound dressing, gauze nonstick bandages, sterile towels, oral syringes for administering medications, and sterile latex gloves.

All the products are branded as Mookie The Beagle Concierge products and can be ordered through the app with delivery scheduled with a Mookie The Beagle Concierge pet care visit or immediate delivery by Mookie The Beagle Concierge delivery services. Mookie The Beagle Concierge has asked for your assistance in QBO to account for inventory.

QBO SatNav

Project 7.1 focuses on the QBO Transactions, specifically on QBO Sales (Customer) and Expense (Vendor) Transactions as shown in the following partial QBO SatNav.

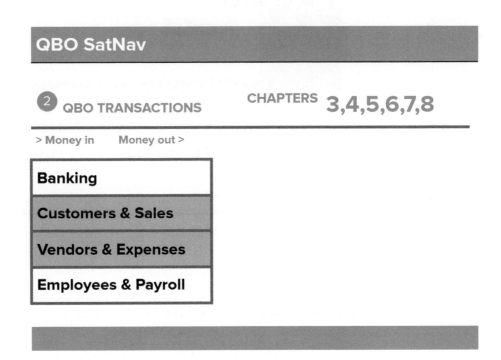

How to LOG into QBO+

To log into QBO, complete the following steps.

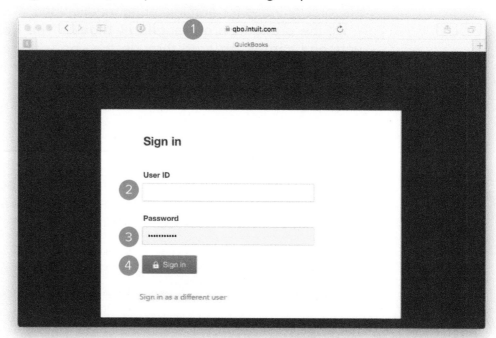

①   Using a web browser go to qbo.intuit.com

②   Enter **User ID** (the email address you used to set up your QBO Account)

③   Enter **Password** (the password you used to set up your QBO Account)

④   Select **Sign in**

> If you are **not** using a public or shared computer, to speed up login, you can save your login to your desktop and select Remember Me. If you are using a public computer or shared computer, do not save to your desktop and unselect Remember Me.

> The new QBO company we created in Project 1.1 will carry all work forward into future chapters. So it is important to check and crosscheck your work to verify it is correct before clicking the Save button. Any errors entered are carried forward in the QBO company you create for text projects.

P7.1.1 Products and Services List

> Before starting P7.1.1 verify that QBO Inventory Tracking is turned on. Go to Gear icon > Account and Settings > Sales > Products and Services > Track quantity and price/rate On > Track inventory quantity on hand > On.

To access the Products and Services List to enter the following, from the Navigation Bar select **Sales > Products and Services > New > Inventory.** Use the following when entering inventory:

- Inventory asset account: Inventory Asset

- Income account: Sales of Product Income

- Expense account: Cost of Goods Sold

- Initial quantity on hand: -0-

- As of Date: 01/01/2018

Enter the following information about Mookie The Beagle Concierge branded products.

CATEGORY	NAME	TYPE	SALES DESCRIPTION	SALES PRICE	COST
Pet Food Supplies	MookieTheBeagle Bon Appetite Organic Doggie Food	Inventory	MookieTheBeagle Bon Appetite Organic Doggie Food	$ 30	$13
Doggie Hammocks	MookieTheBeagle Hammock Small	Inventory	MookieTheBeagle Doggie Hammock Small	$100	$40
Doggie Hammocks	MookieTheBeagle Hammock Medium	Inventory	MookieTheBeagle Doggie Hammock Medium	$150	$60
Doggie Hammocks	MookieTheBeagle Hammock Large	Inventory	MookieTheBeagle Doggie Hammock Large	$200	$80
Pet Healthcare Supplies	E-Collar Cone	Inventory	E-Collar Cone Adjustable to fit various size doggie necks to permit wound healing	$ 20	$ 8
Pet Healthcare Supplies	Activated Charcoal	Inventory	Activated Charcoal for Suspected Poisoning	$ 18	$ 5
Pet Healthcare Supplies	Gauze Bandages	Inventory	Gauze Bandages for Wound Dressing	$ 12	$ 3
Pet Healthcare Supplies	Sterile Towels	Inventory	Sterile Towels for Wound Cleaning	$ 15	$ 4
Pet Healthcare Supplies	Oral Syringes	Inventory	Oral Syringes for Medication Administration (10 pack)	$ 10	$ 2
Pet Healthcare Supplies	Sterile Latex Gloves	Inventory	Sterile Latex Gloves (50 pack)	$ 36	$12

1. Export the Products and Services List to PDF.

   a. From the Products and Services List screen select **Run Report.** (If Run Report doesn't appear on the screen, select the More drop-down menu, then select Run Report.)

   b. Select **Export drop-down arrow > Export to PDF**

2. Update Mookie The Beagle Concierge Shipping Address.

   a. Go to **Gear** icon > **Account and Settings** > **Company** > **Address** > **Company Address**

   b. Enter Address: **432 Phoenician Way**

   c. Enter City: **Mountain View**

   d. Enter State: **CA**

   e. Enter Zip: **94043**

   f. Select Customer-facing address: **Same as company address**

   g. Select Legal address: **Same as company address**

   h. Select **Save**

P7.1.2 Vendor Transaction: Purchase Order

Complete the following Mookie The Beagle Concierge purchase order to order Mookie The Beagle doggie hammocks.

1. Create Purchase Order.

   a. From the Create (+) icon select **Purchase Order**

   b. Add New Vendor: **Maddy's Marvels**

   c. Select Purchase Order Date **01/18/2018**

   d. Verify Shipping Address: **Mookie The Beagle Concierge 432 Phoenician Way Mountain View CA 94043**

   e. Select Item Details Line 1: PRODUCT/SERVICE: **Doggie Hammocks: MookieTheBeagle Hammock Small**

   f. Enter QTY: **2**

   g. RATE and AMOUNT fields should autofill

   h. What is the RATE that autofills?

   i. What is the Total AMOUNT for Line 1?

2. Enter PO Line 2.

   a. Select Item Details Line 2: PRODUCT/SERVICE: **Doggie Hammocks: MookieTheBeagle Hammock Medium**

   b. Enter QTY: **3**

   c. RATE and AMOUNT fields should autofill

   d. What is the RATE that autofills?

   e. What is the Total AMOUNT for Line 2?

3. Enter PO Line 3.

    a. Select Item Details Line 3: PRODUCT/SERVICE: **Doggie Hammocks: MookieTheBeagle Hammock Large**

    b. Enter QTY: **1**

    c. RATE and AMOUNT fields should autofill

    d. What is the RATE that autofills?

    e. What is the Total AMOUNT for Line 3?

4. Total PO.

    a. What is the Total Amount for the Purchase Order?

    b. Select **Save and New**

P7.1.3 Vendor Transaction Purchase Order

Complete the following Mookie The Beagle Concierge purchase order to order Mookie The Beagle Concierge pet healthcare inventory.

1. Create Purchase Order.

    a. From the Create (+) icon select **Purchase Order**

    b. Add New Vendor: **Cathy PetCare Supplies**

    c. Select Date **01/18/2018**

    d. Select Item Details Line 1: PRODUCT/SERVICE: **Pet Healthcare Supplies: E-Collar Cone**

    e. Enter QTY: **1**

    f. RATE and AMOUNT fields should autofill

    g. What is the RATE that autofills?

    h. What is the Total AMOUNT for Line 1?

2. Enter PO Line 2.

    a. Select Item Details Line 2: PRODUCT/SERVICE: **Pet Healthcare Supplies: Activated Charcoal**

    b. Enter QTY: **5**

    c. RATE and AMOUNT fields should autofill

    d. What is the RATE that autofills?

    e. What is the Total AMOUNT for Line 2?

3. Enter PO Line 3.

   a. Select Item Details Line 3: PRODUCT/SERVICE: **Pet Healthcare Supplies: Gauze Bandages**

   b. Enter QTY: **4**

   c. RATE and AMOUNT fields should autofill

   d. What is the RATE that autofills?

   e. What is the Total AMOUNT for Line 3?

4. Enter PO Line 4.

   a. Select Item Details Line 4: PRODUCT/SERVICE: **Pet Healthcare Supplies: Sterile Towels**

   b. Enter QTY: **6**

   c. RATE and AMOUNT fields should autofill

   d. What is the RATE that autofills?

   e. What is the Total AMOUNT for Line 4?

5. Enter PO Line.

   a. Select Item Details Line 4: PRODUCT/SERVICE: **Pet Healthcare Supplies: Oral Syringes**

   b. Enter QTY: **2**

   c. RATE and AMOUNT fields should autofill

   d. What is the RATE that autofills?

   e. What is the Total AMOUNT for Line 5?

6. Enter PO Line 6.

   a. Select Item Details Line 4: PRODUCT/SERVICE: **Pet Healthcare Supplies: Sterile Latex Gloves**

   b. Enter QTY: **6**

   c. RATE and AMOUNT fields should autofill

   d. What is the RATE that autofills?

   e. What is the Total AMOUNT for Line 6?

7. Total PO.

   a. What is the Total Amount for the Purchase Order?

   b. Select **Save and New**

P7.1.4 Purchase Order

Complete the following purchase order to order MookieTheBeagle Bon Appetite Organic Doggie Food.

1. Create Purchase Order.

    a. From the Create (+) icon select **Purchase Order**

    b. Select Date **01/18/2018**

    c. Add New Vendor: **Only The Best Pet Food**

    d. Select Item Details Line 1: PRODUCT/SERVICE: **Pet Food Supplies: MookieTheBeagle Bon Appetite Organic Doggie Food**

    e. Enter QTY: **10**

    f. RATE and AMOUNT fields should autofill

    g. What is the RATE that autofills?

    h. What is the Total AMOUNT for Line 1?

2. Total PO.

    a. What is the Total Amount for the Purchase Order?

    b. Select **Save and Close**

P7.1.5 Vendor Transaction: Bill

Complete the following to record a bill received for the MookieTheBeagle Doggie Hammocks ordered.

1. Create Bill.

    a. From the Create (+) icon select **Bill**

    b. Select Choose a payee: **Maddy's Marvels**

    c. Select Bill Date **01/21/2018**

    d. The Purchase Order entered previously should appear on the Right side of the screen. Select **Add** to add the PO to the bill. Item Details should now show the items from the POs.

    e. What is the Total for the Bill?

    f. Select **Save**

2. View the Transaction Journal for the Bill.

    a. From the bottom of the Maddy's Marvels Bill select **More > Transaction Journal**

    b. What are the Accounts and Amounts Debited?

    c. What Account and Amount is Credited?

P7.1.6 Vendor Transaction: Bill

Complete the following to record a bill received for the Mookie The Beagle Concierge Pet Healthcare supplies ordered.

1. Create Bill.

   a. From the Create (+) icon select **Bill**

   b. Select Choose a payee: **Cathy PetCare Supplies**

   c. Select Bill Date: **01/22/2018**

   d. The Purchase Order entered previously should appear on the Right side of the screen. Select **Add** to add the PO to the bill. Item Details should now show the items from the POs.

   e. What is the Total for the Bill?

   f. Select **Save**

2. View the Transaction Journal for the Bill.

   a. From the bottom of the Cathy's PetCare Supplies Bill select **More > Transaction Journal**

   b. What are the Accounts and Amounts Debited?

   c. What Account and Amount is Credited?

P7.1.7 Vendor Transaction: Bill

Complete the following to record a bill received for the MookieTheBeagle Doggie Organic Doggie Food ordered.

1. Create Bill.

   a. From the Create (+) icon select **Bill**

   b. Select Choose a payee: **Only the Best Pet Food**

   c. Select Bill Date: **01/22/2018**

   d. The Purchase Order entered previously should appear on the Right side of the screen. Select **Add** to add the PO to the bill. Item Details should now show the items from the POs.

   e. What is the Total for the Bill?

   f. Select **Save**

2. View the Transaction Journal for the Bill.

   a. From the bottom of the Only the Best Pet Food Bill select **More > Transaction Journal**

   b. What are the Accounts and Amounts Debited?

   c. What Account and Amount is Credited?

P7.1.8 Vendor Transaction: Pay Bills

Complete the following to pay Mookie The Beagle Concierge bills.

1. Pay Bills.

   a. From the Create (+) icon select **Pay Bills**

   b. Select Payment account: **Checking**

   c. Select Payment Date: **01/23/2018**

   d. Select Payee: **Maddy's Marvels**

   e. Select Payee: **Only the Best Pet Food**

   f. What is the Total Payment Amount?

   g. Select **Save and Close**

2. View the Transaction Journal for Pay Bills.

   a. From the Navigation Bar select **Expenses**

   b. From the Expense Transactions List select **Bill Payment to Maddy's Marvels**

   c. From the bottom of Maddy's Marvels Bill Payment select **More > Transaction Journal**

   d. What Account and Amount is Debited?

   e. What Account and Amount is Credited?

3. View the Transaction Journal for Pay Bills.

   a. From the Navigation Bar select **Expenses**

   b. From the Expense Transactions List select **Bill Payment to Only the Best Pet Food**

   c. From the bottom of Only the Best Pet Food Bill Payment select **More > Transaction Journal**

   d. What Account and Amount is Debited?

   e. What Account and Amount is Credited?

P7.1.9 Customer Transaction: Invoice

Complete the following to record the sale of a MookieTheBeagle Doggie Hammock to Graziella for Bella, her pet Italian Greyhound.

1. Set up Sales Tax Rate.

   a. From the Navigation Bar select **Sales Tax**

   b. From the Sales Tax Center select **Set Up Sales Tax Rates**

    c. Select Sales Tax Settings: **Mark all new customers taxable**

    d. Select Sales Tax Settings: **Mark all new products and services taxable**

    e. Select Sales Tax Rates and Agencies: **Single Tax Rate**

    f. Enter Tax name: **California**

    g. Enter Agency name: **Board of Equalization**

    h. Enter Rate **8.00%**

    i. Select **Save**

2. Create Invoice.

    a. From the Create (+) icon select **Invoice**

    b. Select Choose a customer **Bella Graziella**

    c. Select Date **01/25/2018**

    d. Select Item Details Line 1: PRODUCT/SERVICE: **Doggie Hammocks: MookieTheBeagle Hammocks Medium**

    e. Enter QTY: **1**

    f. RATE and AMOUNT fields should autofill

    g. What is the AMOUNT?

    h. **Check** TAX

    i. Select a Sales Tax Rate: **California (8%)**

    j. What is the Total for the Invoice?

    k. Select **Save** and leave the Invoice displayed

3. View the Transaction Journal for the Invoice.

    a. From the bottom of the Bella Graziella Invoice select **More > Transaction Journal**

    b. What are the Accounts and Amounts Debited?

    c. What are the Accounts and Amounts Credited?

P7.1.10 Customer Transaction Invoice

While Mimi's pet French Bulldog, Bebe, is recovering from her paw injury at Doggie Day Care, Bebe needs in home care. So Mimi ordered the following products and services using the Mookie The Beagle Concierge app.

- 1 MookieTheBeagle Doggie Hammock Small
- 1 MookieTheBeagle E-Collar Cone

- 3 Gauze Bandages
- 2 Sterile Towels
- 1 Oral Syringes
- 1 Sterile Latex Gloves (50 pack)
- 1 Pet Care Errand Service (to deliver the Mookie The Beagle Concierge supplies ordered)
- 2 Pet Health Care Medium Visit Service (to administer medication and change wound dressings)

1. Create Invoice.

   a. From the Create (+) icon select **Invoice**

   b. Select Choose a customer: **Bebe Mimi**

   c. Select Date **01/27/2018**

   d. Select Item Details Line 1: PRODUCT/SERVICE: **Doggie Hammocks: MookieTheBeagle Hammock Small**

   e. Enter QTY: **1**

   f. RATE and AMOUNT fields should autofill

   g. What is the AMOUNT on Line 1?

   h. **Check** TAX

2. Enter Invoice Line 2.

   a. Select Item Details Line 2: PRODUCT/SERVICE: **Pet Healthcare Supplies: E-Collar Cone**

   b. Enter QTY: **1**

   c. RATE and AMOUNT fields should autofill

   d. What is the AMOUNT on Line 2?

   e. **Check** TAX

3. Enter Invoice Line 3.

   a. Select Item Details Line 3: PRODUCT/SERVICE: **Pet Healthcare Supplies: Gauze Bandages**

   b. Enter QTY: **3**

   c. RATE and AMOUNT fields should autofill

   d. What is the AMOUNT on Line 3?

   e. **Check** TAX

4. Enter Invoice Line 4.

    a. Select Item Details Line 4: PRODUCT/SERVICE: **Pet Healthcare Supplies: Sterile Towels**

    b. Enter QTY: **2**

    c. RATE and AMOUNT fields should autofill

    d. What is the AMOUNT on Line 4?

    e. **Check** TAX

5. Enter Invoice Line 5.

    a. Select Item Details Line 5: PRODUCT/SERVICE: **Pet Healthcare Supplies: Oral Syringes**

    b. Enter QTY: **1**

    c. RATE and AMOUNT fields should autofill

    d. What is the AMOUNT on Line 5?

    e. **Check** TAX

6. Enter Invoice Line 6.

    a. Select Item Details Line 6: PRODUCT/SERVICE: **Pet Healthcare Supplies: Sterile Latex Gloves**

    b. Enter QTY: **1**

    c. RATE and AMOUNT fields should autofill

    d. What is the AMOUNT on Line 6?

    e. **Check** TAX

7. Enter Invoice Line 7.

    a. Select Item Details Line 7: PRODUCT/SERVICE: **Pet Care: Errand**

    b. Enter QTY: **1**

    c. RATE and AMOUNT fields should autofill

    d. What is the AMOUNT on Line 7?

    e. **Uncheck** TAX

8. Enter Invoice Line 8.

    a. Select Item Details Line 8: PRODUCT/SERVICE: **Pet Health Care: Medium Visit**

    b. Enter QTY: **2**

    c. RATE and AMOUNT fields should autofill

    d. What is the AMOUNT on Line 8?

    e. **Uncheck** TAX

9. Select Tax Rate.

    a. What is the Subtotal for the Invoice?

    b. Select a Sales Tax Rate: **California (8%)**

    c. What is the amount of tax?

    d. What is the Total for the Invoice?

    e. Select **Save** and leave the Invoice displayed

10. View the Transaction Journal for the Invoice.

    a. From the bottom of the Bebe Mimi Invoice select **More > Transaction Journal**

    b. What are the Accounts and Amounts Debited?

    c. What are the Accounts and Amounts Credited?

P7.1.11 Customer Transaction Invoice

TJ Ryan, a successful interior designer, used the Mookie The Beagle Concierge app to purchase the following products and services for his pet Golden Retriever, Baxter when TJ was detained for hours longer than planned on an interior design job gone awry.

- **1** MookieTheBeagle Doggie Hammock Large
- **2** bags of MookieTheBeagle Bon Appetite Organic Doggie Food
- **1** Pet Care Errand Service (to deliver the Mookie The Beagle Concierge supplies ordered)
- **2** Pet Care Short Visit Service (to feed Baxter and take him on a couple of short walks)

1. Create Invoice and enter products purchased.

    a. From the Create (+) icon select **Invoice**

    b. Add New Customer **Baxter TJ Ryan**

    c. Select Date **01/27/2018**

    d. Select Item Details Line 1: PRODUCT/SERVICE: **Doggie Hammocks: MookieTheBeagle Hammock Medium**

e. Enter QTY: **1**

f. RATE and AMOUNT fields should autofill

g. What is the AMOUNT for Line 1?

h. **Check** TAX

i. Select Item Details Line 2: PRODUCT/SERVICE: **Pet Food Supplies: Mookie Bon Appetite Organic Doggie Food**

j. Enter QTY: **2**

k. RATE and AMOUNT fields should autofill

l. What is the AMOUNT for Line 2?

m. **Check** TAX

n. Select **Save** and leave the Invoice displayed

2. Enter services purchased on Invoice.

a. Select Item Details Line 3: PRODUCT/SERVICE: **Pet Care: Errand**

b. Enter QTY: **1**

c. RATE and AMOUNT fields should autofill

d. What is the AMOUNT for Line 3?

e. **Uncheck** TAX

f. Select Item Details Line 4: PRODUCT/SERVICE: **Pet Care: Short Visit**

g. Enter QTY: **2**

h. RATE and AMOUNT fields should autofill

i. What is the AMOUNT for Line 4?

j. **Uncheck** TAX

k. Select a Sales Tax Rate: **California (8%)**

l. What is the Subtotal for the Invoice?

m. What is the Taxable Subtotal for the Invoice?

n. What is the amount of tax on the invoice?

o. What is the Total for the Invoice?

p. Select **Save** and leave the Invoice displayed

3. View the Transaction Journal for the Invoice.

    a. From the bottom of the Baxter TJ Ryan Invoice select **More > Transaction Journal**

    b What are the Accounts and Amounts Debited?

    c. What are the Accounts and Amounts Credited?

P7.1.12 Customer Transaction: Receive Payment

Complete the following to record a customer payment from TJ Ryan.

1. Create Receive Payment.

    a. From the Create (+) icon select **Receive Payment**

    b. Select Choose a customer: **Baxter TJ Ryan**

    c. Select Payment Date: **01/30/2018**

    d. Select Payment Method: **Credit Card**

    e. Select Deposit to: **Checking**

    f. Select the Invoice just entered for **Baxter TJ Ryan**

    g. What is the Amount Received?

    h. Select **Save and Close**

2. View the Transaction Journal for Receive Payments.

    a. From the Navigation Bar select **Sales**

    b. From the Sales Transactions List select **Baxter TJ Ryan Payment** just entered

    c. From the bottom of Baxter TJ Ryan Receive Payment select **More > Transaction Journal**

    d. What Account and Amount is Debited?

    e. What Account and Amount is Credited?

www.my-quickbooksonline.com

Go to www.My-QuickBooksOnline.com for additional resources for you including QBO Help, QBO Videos, and more.

Chapter 8

Employees and Payroll

Chapter 8 focuses on recording employee and payroll transactions. Payroll involves preparing employee paychecks, withholding the appropriate amount in taxes, and paying the company's share of payroll taxes. To assist in processing payroll, QBO offers a time-tracking feature that permits us to track the amount of time worked.

Section 8.1

QBO SatNav

QBO SatNav is your satellite navigation for QuickBooks Online, assisting you in navigating QBO

Chapter 8 focuses on QuickBooks Online Employee transactions which are considered payroll expenses.

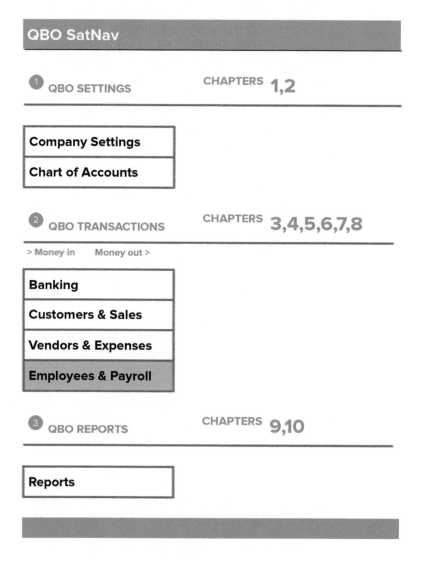

Section 8.2

QBO LOGIN TO SAMPLE COMPANY

To log into the QBO Sample Company:

1. Open a web browser. (Note: Intuit recommends using Google Chrome.)
2. Go to the https://qbo.intuit.com/redir/testdrive
3. Follow onscreen instructions for security verification.

Craig's Design and Landscaping Services should appear on your screen.

We use the Sample Company for practice throughout the chapter and exercises. The Sample Company will reset each time it is reopened. So make certain to allow enough time to complete all chapter activities before closing the Sample Company. Otherwise, you will lose the work you have entered when you reopen the Sample Company.

Section 8.3

NAVIGATING EMPLOYEE TRANSACTIONS

There are two main aspects to using QBO for Employee and Payroll purposes:

- Setting up payroll
- Processing payroll

PAYROLL SETUP

Payroll setup requires:

1. Set up **Employees List**
2. Turn on **Time Tracking** preference
3. Turn on **QBO Payroll**

PAYROLL PROCESSING

Payroll processing consists of the following four main types of tasks:

1. **Enter Time.** QBO permits us to track employee time worked to use in processing payroll and billing customers.
2. **Pay Employees.** Select employees to pay and create their paychecks.
3. **Pay Payroll Liabilities.** Pay payroll tax liabilities due governmental agencies such as the IRS. Payroll tax liabilities include federal income taxes withheld, state income taxes withheld, FICA (Social Security and Medicare), and unemployment taxes.
4. **Process Payroll Forms.** Process payroll forms including Forms 940, 941, W-2, and W-3 that must be submitted to governmental agencies.

Section 8.4

EMPLOYEES LIST

The Employees List contains employee information such as address, telephone, salary or wage rate, and Social Security number.
To use the Employees List:

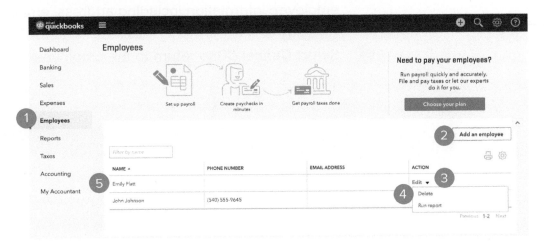

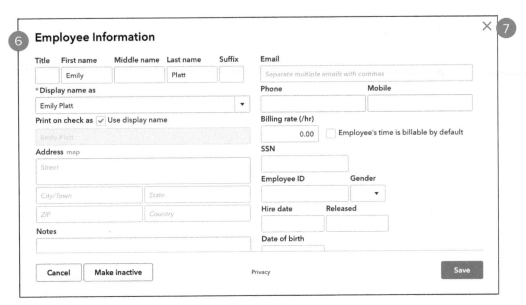

1. To view the Employees List select **Employees** from the Navigation Bar

2. To add a new Employee select **Add Employee**

3. To edit an Employee, select **Edit** for the employee

4. To delete an Employee from the Employees List select **Delete** from the drop-down menu

5. To view Employee information, click on the **Employee's Name**

6. **View** the Employee Information screen contains detailed employee information including address, email, phone, social security number, Employee ID, and date of birth

7. Select **Cancel (X)** to return to the Employees List

Section 8.5

TIME TRACKING

QBO time tracking permits us to track the amount of time worked. QBO uses time tracked to:

1. Calculate employee paychecks
2. Transfer time to sales invoices to bill customers for work performed

Although this chapter focuses on time worked by employees, work can be performed by employees, subcontractors, or owners. The time-tracking feature can be used to track time worked by any of the three. How we record the payment, however, depends upon who performs the work: employee, subcontractor, or business owner.

It is important that we determine the status of the individual performing the work. The status determines whether we record payments to the individual as an employee paycheck, vendor payment, or owner withdrawal.

Status	QBO Payment	Tax Form
Employee	Employee Paycheck	Form W-2
Contractor	Vendor Payment	Form 1099-MISC
Owner	Owner Dividend or Distribution	Owner's Tax Return

TURN ON TIME-TRACKING PREFERENCES

To turn on QBO time-tracking preferences:

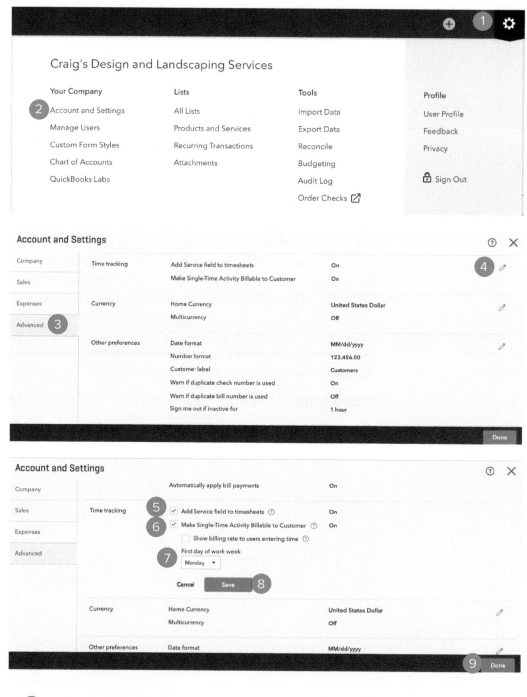

1 Select **Gear** icon

2 Under Your Company select **Account and Settings**

③ From the Account and Settings screen, select **Advanced**

④ Scroll down to the Time tracking section and select the **Edit Pencil**

⑤ Check **Add Service field to timesheets** to display **On**

⑥ Check **Make Single-Time Activity Billable to Customer** to display **On**

⑦ Select First day of work week: **Monday**

⑧ Select **Save**

⑨ Select **Done**

After turning on time-tracking preferences, we are ready to enter time.

ENTER TIME TRACKING

When employees use time tracking, the employee records total time worked and any time that is billable to a specific customer. Time data is then used to:

1. Prepare paychecks
2. Invoice customers for billable time

QBO provides two different ways to track time.

1. **Single Time Activity.** Use Single Time Activity time tracking to time one activity and enter the time data. QBO automatically records the time on the employee's weekly timesheet.
2. **Weekly Timesheet.** Use the weekly timesheet to enter time worked by each employee during the week, including time that is billable to specific customers.

SINGLE TIME ACTIVITY

The Single Time Activity for tracking time tracks the time for one activity. We will use the QBO Single Time Activity feature to time how long it takes to complete payroll activities in this chapter.

To use the Single Time Activity feature:

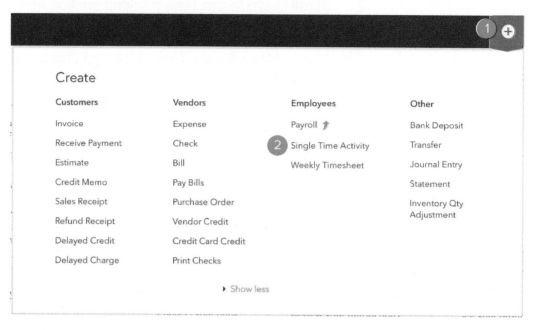

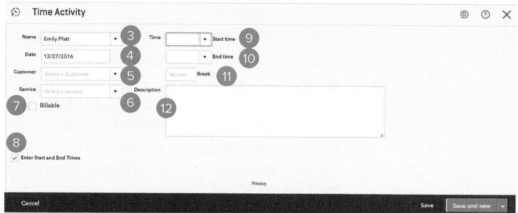

1. Select **Create (+)** icon

2. Under Employees select **Single Time Activity**

3. From the Time Activity screen, select **+ Add new** and enter your name

4. Enter **Date**

5. If the work was billable to a particular customer, we would select the Customer Name from the drop-down Customers List. In this case, your time is not billable to a particular customer's job, so **leave Customer blank.**

6. If the work was billable to a particular customer, we would select the Service from the drop-down Services List. In this case, your time is not billable to a particular customer's job, so **leave Service blank.**

7. If the work was billable to a particular customer, we would check Billable. In this case, your time is not billable to a particular customer's job, so **uncheck Billable.**

8. Select **Enter Start and End Times**

9. Select **Start Time**

10. When finished with the payroll activities in this chapter, you will select End time. For now, **leave End time blank.**

11. Enter **Break** when you take a break from QBO payroll chapter

12. Enter **Description** of your payroll activities in this chapter

Continue on with the remaining payroll activities in this chapter. When finished, you will enter your End Time to track your time.

WEEKLY TIMESHEET

The weekly timesheet can be used to enter the hours worked during the week. If time is billable to a specific customer, this is indicated on the weekly timesheet. Later, billable time can be transferred to a specific customer's invoice.

To use QBO weekly timesheet feature:

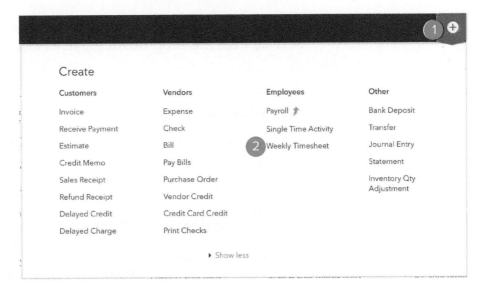

1. Select **Create (+)** icon

2. Under Employees select **Weekly Timesheet**

3. From the Weekly Timesheet screen, select **Employee Name**

4. Enter **Dates** for weekly timesheet

5. If the work was billable to a specific customer, we would select the **Customer** Name from the drop-down Customers List. Otherwise, leave Customer blank.

6. If the work was billable to a specific customer, we would select the **Service** from the drop-down Services List

7. If the work was billable to a specific customer, we would **check Billable**

8. Enter **Description**

9. Enter **Time** worked on specific days corresponding to the specific customer and service. Each time the specific customer or specific service changes, then we will move to the next line of the timesheet.

10. Verify the **Total for the Timesheet Line** that QBO calculates is correct

11. Verify the **Total for the Timesheet** that QBO calculates is correct

(12) If more lines are needed on the weekly timesheet, select **Add lines**

(13) If the weekly timesheets are similar from week to week, select **Copy last timesheet**

(14) If we need to delete a line on the timesheet, select the **Trashcan** for that line

(15) Normally we would select Save and New or Save and Close, but in this case select **Cancel.** We will enter new time tracking in the exercises at the end of the chapter.

Section 8.6

SET UP PAYROLL

To use QBO payroll requires a subscription to QBO payroll service.

If we had QBO payroll service, to turn on the QBO payroll we would complete the following.

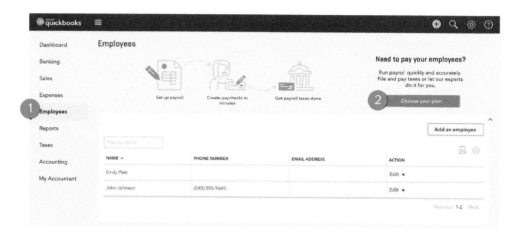

1. If we had QuickBooks Online Payroll Service, we would select **Employees** from the Navigation Bar

2. Then on the Employees screen we would select **Choose your plan.** If we were not using the Sample Company, next we would follow the onscreen instructions to complete payroll setup.

Section 8.7

PAY EMPLOYEES

PAY EMPLOYEES USING DIRECT DEPOSIT OR PRINT CHECKS

After entering time worked and setting up payroll, we would pay employees on a scheduled payroll payday. QBO Payroll will send email reminders when payroll should be run.

If we had QuickBooks Online Payroll Service, to run QBO payroll we would complete the following.

1. If we had QuickBooks Online Payroll Service, we would select **Employees** from the Navigation Bar. Since this is the Sample Company, next we must select **Choose your plan.**

2. Then when the Employees screen appears we would select **Run Payroll.** After selecting Run Payroll, we would follow the onscreen instructions to process and preview the employee paychecks.

QBO Payroll offers the options of printing checks or using direct deposit to employees' bank accounts.

QBO MOBILE PAYROLL APP

The QBO Mobile Payroll app for Apple iPhone/iPad and Android offers employers the convenience of running payroll from their mobile devices. Then the payroll information is synced with QuickBooks Online.

Section 8.8

PAY PAYROLL LIABILITIES

Payroll liabilities include amounts for:

- Federal income taxes withheld from employee paychecks
- State income taxes withheld from employee paychecks
- FICA (Social Security and Medicare, including both the employee and the employer portions)
- Unemployment taxes

Federal income taxes, state income taxes, and the employee portion of FICA are withheld from the employee, and the company has an obligation (liability) to remit these amounts to the appropriate tax agency. The employer share of FICA and unemployment taxes are payroll taxes the employer owes.

QuickBooks Online Full Service Payroll offers companies the ability to e-pay payroll liabilities. The company sets up e-pay by selecting which company bank accounts from which to pay the payroll liabilities. The appropriate federal and state agencies are selected to receive the payments. QB Online Payroll even sends email reminders when it is time to e-pay the payroll liabilities.

Section 8.9

FILE PAYROLL FORMS

Payroll forms summarize the amount of payroll withholdings that have been collected and remitted.

Payroll tax forms include:

- Federal Form 940: Employer's Annual Federal Unemployment (FUTA) Tax Return. This form summarizes the amount of unemployment tax paid and due by the employer.

- Federal Form 941: Employer's Quarterly Federal Tax Return. Filed with the IRS, this form summarizes the amount of federal income tax, Social Security, and Medicare withheld from employee paychecks for the quarter.

- Federal Form 944: Employer's Annual Federal Tax Return. Filed with the IRS, this form summarizes the amount of federal income tax, Social Security, and Medicare withheld from employee paychecks for the year. Form 944 is used by very small employers instead of filing Form 941 each quarter.

- Form W-2: Wage and Tax Statement. Before the end of January, an employer must provide W-2s to employees that summarize amounts paid for salaries, wages, and withholdings for the year.

- Form W-3: Transmittal of Wage and Tax Statements. Filed with the Social Security Administration, this form is a summary of all an employer's W-2 forms.

QB Online Full Service Payroll offers companies the ability to e-file payroll tax forms. The company must set up this feature for e-filing, but once set up is completed with all the appropriate agencies, it simply requires a click of a button to e-file. QB Online Payroll sends email reminders when it is time to e-file the various payroll forms and sends confirmations once the e-filing has been completed.

> **STOP** the Stopwatch now by clicking the Stop button. How long did it take you to complete the payroll activities? Click Clear then Close the Stopwatch.

Section 8.10

ACCOUNTING ESSENTIALS

Payroll Liabilities and Payroll Taxes

Accounting Essentials summarize important foundational accounting knowledge you may find useful when using QBO

What are payroll liabilities?

- Payroll liabilities include two types of amounts:
    1. Amounts withheld from employee paychecks that must be paid to third parties
    2. Payroll tax expenses owed by the business
- Payroll liabilities include:
    - Federal income taxes withheld from employee paychecks
    - State income taxes withheld from employee paychecks
    - FICA (Social Security and Medicare, including both the employee and the employer portions)
    - Unemployment taxes
- Federal income taxes, state income taxes, and the employee portion of FICA are withheld from the employee, and the company has an obligation (liability) to remit these amounts to the appropriate tax agency. The employer share of FICA and unemployment taxes are payroll taxes the employer owes.

Payroll Liabilities (Federal)	Withheld from Employee Pay	Payroll Tax Expense Owed by Business	Reported on Tax Form
Federal Income Taxes	X		941 Quarterly 944 Annual
FICA (SS + MEDICARE)	X	X	941 Quarterly 944 Annually
Federal Unemployment Tax		X	940 Annual

What are payroll tax forms?

- Basically, payroll forms summarize the amount of payroll withholdings that have been collected and remitted.

- Payroll tax forms include:

  - Federal Form 940: Employer's Annual Federal Unemployment (FUTA) Tax Return. This form summarizes the amount of unemployment tax paid and due by the employer.

  - Federal Form 941: Employer's Quarterly Federal Tax Return. Filed with the IRS, this form summarizes the amount of federal income tax, Social Security, and Medicare withheld from employee paychecks for the quarter.

  - Federal Form 944: Employer's Annual Federal Tax Return. Filed with the IRS, this form summarizes the amount of federal income tax, Social Security, and Medicare withheld from employee paychecks for the year. Form 944 is used by very small employers instead of filing Form 941 each quarter.

  - Form W-2: Wage and Tax Statement. Before the end of January, an employer must provide W-2s to employees that summarize amounts paid for salaries, wages, and withholdings for the year.

  - Form W-3: Transmittal of Wage and Tax Statements. Filed with the Social Security Administration, this form is a summary of all an employer's W-2 forms.

PRACTICE QUIZ 8

Q8.1

A company is not required to withhold payroll taxes for:

a. Employees paid by the hour

b. Salaried employees

c. Out-of-state employees

d. Independent contractors

Q8.2

A payment to a stockholder is recorded as a(n):

a. Employee paycheck

b. Vendor payment

c. Dividend

d. None of the above

Q8.3

In the Weekly Timesheet window you can record:

a. Time billable to a specific vendor

b. Time billable to a specific customer

c. How many shipments of inventory items were received

d. Number of purchase orders from each supplier

Q8.4

A company completes Form _____ to summarize for the IRS, the amount of federal income tax, Social Security, and Medicare withheld from employee paychecks for the year.

a. W-3

b. 940

c. 944

d. None of the above

Q8.5

Which one of the following is not a payroll liability?

   a. Property taxes

   b. Unemployment taxes

   c. State income taxes withheld

   d. Federal income taxes withheld from employee paychecks

Q8.6

QuickBooks permits you to track employee time using which of the two following:

   a. Weekly Timesheet

   b. Paycheck

   c. Single Time Activity

   d. Monthly Timesheet

Q8.7

The employer must match which one of the following taxes paid by an employee?

   a. State Income

   b. Medicare

   c. Federal Income

   d. Federal Unemployment

Q8.8

All of the following are payroll liabilities owed to outside agencies except:

   a. Net Pay

   b. Federal Income taxes

   c. State Income taxes

   d. Unemployment taxes

Q8.9

The following taxes are reported on Form 941 except:

a. FICA-Medicare (employer and employee)

b. State income taxes withheld from the employee paychecks

c. Federal income taxes withheld from the employee paychecks

d. FICA-Social Security (employer and employee)

Q8.10

Net Pay is equal to:

a. Gross pay minus deductions for federal and state income taxes and unemployment taxes

b. Gross pay minus federal and state income taxes, but not FICA taxes

c. Gross pay plus deductions for FICA taxes and federal and state income taxes

d. Gross pay minus deductions for FICA taxes and federal and state income taxes

Q8.11

QuickBooks Online Full Service payroll can:

a. E-file payroll tax forms

b. E-pay payroll taxes from your company checking account

c. Direct deposit employee paychecks

d. All of the above

Q8.12

Payroll liabilities include the following two types of amounts:

a. Amounts withheld from employees paychecks that must be paid to third parties, such as federal income tax withheld

b. Payroll tax expenses owed by the business, such as unemployment tax

c. Net paycheck amount paid to employees

d. Purchases from vendors

Q8.13

To turn on QBO payroll:

   a. From the Gear icon select Employees > Turn on Payroll

   b. From the Navigation Bar select Transactions > Expenses > Turn on Payroll

   c. From the Gear icon select Transactions > Payroll

   d. From the Navigation Bar select Employees > Turn on Payroll

Q8.14

After turning on QBO payroll, to run QBO payroll:

   a. From the Navigation Bar select Employees > Run Payroll

   b. From the Gear icon select Employees > Run Payroll

   c. From the Navigation Bar select Transactions > Expenses

   d. From the Gear icon select Transactions > Run Payroll

EXERCISES 8

> We use the QBO Sample Company, Craig's Design and Landscaping Services for practice throughout the exercises. The Sample Company will reset each time it is reopened. So make certain to allow enough time to complete exercises before closing the Sample Company. Otherwise, you will lose the work you have entered when you reopen the Sample Company.

To access the QBO Sample Company, complete the following steps.

1. Open a web browser. (Note: Intuit recommends using Google Chrome.)

2. Go to the https://qbo.intuit.com/redir/testdrive

3. Follow onscreen instructions for security verification.

Craig's Design and Landscaping Services should appear on your screen.

E8.1 Employee and Payroll Activities

Match the following activities with the following framework for navigating QBO payroll.

Employee and Payroll Activities

a. Enter Time to track employee time worked to use in processing payroll and billing customers

b. Process Payroll Forms including Forms 940, 941, W-2, and W-3 that must be submitted to governmental agencies

c. Turn on QBO Payroll

d. Pay Employees by selecting employees to pay and creating their paychecks

e. Turn on Time Tracking preference

f. Set up Employees List

g. Pay Payroll Liabilities, such as federal income taxes withheld, state income taxes withheld, FICA (Social Security and Medicare), and unemployment taxes due to governmental agencies

Navigating Employee and Payroll Activities

PAYROLL SETUP

1. _____
2. _____
3. _____

PAYROLL PROCESSING

1. _____
2. _____
3. _____
4. _____

E8.2 Time Tracking and Status

Match the following items with the appropriate status of the individual performing work using time tracking.

Items

- Dividend or distribution
- Form W-2
- Paycheck

- Form 1099-MISC
- Owners Tax Return
- Vendor Payment

Status	QBO Payment	Tax Form
Employee	_____	_____
Contractor	_____	_____
Owner	_____	_____

E8.3 Payroll Liabilities

Place an X in the following appropriate boxes to indicate whether the federal payroll item is paid by the employee or the employer.

Payroll Liabilities (Federal)	Withheld from Employee Pay	Payroll Tax Expense Owed by Business
Federal Income Taxes		
FICA (SS + MEDICARE)		
Federal Unemployment Tax		

E8.4 Time Tracking Preferences

Answer the following questions about the Time Tracking preferences if a company plans to use QBO for time tracking.

1. If a company wants to turn on Time Tracking preferences, go to _____ icon > _____ > _____
2. What should be the setting for Add Service field to timesheets?
3. What should be the setting for Make Single-Time Activity Billable to Customer?

E8.5 Single Time Activity

Using the QBO Sample Company, Craig's Design and Landscaping Company, complete the following to track time by entering a single time activity.

1. Create Single Time Activity.
   a. From the Create (+) icon select **Single Time Activity**
   b. Select a Name: **+ Add new** > enter **your own name** > **Employee Type** > **Save**

  c. Select Customer: **Cool Cars**

  d. Enter Service: **Landscaping: Installation**

  e. **Check** Bill at **$50.00** per hour

  f. **Check** Enter Start and End Times

  g. Select Start time: **8:00 AM**

  h. Select End time: **11:45 AM**

  i. What is the summary of time worked in hours and minutes?

  j. What is the total cost of the time worked?

  k. Select **Save and New**

E8.6 Single Time Activity

Using the QBO Sample Company, Craig's Design and Landscaping Company, complete the following to track time by entering a single time activity.

  1. Create Single Time Activity.

  a. From the Create (+) icon select **Single Time Activity**

  b. Select a Name: **+ Add new** > enter **your own name** > **Employee** Type > **Save**

  c. Select Customer: **Cool Cars**

  d. Enter Service: **Landscaping: Installation**

  e. **Check** Bill at **$50.00** per hour

  f. **Check** Enter Start and End Times

  g. Select Start time: **1:00 PM**

  h. Select End time: **5:00 PM**

  i. What is the summary of time worked in hours and minutes?
  j. What is the total cost of the time worked?

  k. Select **Save and New**

E8.7 Single Time Activity

Using the QBO Sample Company, Craig's Design and Landscaping Company, complete the following to track time by entering a single time activity.

  1. Create Single Time Activity.

  a. From the Create (+) icon select **Single Time Activity**

  b. Select a Name: **+ Add new** > enter **your own name** > **Employee** Type > **Save**

c. Select Customer: **Red Rock Diner**

d. Enter Service: **Landscaping: Installation**

e. **Check** Bill at **$50.00** per hour

f. **Check** Enter Start and End Times

g. Select Start time: **5:30 PM**

h. Select End time: **7:00 PM**

i. What is the summary of time worked in hours and minutes?

j. What is the total cost of the time worked?

k. Select **Save and Close**

E8.8 Invoice and Time Tracking

This assignment is a continuation of E8.5 to E8.7

Using the QBO Sample Company, Craig's Design and Landscaping Company, complete the following.

1. Create Invoice with Tracked Time.

    a. From the Create (+) icon select **Invoice**

    b. Select Choose a customer: **Cool Cars**

    c. From the Add to Invoice drawer on the right side of the screen, select: **Don't group time > Add all**

    d. What is the Balance due on the Invoice?

    e. Select **Save** and leave the Invoice displayed

2. View the Transaction Journal for the Invoice.

    a. From the bottom of the Cool Cars Invoice select **More > Transaction Journal**

    b. What are the Accounts and Amounts Debited?

    c. What are the Accounts and Amounts Credited?

E8.9 Weekly Timesheet

This assignment is a continuation of E8.5 to E8.7

Using the QBO Sample Company, Craig's Design and Landscaping Company, complete the following to track time using the QBO Weekly Timesheet.

1. Create Weekly Timesheet.

   a. From the Create (+) icon select **Weekly Timesheet**

   b. Select: **Your Name**

   c. Total Hours should be: **9:15**

   d. If needed, select **Add Lines**

   e. On the next open line, select Customer Name: **Red Rock Diner**

   f. Select Service item: **Landscaping: Installation**

   g. **Check** Bill at **$50.00** per hour

   h. Enter **8 hours for the next 2 days**

   i. What are the Total Hours for the Weekly Timesheet?

   j. Select **Save and Close**

E8.10 Time Activity

This assignment is a continuation of E8.5, E8.6, E8.7, and E8.9

Using the QBO Sample Company, Craig's Design and Landscaping Company, complete the following.

1. View Time Activity for Cool Cars.

   a. From the Navigation Bar select **Employees**

   b. From the Employees List select the **drop-down arrow** by Edit for **your own name > Run report**

   c. Select **Time Activity Date** to include all dates for which you entered time on the weekly timesheet, then select **Run Report**

   d. What is the Total Amount for Billable Time for Cool Cars?

   e. What is the Total Duration for Cool Cars?

2. View Time Activity for Red Rock Diner.

   a. From the Time Activity Report from requirement 1, what is the Total Amount for Billable Time for Red Rock Diner?

   b. What is the Total Duration for Red Rock Diner?

PROJECT 8.1

Project 8.1 is a continuation of Project 7.1. You will use the QBO client company you created for Project 1.1 and updated in subsequent Projects 2.1 through 7.1. Keep in mind the QBO company for Project 8.1 does not reset and carries your data forward, including any errors. So it is important to check and crosscheck your work to verify it is correct before clicking the Save button.

BACKSTORY

Mookie The Beagle™ Concierge provides convenient, high-quality pet care on demand. CK is the only employee of Mookie The Beagle Concierge. The other pet care providers are hired as independent contractors, meeting all IRS requirements to be classified as such. Mookie The Beagle Concierge would like to use the QBO weekly timesheet to track time spent on specific customers (pets).

Mookie The Beagle Concierge has asked for your assistance with the following QBO employee and payroll tasks.

QBO SatNav

Project 8.1 focuses on the QBO Transactions, specifically QBO Expense Transactions as shown in the following partial QBO SatNav.

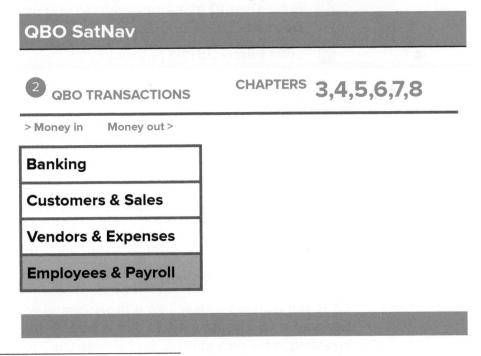

HOW TO LOG INTO QBO+

To log into QBO, complete the following steps.

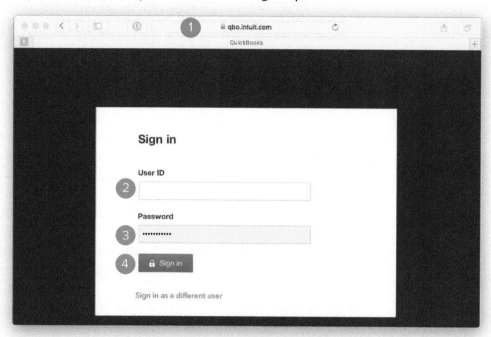

1. Using a web browser go to qbo.intuit.com

2. Enter **User ID** (the email address you used to set up your QBO Account)

3. Enter **Password** (the password you used to set up your QBO Account)

4. Select **Sign in**

> If you are <u>not</u> using a public or shared computer, to speed up login, you can save your login to your desktop and select Remember Me. If you are using a public computer or shared computer, do not save to your desktop and unselect Remember Me.

> The new QBO company we created in Project 1.1 will carry all work forward into future chapters. So it is important to check and crosscheck your work to verify it is correct before clicking the Save button. Any errors entered are carried forward in the QBO company you create for text projects.

P8.1.1 Single Time Activity

CK is still working as a full-time professional while launching Mookie The Beagle Concierge and would like a better idea of how many hours he is investing in his new startup. So he uses QBO to track his time spent working on coding his Mookie The Beagle Concierge app and other time spent on administrative and management tasks for his startup. Complete the following to enter a single time activity for CK.

1. Turn on Service Field on Timesheet.

   a. Select **Gear** icon > **Account and Settings** > **Advanced**

   b. Select the **Time Tracking Edit pencil**

   c. **Check Add Service field to time sheets** to change the setting to **On**

   d. **Check Make Single Time Activity Billable to Customers** to change the setting to **On**

   e. Select **Save**

2. Create Single Time Activity.

   a. From the Create (+) icon select **Single Time Activity**

   b. Select a Name: **+ Add new** > enter **CK Walker** > **Employee** Type > **Save**

   c. Enter Date **01/18/2018**

   d. Depending on your screen display: **Uncheck** Bill at **$0.00** per hour or Leave Billable **Unchecked**

   e. **Check** Enter Start and End Times

   f. Select Start time: **7:00 PM**

   g. Select End time: **9:00 PM**

   h. What is the summary of time worked?

   i. Select **Save and New**

3. Create Single Time Activity.

   a. Select a Name: **CK Walker**

   b. Enter Date **01/19/2018**

   c. Depending on your screen display: **Uncheck** Bill at **$0.00** per hour or Leave Billable **Unchecked**

   d. **Check** Enter Start and End Times

   e. Select Start time: **7:00 PM**

   f. Select End time: **9:30 PM**

   g. What is the summary of time worked?

   h. Select **Save and Close**

P8.1.2 Weekly Timesheet

Next CK tests using the QBO weekly timesheet feature to track his time.

1. Create Weekly Timesheet.

   a. From the Create (+) icon select **Weekly Timesheet**

   b. Select: **CK Walker**

   c. Select Date: 01/14/2018 to 01/20/2018

   d. On Line 1 where time previously entered should appear enter the following hours:

      - **2 hours for Monday 15**
      - **2 hours Tuesday 16**
      - **3 hours Wednesday 17**
      - **8 hours for Saturday January 20**

   e. What are the Total Hours for the Weekly Timesheet?

   f. Select **Save and Close**

P8.1.3 Single Time Activity

After testing the QBO time tracking feature, CK decides he would like to have a subcontractor test tracking subcontractor time to streamline billing customers and paying the subcontractors. Jean Paulny, a vet student and Mookie The Beagle Concierge subcontractor, volunteers to participate in testing the time tracking feature. Jean Paulny will be providing pet care services Monday through Thursday for TJ Ryan's Golden Retriever Baxter. TJ is tied up each evening with an intensive interior design job so Jean Paulny will be stopping by Baxter's home each evening to check on him, feed and walk him.

Complete the following Single Time Activity for Jean Paulny for Monday.

1. Create Single Time Activity.

   a. From the Create (+) icon select **Single Time Activity**

   b. Select a Name: **+ Add new** > enter **Jean Paulny** > **Vendor** Type > **Save**

   c. Enter Date **01/22/2018**

   d. Select Customer: **Baxter TJ Ryan**

   e. Enter Service: **Pet Care: Short Visit**

   f. **Check** Bill at **$20.00** per hour

g. **Check** Enter Start and End Times

h. Select Start time: **5:00 PM**

i. Select End time: **6:00 PM**

j. What is the summary of time worked in hours and minutes?

k. What is the total cost of the time worked?

l. Select **Save and New**

P8.1.4 Single Time Activity

Complete the following Single Time Activity for Jean Paulny when he provides services to TJ Ryan's Golden Retriever Baxter for Tuesday.

1. Create Single Time Activity.

   a. From the Create (+) icon select **Single Time Activity**

   b. Select a Name: **Jean Paulny**

   c. Enter Date **01/23/2018**

   d. Select Customer: **Baxter TJ Ryan**

   e. Enter Service: **Pet Care: Short Visit**

   f. **Check** Bill at **$20.00** per hour

   g. **Check** Enter Start and End Times

   h. Select Start time: **5:15 PM**

   i. Select End time: **6:15 PM**

   j. What is the summary of time worked in hours and minutes?

   k. What is the total cost of the time worked?

   l. Select **Save and New**

P8.1.5 Single Time Activity

Complete the following Single Time Activity for Jean Paulny when he provides services to TJ Ryan's Golden Retriever Baxter for Wednesday.

1. Create Single Time Activity.

   a. From the Create (+) icon select **Single Time Activity**

   b. Select a Name: **Jean Paulny**

   c. Enter Date **01/24/2018**

   d. Select Customer: **Baxter TJ Ryan**

e. Enter Service: **Pet Care: Short Visit**

f. **Check** Bill at **$20.00** per hour

g. **Check** Enter Start and End Times

h. Select Start time: **5:30 PM**

i. Select End time: **6:30 PM**

j. What is the summary of time worked in hours and minutes?

k. What is the total cost of the time worked?

l. Select **Save and Close**

P8.1.6 Weekly Timesheet

Complete the following Weekly Timesheet for Jean Paulny to summarize Single Time Activities previously entered and add services he provided to TJ Ryan's Golden Retriever Baxter for Thursday.

1. Create Weekly Timesheet.

    a. From the Create (+) icon select **Weekly Timesheet**

    b. Select Name **Jean Paulny**

    c. Select Date **01/21/2018 to 01/27/2018**

    d. On Line 1 where time previously entered for Baxter should appear enter **1 hour for Thursday January 25, 2018**

    e. What are the Total Hours for the Weekly Timesheet?

    f. What is the Total Billable Amount for the Weekly Timesheet for Jean Paulny?

    g. Select **Save and Close**

P8.1.7 Invoice and Time Tracking

Using tracked time, complete the following to create an invoice for services provided to Baxter, TJ Ryans' pet Golden Retriever.

1. Create Invoice with Tracked Time.

    a. From the Create (+) icon select **Invoice**

    b. Select Choose a customer: **Baxter TJ Ryan**

    c. Select Date **01/29/2018**

    d. From the Add to Invoice drawer on the right side of the screen, select: **Don't group time > Add all**

  e. What is the Balance due on the Invoice?

  f. Select **Save** and leave the Invoice displayed

2. View the Transaction Journal for the Invoice.

  a. From the bottom of the Baxter TJ Ryan Invoice just prepared select **More > Transaction Journal**

  b. What are the Accounts and Amounts Debited?

  c. What are the Accounts and Amounts Credited?

www.my-quickbooksonline.com

Go to www.My-QuickBooksOnline.com for additional resources for you including QBO Help, QBO Videos, and more.

Chapter 9

QBO Adjustments

Adjustments are often required to bring our accounts up to date and show the correct account balances on financial reports. Adjustments are typically made at the end of the accounting period so accounts are up to date before year-end reports are prepared.

Section 9.1

QBO SatNav

QBO SatNav is your satellite navigation for QuickBooks Online, assisting you in navigating QBO

Chapter 9 covers adjustments which are required to ensure we have reliable reports, shown in the following QBO SatNav.

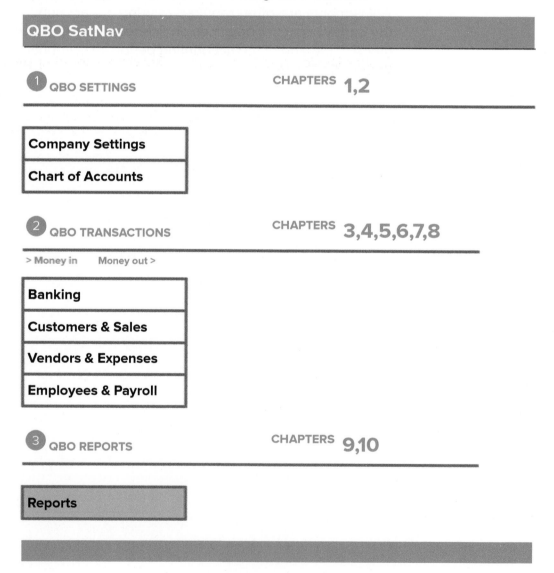

QBO SatNav

1 QBO SETTINGS   CHAPTERS **1,2**

| Company Settings |
| Chart of Accounts |

2 QBO TRANSACTIONS   CHAPTERS **3,4,5,6,7,8**

> Money in   Money out >

| Banking |
| Customers & Sales |
| Vendors & Expenses |
| Employees & Payroll |

3 QBO REPORTS   CHAPTERS **9,10**

| Reports |

Section 9.2

QBO LOGIN TO SAMPLE COMPANY

To log into the QBO Sample Company:

1. Open a web browser. (Note: Intuit recommends using Google Chrome.)

2. Go to the https://qbo.intuit.com/redir/testdrive

3. Follow onscreen instructions for security verification.

Craig's Design and Landscaping Services should appear on your screen.

> **We use the Sample Company** for practice throughout the chapter and exercises. The Sample Company will reset each time it is reopened. So make certain to allow enough time to complete all chapter activities before closing the Sample Company. Otherwise, you will lose the work you have entered when you reopen the Sample Company.

Section 9.3

ACCOUNTING CYCLE

The accounting cycle is a series of accounting activities that a business performs each accounting period.

> An accounting period **can be one month, one quarter, or one year.**

The accounting cycle usually consists of the following steps.

- **Chart of Accounts.** The Chart of Accounts is a list of all accounts used to accumulate information about assets, liabilities, owners' equity, revenues, and expenses. Create a Chart of Accounts when the business is established and modify the Chart of Accounts as needed over time.

- **Transactions.** During the accounting period, record transactions with customers, vendors, employees, and owners.

- **Trial Balance.** A Trial Balance is also referred to as an unadjusted Trial Balance because it is prepared before adjustments. A Trial Balance lists each account and the account balance at the end of the accounting period. Prepare a Trial Balance to verify that the accounting system is in balance—total debits should equal total credits.

- **Adjustments.** At the end of the accounting period before preparing financial statements, make any adjustments necessary to bring the accounts up to date. Adjustments are entered in the Journal using debits and credits.

- **Adjusted Trial Balance.** Prepare an Adjusted Trial Balance (a Trial Balance after adjustments) to verify that the accounting system still balances. If additional account detail is required, print the general ledger (the collection of all the accounts listing the transactions that affected the accounts).

- **Financial Statements.** Prepare financial statements for external users (Profit & Loss, Balance Sheet, and Statement of Cash Flows). Prepare income tax summary reports and management reports.

Section 9.4

ADJUSTING ENTRIES

WHY DO WE MAKE ADJUSTING ENTRIES?

Adjusting entries record adjustments necessary to bring the accounts up to date at the end of an accounting period. We want to make adjusting entries before preparing financial reports so the accounts reflected on the reports are up to date.

HOW DO WE MAKE ADJUSTING ENTRIES?

Adjustments are also called Adjusting Entries because the way we enter adjustments is by making entries in the Journal. Adjusting entires are entered in the onscreen QBO Journal using debits and credits.

> The onscreen Journal **using debits and credits to enter transactions is accessed from the Create (+) icon > Other > Journal Entry.**

Some companies use QBO to maintain their financial system throughout the year and then have an accountant prepare the adjusting entries at year end to enter into QBO.

WHEN DO WE MAKE ADJUSTING ENTRIES?

Adjusting entries are dated the last day of the accounting period. Typically, we prepare adjusting entries after we prepare a Trial Balance to verify that our accounts are in balance. The Trial Balance lists all accounts with their debit and credit balances. This permits us to see that our total debits equal our total credits. The Trial Balance is discussed in more detail in the next chapter, Chapter 10.

Section 9.5

USING QBO TO MAKE ADJUSTING ENTRIES

USING THE ONSCREEN JOURNAL TO RECORD ADJUSTING ENTRIES

We can use the QBO onscreen Journal to enter adjusting entries. To make adjusting entries:

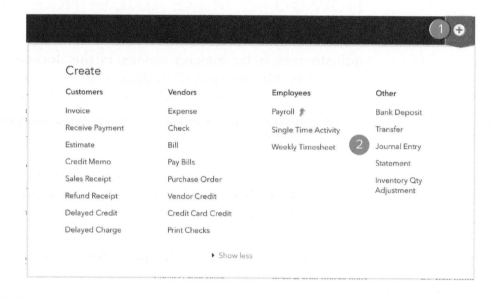

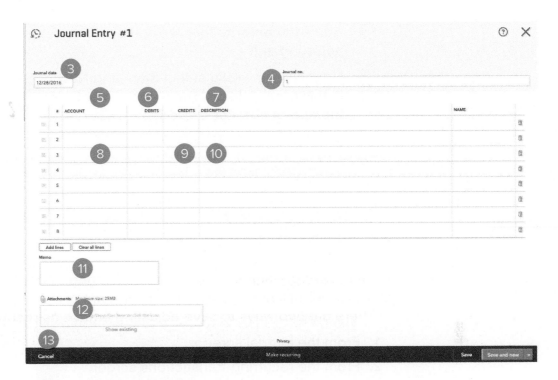

Journal Entry #1

1. Select **Create (+)** icon

2. Select **Journal Entry** to access the onscreen Journal

3. Enter **Journal date**

4. Enter **Journal no.** QBO will automatically number Journal entries consecutively unless we modify the Journal no. Often we label adjusting entries as ADJ 1, ADJ 2, and so on. Then we can clearly see which Journal entries are adjusting entries.

5. On Line 1 select **Account** to debit from the drop-down list of accounts

6. Enter the **Debit Amount**

7. Enter **Description**

8. On Line 2 select **Account** to credit

9. Enter the **Credit Amount**

10. Enter **Description**

11. Enter **Memo,** such as Adjusting entry to record amount of insurance expired. If we had to make any calculations to determine the adjusting entry amounts, then we should include those calculations in the Memo field.

(12) Add **Attachments** that are source documents related to the adjusting entry

(13) Normally we would select Save and New or Save and Close, but in this case, select **Cancel.** We will enter new adjusting entries in the end-of-chapter exercises.

> When making journal entries, including adjusting entries, accountants generally list Debits before Credits. **Note that QBO may not always list Debits before Credits in journal entries.**

USING RECURRING TRANSACTIONS FOR ADJUSTING ENTRIES

We can save our adjusting entries as recurring transactions. This saves us time. We will still need to update the amount of the adjustment, if needed.

There are two ways to save adjusting entries as recurring transactions:

1. From the journal screen
2. From the recurring transactions screen

To save an adjusting entry as a recurring transaction from the journal screen:

(1) Enter the **adjusting entry** in the onscreen journal

(2) Select **Save** to save the adjusting entry for the current period

(3) Select **Make recurring** to save the adjusting entry as a recurring transaction

④ Enter **Template name,** such as Adjusting Entry Prepaid Insurance. Since the Recurring Transactions are listed alphabetically, we want to name the Template so it automatically sorts in a way that is easy for us to find it.

⑤ Select Type: **Reminder** so we will be reminded to use the Recurring Transaction Template to make the adjusting entry.

⑥ Enter the **number of days** to be reminded before the transaction date

⑦ Enter Interval **Yearly**

⑧ Select Month **December**

⑨ Select Date **Last**

⑩ Enter **Start date**

⑪ Enter End **None**

⑫ Enter **Line 1 of the adjusting entry** including Account, Debit Amount, and Description

⑬ Enter **Line 2 of the adjusting entry** including Account, Credit Amount, and Description

⑭ Enter **Memo**

⑮ Add **Attachments** if any

⑯ Normally we would select **Save Template.** In this case, select **Cancel.**

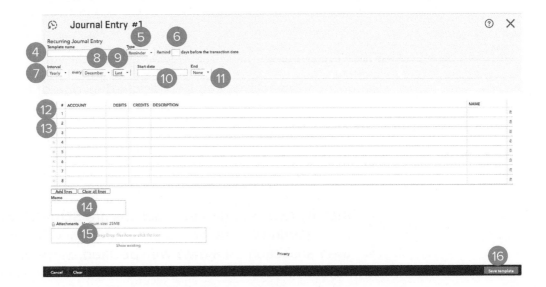

Another way to save an adjusting entry as a recurring transaction is by accessing Recurring Transactions from the Gear icon:

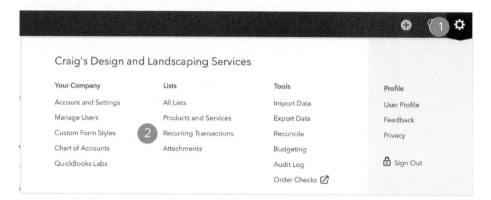

1. Select **Gear** icon

2. Select **Recurring Transactions**

3. Select **New** to add a new recurring transaction

4. Select **Edit** to update the recurring transaction previously entered

5. Select **Use** to use the recurring transaction to enter a new transaction

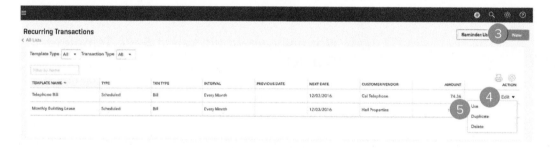

Recurring transactions can be classified as one of three types:

1. Scheduled

2. Unscheduled

3. Reminder

1. **Scheduled Recurring Transactions.** Notice in the Type column above that the two recurring transactions are **Scheduled.** This indicates that the recurring transaction is scheduled for QBO to automatically enter the transaction on a date we specified. Since we need to update the adjusting entry amounts each year, Scheduled is not a good option to use for adjusting entry Recurring Transactions.

2. **Unscheduled Recurring Transactions.** Unscheduled transactions will appear in the Recurring Transaction List but QBO will not automatically enter the transaction. Instead, we must go to the Recurring Transaction List and select Use. Although we could use Unscheduled for an adjusting entry Recurring Transaction, this option will not remind us to make the adjusting entry.

3. **Reminder Recurring Transactions.** Recurring Transactions with Reminder option will alert us with a reminder when we should use a recurring transaction to enter a new transaction. Since we need to update the amounts for adjusting entries each year, select Reminder for adjusting entry Recurring Transactions.

Section 9.6

TYPES OF ADJUSTING ENTRIES

If we use the accrual basis of accounting to calculate profits, the following four types of adjusting entries may be necessary.

1. **Prepaid items.** Items that are prepaid, such as prepaid insurance or prepaid rent.

2. **Unearned items.** Items that a customer has paid us for, but we have not provided the product or service.

3. **Accrued expenses.** Expenses that are incurred but not yet paid or recorded.

4. **Accrued revenues.** Revenues that have been earned but not yet collected or recorded.

> **The accrual basis of accounting** attempts to match expenses with the revenue (income) they generate. The cash basis records revenues (income) when cash is received and records expenses when cash is paid. The accrual basis attempts to record revenue (income) in the accounting period when it is earned (the product or service is provided) regardless of when the cash is received. The accrual basis attempts to record expenses in the accounting period it is incurred regardless of when the cash is paid.

> **Depreciation** is a special type of prepaid item involving fixed assets, such as equipment. Depreciation is the allocation of an asset's cost over its useful life. Depreciation can be calculated in a number of different ways. For more information about calculating depreciation for tax purposes, go to www.irs.gov.

Section 9.7

PREPAID ITEMS: RELATED EXPENSE/ASSET ACCOUNTS

Prepaid items are items that are paid in advance, such as prepaid insurance or prepaid rent. An adjustment may be needed to record the amount of the prepaid item that has not expired at the end of the accounting period. For example, an adjustment may be needed to record the amount of insurance that has not expired as Prepaid Insurance (an asset with future benefit) and the amount of insurance that has expired as Insurance Expense.

Adjusting entries for prepaid items typically affect an Expense account and an Asset account. Examples or related Expense and Asset accounts used for prepaid item adjusting entries are as follows.

Prepaid Items	Expense Account	Asset Account
Prepaid Insurance	Insurance Expense	Prepaid Insurance
Prepaid Rent	Rent Expense	Prepaid Rent
Office Supplies	Office Supplies Expense	Office Supplies

Basically we want to make certain that the amounts in the related Expense (such as Insurance Expense) and Asset account (Prepaid Insurance) are appropriate.

The adjusting entry is a Journal entry recording the amount that needs to be transferred between the two accounts, an Expense account and an Asset account, to show the appropriate balance in each account.

Whether a debit or credit increases or decreases an account depends upon the type of account.

Account Type	Debit	Credit
Asset	Increase	Decrease
Liabilities	Decrease	Increase
Equity	Decrease	Increase
Revenues (Income)	Decrease	Increase
Expenses	Increase	Decrease

For example, if we need to make an adjusting entry to increase Insurance Expense and decrease Prepaid Insurance for $1,000, we would determine whether to debit or credit the accounts as follows:

Account	Account Type	Increase or Decrease?	Debit or Credit?	Amount
Insurance Expense	Expense	Increase	Debit	$1,000
Prepaid Insurance	Asset	Decrease	Credit	$1,000

An example of an adjusting entry for a prepaid item using the QBO Journal follows.

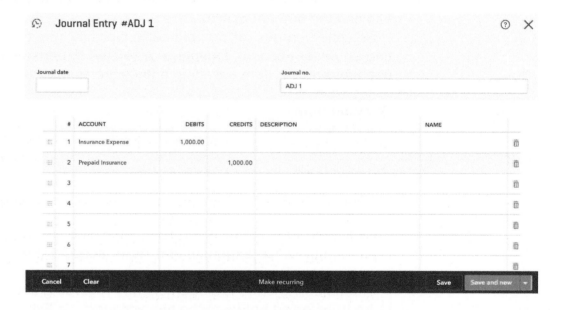

Section 9.8

UNEARNED ITEMS: RELATED REVENUE/LIABILITY ACCOUNTS

Unearned items consist of revenue that we have not earned. If a customer pays in advance of receiving a service, such as when a customer makes a deposit, our business has an obligation (liability) to either provide the service in the future or return the customer's money. An adjustment may be necessary to bring the revenue account and unearned revenue (liability) account up to date.

Unearned Items	Revenue Account	Liability Account
Unearned Rent Revenue	Rent Revenue	Unearned Revenue
App Subscription	App Subscription Revenue	Unearned App Subscription Revenue

The adjusting entry is a Journal entry recording the amount that needs to be transferred between the two accounts, a Revenue account and a Liability account, to show the appropriate balance in each account.

If we need to make an adjusting entry to increase Rent Revenue and decrease Unearned Revenue for $2,000, we would determine whether to debit or credit the accounts as follows:

Account	Account Type	Increase or Decrease?	Debit or Credit?	Amount
Rent Revenue	Revenue	Increase	Credit	$2,000
Unearned Revenue	Liablity	Decrease	Debit	$2,000

An example of an adjusting entry for unearned revenue using the QBO Journal follows.

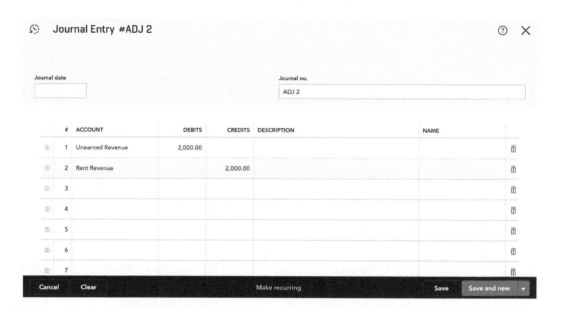

Section 9.9

ACCRUED EXPENSES: RELATED EXPENSE/LIABILITY ACCOUNTS

Accrued expenses are expenses that are incurred but not yet paid or recorded. Examples of accrued expenses include accrued interest expense (interest expense that has been incurred but not yet paid).

Accrued Expenses	Expense Account	Liability Account
Accrued Interest Incurred	Interest Expense	Interest Payable
Accrued Taxes Payable	Tax Expense	Taxes Payable

The adjusting entry is a Journal entry recording the amount that needs to be transferred between the two accounts, an Expense account and a Liability account, to show the appropriate balance in each account.

If we need to make an adjusting entry to increase Interest Expense and increase Interest Payable for $3,000, we would determine whether to debit or credit the accounts as follows:

Account	Account Type	Increase or Decrease?	Debit or Credit?	Amount
Interest Expense	Expense	Increase	Debit	$3,000
Interest Payable	Liablity	Increase	Credit	$3,000

An example of an adjusting entry for accrued interest expense using the QBO Journal follows.

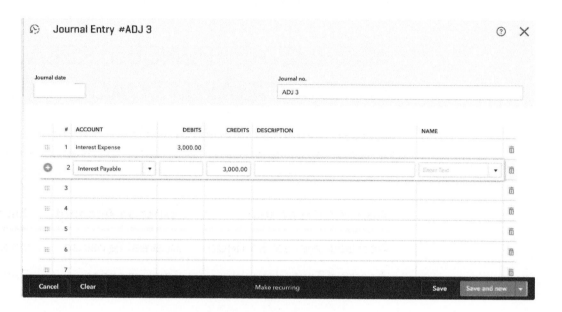

Section 9.10

ACCRUED REVENUES: RELATED REVENUE/ASSET ACCOUNTS

Accrued revenues are revenues that have been earned but not yet collected or recorded. Examples of accrued revenues include interest revenue that has been earned but not yet collected or recorded.

Accrued Revenues	Revenue Account	Asset Account
Accrued Interest Earned	Interest Revenue	Interest Receivable
Accrued Rent Revenue	Rent Revenue	Rent Receivable

The adjusting entry is a Journal entry recording the amount that needs to be transferred between the two accounts, a Revenue account and an Asset account, to show the appropriate balance in each account.

If we need to make an adjusting entry to increase Interest Revenue and increase Interest Receivable for $4,000, we would determine whether to debit or credit the accounts as follows:

Account	Account Type	Increase or Decrease?	Debit or Credit?	Amount
Interest Revenue	Revenue	Increase	Credit	$4,000
Interest Receivable	Asset	Increase	Debit	$4,000

An example of an adjusting entry for accrued interest revenue using the QBO Journal follows.

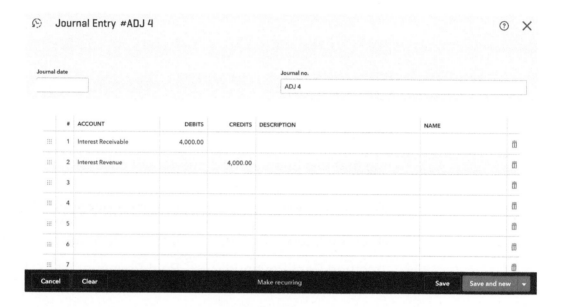

Section 9.11

ACCOUNTING ESSENTIALS

Accounting Adjustments and Corrections

Accounting Essentials summarize important foundational accounting knowledge you may find useful when using QBO

Why are adjusting entries necessary?

- When the accrual basis of accounting is used, adjusting entries are often necessary to bring the accounts up to date at the end of the accounting period. The accrual basis records revenue (income) when it is earned (when products and services are provided to customers) regardless of when the cash is received from customers. So at year-end there may be revenue that has not been recorded that has been earned, such as interest revenue. The accrual basis records expenses when they are incurred (the benefits have expired) regardless of when the cash is paid. So again, at year-end there may be expenses that have been incurred, but not recorded, such as interest expense.

- The accrual basis is often viewed as a better measure of profit than the cash basis. The cash basis records revenue (income) when the cash is received and records expenses when the cash is paid.

In double-entry accounting, how do we know whether to use a debit or credit for adjusting entries?

- Whether a debit or credit increases or decreases an account depends upon the type of account.

Account Type	Debit	Credit
Assets	Increase	Decrease
Liabilities	Decrease	Increase
Equity	Decrease	Increase
Revenues (Income)	Decrease	Increase
Expenses	Increase	Decrease

What are corrections?

- Corrections, or correcting entries, fix mistakes in the accounting system. Adjusting entries, on the other hand, are not mistakes, but updates that are required to bring accounts to their correct balance as of a certain date.

How do we make a correction using journal entries?

- For example, assume the Cash account should have been debited for $200.00 and the Professional Fees Revenue account credited for $200.00. However, the following incorrect entry was made for $2,000.00 instead of $200.00.

Incorrect Entry	Account	Amount
Debit	Cash	$2,000.00
Credit	Professional Fees Revenue	$2,000.00

- Often the easiest way for us to correct an error is to make two correcting entries in the Journal:

1. **Eliminate the effect of the incorrect entry by making the opposite journal entry with Correcting Entry 1:**

Correcting Entry 1	Account	Amount
Debit	Professional Fees Revenue	$2,000.00
Credit	Cash	$2,000.00

2. **After eliminating the effect of the incorrect entry, make the following Correcting Entry 2 that should have been made initially:**

Correcting Entry 2	Account	Amount
Debit	Cash	$200.00
Credit	Professional Fees Revenue	$200.00

How do we correct errors on saved documents, such as invoices or purchase orders?

- Once a document has been saved, we can use one of three approaches to correct the error:
  1. **Display** the document, correct the error, then save the document again.
  2. **Void** the erroneous document, then create a new document. Voiding keeps a record of the document, but changes the amounts to zero.
  3. **Delete** the erroneous document, then create a new document. Deleting the document erases the document from our system.
- Typically, options 1 or 2 are preferable because we have a better audit trail showing changes.

PRACTICE QUIZ 9

Q9.1

QuickBooks uses which basis of bookkeeping?

- a. Accrual
- b. Cash
- c. Both a and b
- d. Neither a nor b

Q9.2

At the end of an accounting period, adjusting entries are made to:

- a. Ensure a profit
- b. Bring the accounts up to date
- c. Debit or credit the checking account
- d. Prove that debits equal credits

Q9.3

Accrued Revenues are:

  a. Revenues that have been earned, but not collected

  b. Payment received in advance of receiving the service

  c. Revenues that have been collected, but not yet earned

  d. Revenues that have been recorded

Q9.4

Sales are recorded under cash basis accounting when:

  a. The goods or services are provided regardless of whether the payment is collected from customers

  b. The costs are incurred to earn the revenue

  c. The cash is collected from customers

  d. The bookkeeper has time to record the transactions

Q9.5

Sales are recorded under accrual basis accounting when:

  a. The goods or services are provided regardless of whether the payment is collected from customers

  b. The costs are incurred to earn the revenue

  c. The actual cash is collected from customers

  d. The bookkeeper has time to record the transactions

Q9.6

Adjusting entries are typically made:

  a. At the beginning of the accounting period

  b. Whenever an error is found and a correction is required

  c. At the beginning of each month

  d. On the last day of the accounting period

Q9.7

The Journal entry to update the Office Supplies account for office supplies used is which of the following types of adjusting entry?

a. Prepaid item

b. Unearned Revenue

c. Accrued Expense

d. Accrued Revenue

e. Not an adjusting entry

Q9.8

The Journal entry to update the accounts for interest expense incurred but not recorded is which of the following types of adjusting entries?

a. Prepaid item

b. Unearned Revenue

c. Accrued Expense

d. Accrued Revenue

e. Not an adjusting entry

Q9.9

The Journal entry to update the accounts for interest earned but not recorded is which of the following types of adjusting entries?

a. Prepaid item

b. Unearned Revenue

c. Accrued Expense

d. Accrued Revenue

e. Not an adjusting entry

Q9.10

The Journal entry to update the accounts for customer subscriptions that are prepaid but not yet earned is which of the following types of adjusting entries?

a. Prepaid item

b. Unearned Revenue

c. Accrued Expense

d. Accrued Revenue

e. Not an adjusting entry

Q9.11

The Journal entry to update the accounts for prepaid insurance that has expired is which of the following types of adjusting entries?

a. Prepaid item

b. Unearned Revenue

c. Accrued Expense

d. Accrued Revenue

e. Not an adjusting entry

Q9.12

The Journal entry to update the accounts for customer services provided but not yet recorded is which of the following types of adjusting entries?

a. Prepaid item

b. Unearned Revenue

c. Accrued Expense

d. Accrued Revenue

e. Not an adjusting entry

Q9.13

The Journal entry to record payment of cash for office supplies is which of the following types of adjusting entries?

a. Prepaid item

b. Unearned Revenue

c. Accrued Expense

d. Accrued Revenue

e. Not an adjusting entry

Q9.14

The Journal entry to update the accounts for rent expense recorded that has not expired is which of the following types of adjusting entries?

a. Prepaid item

b. Unearned Revenue

c. Accrued Expense

d. Accrued Revenue

e. Not an adjusting entry

EXERCISES 9

We use the QBO Sample Company, Craig's Design and Landscaping Services for practice throughout the exercises. The Sample Company will reset each time it is reopened. So make certain to allow enough time to complete exercises before closing the Sample Company. Otherwise, you will lose the work you have entered when you reopen the Sample Company.

To access the QBO Sample Company, complete the following steps.

1. Open a web browser. (Note: Intuit recommends using Google Chrome.)

2. Go to the https://qbo.intuit.com/redir/testdrive

3. Follow onscreen instructions for security verification.

Craig's Design and Landscaping Services should appear on your screen.

E9.1 Debits and Credits

Enter either Increase or Decrease in the following table to complete it.

- **Increase**
- **Decrease**

Account Type	Debit	Credit
Asset	_____	_____
Liabilities	_____	_____
Equity	_____	_____
Revenues (Income)	_____	_____
Expenses	_____	_____

E9.2 Journal

Identify the labels of the following columns in the QBO Journal.

Item

1. _____
2. _____
3. _____
4. _____

E9.3 Adjusting Entry Prepaid Rent

Using the QBO Sample Company, Craig's Design and Landscaping Company, complete the following.

Craig paid $900 of rent on December 1 for an entire year (12 months). So at the end of the accounting period on December 31, Craig has used 1 month of rent @ $75 ($900/12 months = $75 per month). The balance is Prepaid Rent Expense, an asset account with future benefit. Since Craig recorded the entire $900 as Rent Expense, an adjusting entry is needed to bring accounts up to date at December 31.

1. Complete the following table

Account	Account Type	Increase or Decrease?	Debit or Credit?	Amount
Rent Expense	Expense	_____	_____	$_____
Prepaid Rent Expense	Asset	_____	_____	$_____

2. Create Adjusting Journal Entry.

   a. Add a new Subaccount to Prepaid Expenses for the COA: **Prepaid Rent Expense**

   b. From the Create (+) icon select **Journal Entry**

   c. Enter the adjusting journal entry in QBO.

   d. Complete the following.

1. _____

2. _____

3. _____

4. _____

E9.4 Adjusting Entry Prepaid Insurance

Using the QBO Sample Company, Craig's Design and Landscaping Company, complete the following.

In December Craig paid $241.23 for insurance to cover a 3-month period. So at the end of the accounting period on December 31, 1 month of rent had expired @ $80.41 ($241.23/3 months = $80.41 per month). The balance is Prepaid Insurance Expense, an asset account with future benefit. Since Craig recorded the entire $241.23 as Insurance Expense, an adjusting entry is needed to bring accounts up to date at December 31.

1. Complete the following table

Account	Account Type	Increase or Decrease?	Debit or Credit?	Amount
Insurance Expense	Expense	_____	_____	$_____
Prepaid Insurance Expense	Asset	_____	_____	$_____

2. Create Adjusting Journal Entry.

   a. Add a new Subaccount to Prepaid Expenses for the COA: **Prepaid Insurance Expense**

   b. From the Create (+) icon select **Journal Entry**

   c. Enter the adjusting journal entry in QBO

   d. Complete the following.

1. _____

2. _____

3. _____

4. _____

E9.5 Adjusting Entry Prepaid Equipment Rental

Using the QBO Sample Company, Craig's Design and Landscaping Company, complete the following.

In December Craig paid $112 for equipment rental and recorded it as Equipment Rental, an Expenses account. But the $112 was prepaid to reserve the equipment for use in January of next year. So at the end of the accounting period on December 31, the benefits of the $112 had not expired and would not be Equipment Rental Expense, but Prepaid Rent Expense, an asset with future benefit. Since Craig recorded the entire $112 as Equipment Rental Expense, an adjusting entry is needed to bring accounts up to date at December 31.

1. Complete the following table

Account	Account Type	Increase or Decrease?	Debit or Credit?	Amount
Equipment Rental	Expense	_____	_____	$_____
Prepaid Rent Expense	Asset	_____	_____	$_____

2. Create Adjusting Journal Entry.

   a. From the Create (+) icon select **Journal Entry**

   b. Enter the adjusting journal entry in QBO

   c. Complete the following.

1. _____

2. _____

3. _____

4. _____

E9.6 Adjusting Entry Unearned Revenue

Using the QBO Sample Company, Craig's Design and Landscaping Company, complete the following.

In November Craig received $225 from Kate Whelan as a customer prepayment for design work. Craig recorded the entire $225 as Design Income. At the end of the accounting period on December 31, none of the design work had been provided to Kate, so the $225 had not been earned as of year end. Since it had not been earned, the $225 is a liability because Craig has an obligation to provide the design service or return the $225 to the customer. So an adjusting entry is needed to bring accounts up to date at December 31.

1. Complete the following table

Account	Account Type	Increase or Decrease?	Debit or Credit?	Amount
Design Income	Income	_____	_____	$_____
Unearned Revenue	Liability	_____	_____	$_____

2. Create Adjusting Journal Entry.

    a. Add a new Liability Account to the Chart of Accounts: **Unearned Revenue**

    b. From the Create (+) icon select **Journal Entry**

    c. Enter the adjusting journal entry in QBO

    d. Complete the following.

1. _____

2. _____

3. _____

4. _____

E9.7 Adjusting Entry Accrued Expenses

Using the QBO Sample Company, Craig's Design and Landscaping Company, complete the following.

    PG&E will bill Craig on January 1 for the prior year December utility services provided of $99. Since the Utilities Expense is incurred in December, the $99 must be recorded as an accrued expense and a liability recorded for the amount that Craig is obligated to pay in January. So an adjusting entry is needed to bring accounts up to date at December 31.

1. Complete the following table

Account	Account Type	Increase or Decrease?	Debit or Credit?	Amount
Utilities: Gas and Electric	Expense	_____	_____	$_____
Accounts Payable (A/P)	Liability	_____	_____	$_____

2. Create Adjusting Journal Entry.

   a. From the Create (+) icon select **Journal Entry**

   b. Enter the adjusting journal entry in QBO

   c. Complete the following.

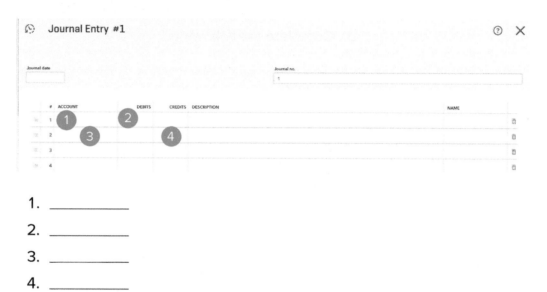

1. _____

2. _____

3. _____

4. _____

E9.8 Adjusting Entry Accrued Expenses

Using the QBO Sample Company, Craig's Design and Landscaping Company, complete the following.

   Interest on Craig's Notes Payable has been incurred, but not recorded or paid. The interest that has been incurred is calculated as principal multiplied by the interest rate multiplied by the time period ($4,000 × 10% × 1/12 = $33.33). Interest Expense of $33.33 must be recorded as an accrued expense and Accounts Payable, a liability, recorded for the amount that Craig is obligated to pay later. So an adjusting entry is needed to bring accounts up to date at December 31.

1. Complete the following table

Account	Account Type	Increase or Decrease?	Debit or Credit?	Amount
Interest Expense	Expense	_____	_____	$_____
Accounts Payable (A/P)	Liability	_____	_____	$_____

2. Create Adjusting Journal Entry.

   a. Add a new Expense Account to the Chart of Accounts: **Interest Expense**

   b. From the Create (+) icon select **Journal Entry**

   c. Enter the adjusting journal entry in QBO

   d. Complete the following.

1. _____

2. _____

3. _____

4. _____

E9.9 Adjusting Entry Accrued Expense

Using the QBO Sample Company, Craig's Design and Landscaping Company, complete the following.

   Interest on Craig's Loan Payable has been incurred, but not recorded or paid. The interest that has been incurred is calculated as principal multiplied by the interest rate multiplied by the time period ($25,000 × 12% × 1/12 = $250.00). Interest Expense of $250.00 must be recorded as an accrued expense and Accounts Payable, a liability, recorded for the amount that Craig is obligated to pay later. So an adjusting entry is needed to bring accounts up to date at December 31.

1. Complete the following table

Account	Account Type	Increase or Decrease?	Debit or Credit?	Amount
Interest Expense	Expense	_____	_____	$_____
Accounts Payable (A/P)	Liability	_____	_____	$_____

2. Create Adjusting Journal Entry.

    a. If needed, add a new Expense Account to the Chart of Accounts: **Interest Expense**

    b. From the Create (+) icon select **Journal Entry**

    c. Enter the adjusting journal entry in QBO

    d. Complete the following.

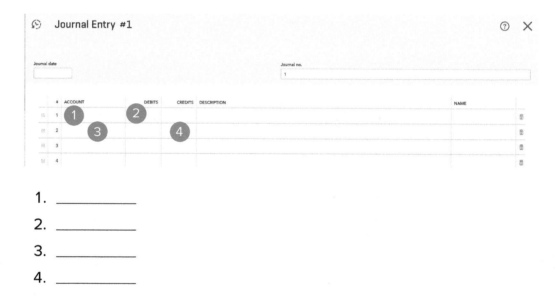

1. _____

2. _____

3. _____

4. _____

E9.10 Adjusting Entry Accrued Revenue

Using the QBO Sample Company, Craig's Design and Landscaping Company, complete the following.

Craig's Design and Landscaping has earned interest of $7.20 on its Saving account. This interest has been earned, but not recorded or received. Interest Earned of $7.20 needs to be recorded as an accrued revenue and Accounts Receivable, an asset, recorded for the amount that Craig will receive later. So an adjusting entry is needed to bring accounts up to date at December 31.

1. Complete the following table

Account	Account Type	Increase or Decrease?	Debit or Credit?	Amount
Interest Earned	Income	_____	_____	$_____
Accounts Receivable (A/R)	Asset	_____	_____	$_____

2. Create Adjusting Journal Entry.

   a. From the Create (+) icon select **Journal Entry**

   b. Enter the adjusting journal entry in QBO

   c. Complete the following.

1. _____

2. _____

3. _____

4. _____

3. How can you save this adjusting entry as a recurring transaction?

PROJECT 9.1

Project 9.1 is a continuation of Project 8.1. You will use the QBO client company you created for Project 1.1 and updated in Projects 2.1 through 8.1. Keep in mind the QBO company for Project 9.1 does not reset and carries your data forward, including any errors. So it is important to check and crosscheck your work to verify it is correct before clicking the Save button.

BACKSTORY

Mookie The Beagle™ Concierge, a provider of convenient, high-quality pet care, has asked for your assistance in making adjusting entries before preparing financial reports for the first month of operations.

   Complete the following for Mookie the Beagle Concierge.

QBO SatNav

Project 9.1 focuses on the QBO Reports as shown in the following partial QBO SatNav.

HOW TO LOG INTO QBO+

To log into QBO, complete the following steps.

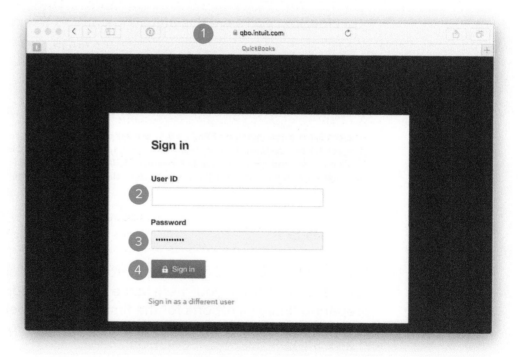

1. Using a web browser go to qbo.intuit.com

2. Enter **User ID** (the email address you used to set up your QBO Account)

3. Enter **Password** (the password you used to set up your QBO Account)

4. Select **Sign in**

If you are <u>not</u> using a public or shared computer, to speed up login, you can save your login to your desktop and select Remember Me. If you are using a public computer or shared computer, do not save to your desktop and unselect Remember Me.

The new QBO company we created in Project 1.1 will carry all work forward into future chapters. So it is important to check and crosscheck your work to verify it is correct before clicking the Save button. Any errors entered are carried forward in the QBO company you create for text projects.

P9.1.1 Adjusting Entry Prepaid Insurance

At January 31, 2018 CK needs to update his accounts before preparing financial statements to review Mookie The Beagle Concierge performance for its first month of operations. CK has asked for your assistance in preparing the adjusting entries. Mookie The Beagle Concierge will be using the accrual basis of accounting.

In January Mookie The Beagle Concierge purchased $300 of liability insurance to cover a 3 month period. So at the end of the accounting period on January 31, 1 month of rent had expired @ $100.00. ($300/3 months = $100 per month). The balance is Prepaid Insurance Expense, an asset account with future benefit. Since Mookie The Beagle Concierge recorded the entire $300 as Insurance Expense, an adjusting entry is needed to bring accounts up to date at January 31.

1. Complete the following table

Account	Account Type	Increase or Decrease?	Debit or Credit?	Amount
Insurance Expense	Expense	_____	_____	$_____
Prepaid Expenses: Insurance	Asset	_____	_____	$_____

2. Create Adjusting Journal Entry.

   a. From the Create (+) icon select **Journal Entry**

   b. Enter the adjusting journal entry in QBO on January 31, 2018.

   c. Complete the following.

Journal Entry   ⑦ ✕

Journal date   Journal no.

#	ACCOUNT	DEBITS	CREDITS	DESCRIPTION	NAME	
1	①	②				🗑
2	③		④			🗑
3						🗑
4						🗑

1. _____

2. _____

3. _____

4. _____

P9.1.2 Adjusting Entry Supplies

Complete the following adjusting entry for Mookie The Beagle Concierge.
Mookie The Beagle Concierge purchased $426 of supplies during January 2018. At the end of the accounting period on January 31, Mookie The Beagle Concierge still had $236 of unused supplies on hand. The $236 of Supplies is an asset with future benefit. Since Mookie The Beagle Concierge recorded the entire $426 as Supplies Expense, an adjusting entry is needed to bring accounts up to date at January 31.

1. Complete the following table

Account	Account Type	Increase or Decrease?	Debit or Credit?	Amount
Supplies Expense	Expense	_____	_____	$_____
Prepaid Expenses: Supplies	Asset	_____	_____	$_____

2. Create Adjusting Journal Entry.

   a. From the Create (+) icon select **Journal Entry**

   b. Enter the adjusting journal entry in QBO on January 31, 2018.

   c. Complete the following.

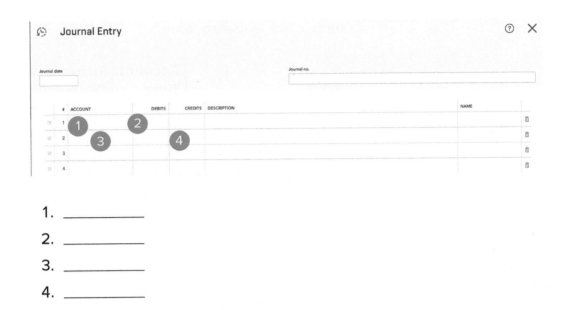

1. _____

2. _____

3. _____

4. _____

P9.1.3 Adjusting Entry Prepaid Rental

When Mookie The Beagle Concierge started stocking Mookie The Beagle Concierge branded inventory, CK rented a centrally located storage locker with digital access. This permitted Mookie The Beagle Concierge subcontracts to access the storage locker for deliveries to customers. CK had digital surveillance and from his smartphone could electronically permit the subcontractors access when they arrived at the storage locker. In addition, all inventory had an RFID chip that was automatically read when the subcontractor passed the storage locker door to exit. This improved inventory control in that CK was immediately notified on his smartphone when any inventory was removed from the storage locker. The storage locker was streamlining operations. The only issue is that CK completely overlooked recording the storage locker rental in QBO.

Complete the following adjusting entry for Mookie The Beagle Concierge.

In anticipation of carrying Mookie The Beagle Concierge branded Inventory, CK charged $432 for 6 months storage locker rental from Lynne's Space to Mookie The Beagle Concierge's VISA credit card on January 1, 2018. So at the end of the accounting period on January 31, Mookie The Beagle Concierge has used 1 month of rent @ $72 ($432/6 months = $72 per month). The balance ($360) is a Prepaid Expense: Prepaid Rent, an asset account with future benefit. Since CK had not recorded anything related to the storage locker rental, an adjusting entry is needed to bring accounts up to date at January 31.

1. Complete the following table

Account	Account Type	Increase or Decrease?	Debit or Credit?	Amount
Rent Expense	Expense	_____	_____	$_____
Prepaid Expenses: Rent	Asset	_____	_____	$_____
VISA Credit Card	Liability	_____	_____	$_____

2. Create Adjusting Journal Entry.

   a. Add a new Subaccount to Prepaid Expenses for the COA: **Rent**

   b. From the Create (+) icon select **Journal Entry**

   c. Enter the adjusting journal entry in QBO on January 31, 2018.

   d. Complete the following.

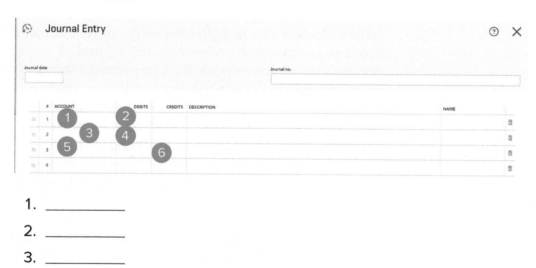

1. _____

2. _____

3. _____

4. _____

5. _____

6. _____

P9.1.4 Adjusting Entry Unearned Revenue

Complete the following adjusting entry for Mookie The Beagle Concierge.
   On January 12, 2018 Julie prepaid $1,600 for pet care services to be provided each Friday for 8 weeks for her Yellow Lab, Honey. Mookie The Beagle Concierge recorded the entire $1,600 as Sales. At the end of the accounting period on January 31, 3 weeks (01/12, 01/19, 01/26) of

the pet care services had been provided to Honey, so 5 weeks of services or $1,000 ($1,600/8 = $200 per week) had not been earned as of the end of January. Since $1,000 had not been earned, the $1,000 is a liability because Mookie The Beagle Concierge has an obligation to provide the pet care service or return the $1,000 to the customer. So an adjusting entry is needed to bring accounts up to date at January 31.

1. Complete the following table

Account	Account Type	Increase or Decrease?	Debit or Credit?	Amount
Sales	Income	_____	_____	$_____
Unearned Revenue	Liability	_____	_____	$_____

2. Create Adjusting Journal Entry.

   a. Add a new Other Current Liabilities Account to the Chart of Accounts: **Unearned Revenue**

   b. From the Create (+) icon select **Journal Entry**

   c. Enter the adjusting journal entry in QBO on January 31, 2018.

   d. Complete the following.

1. _____

2. _____

3. _____

4. _____

P9.1.5 Adjusting Entry Accrued Expenses

Complete the following adjusting entry for Mookie The Beagle Concierge. Interest on Mookie The Beagle Concierge's Loan Payable to CK has been incurred, but not recorded or paid. The interest that has been incurred is calculated as principal multiplied by the interest rate multiplied by the time period ($1,000 × 6% × 1/12 = $5.00). Interest Expense of $5.00 must be recorded as an accrued expense and Accounts Payable, a liability, recorded for the amount that Mookie The Beagle Concierge is obligated to pay later. So an adjusting entry is needed to bring accounts up to date at January 31.

1. Complete the following table

Account	Account Type	Increase or Decrease?	Debit or Credit?	Amount
Interest Expense	Expense	_____	_____	$_____
Accounts Payable (A/P)	Liability	_____	_____	$_____

2. Create Adjusting Journal Entry.

   a. From the Create (+) icon select **Journal Entry**

   b. Enter the adjusting journal entry in QBO on January 31, 2018. If requested, add Mr. CK Walker as a Vendor for the Name field.

   c. Complete the following.

1. _____

2. _____

3. _____

4. _____

P9.1.6 Adjusting Entry Accrued Expenses

Complete the following adjusting entry for Mookie The Beagle Concierge.
   During January Mary Dolan, a subcontractor, provided pet care services to Julie's Honey for three Fridays in January, totaling 24 hours @ $10 per hour. CK overlooked recording this subcontractor expense since Mary

had not been paid for these services yet. So at January 31, an adjusting entry is needed to record Subcontractor Expense that will be paid later. In the future, CK is hoping that the QBO time tracking will assist in avoiding these types of oversights going forward.

1. Complete the following table

Account	Account Type	Increase or Decrease?	Debit or Credit?	Amount
Subcontractor Expense	Expense	_____	_____	$_____
Accounts Payable (A/P)	Liability	_____	_____	$_____

2. Create Adjusting Journal Entry.

   a. From the Create (+) icon select **Journal Entry**

   b. Enter the adjusting journal entry in QBO on January 31, 2018. If requested, select Mary Dolan for the Name field.

   c. Complete the following.

1. _____

2. _____

3. _____

4. _____

P9.1.7 Adjusting Entry Accrued Expense

Complete the following adjusting entry for Mookie The Beagle Concierge.

At January 31 Mookie The Beagle Concierge has incurred $110 of accounting services for assistance with QBO. This amount has not been paid nor recorded by Mookie The Beagle Concierge, so an adjusting entry is needed to record the expense incurred.

1. Complete the following table

Account	Account Type	Increase or Decrease?	Debit or Credit?	Amount
Legal and Professional Fees	Expense	_____	_____	$_____
Accounts Payable (A/P)	Liability	_____	_____	$_____

2. Create Adjusting Journal Entry.

    a. From the Create (+) icon select **Journal Entry**

    b. Enter the adjusting journal entry in QBO on January 31, 2018. If requested, enter Your Name in the Name field.

    c. Complete the following.

1. _____

2. _____

3. _____

4. _____

P9.1.8 Adjusting Entry Renter Insurance

Oops. . . When cleaning out his jacket pocket, CK discovers a receipt for renter insurance for the storage locker rental. The renter insurance was purchased from Temple Insurance to provided insurance coverage for the inventory that CK planned to store in the storage locker. Mookie The Beagle Concierge purchased 1 month of renter insurance coverage for the period January 1 through January 31, 2018. Using the company credit card, Mookie The Beagle Concierge paid $8.00 on January 16, 2018 for 1 month of insurance coverage.

So at the end of the accounting period on January 31, 1 month of rent had expired at $8.00. Since Mookie The Beagle Concierge had not recorded the transaction, the entire $8.00 should be recorded as Renter Insurance Expense with an adjusting entry to bring accounts up to date at January 31.

1. Complete the following table

Account	Account Type	Increase or Decrease?	Debit or Credit?	Amount
Insurance Expense - Renter	Expense	_____	_____	$_____
VISA Credit Card	Liability	_____	_____	$_____

2. Edit the Chart of Accounts to change the Account Title from Insurance - Disability (Expense) to Insurance - Renter (Expense).

   a. From the Navigation Bar select **Transactions** > **Chart of Accounts**

   b. From the Chart of Accounts screen, for the Account 5007 Insurance - Disability select the **down** arrow > **Edit**

   c. Category Type should be **Expenses**

   d. Detail Type should be **Insurance**

   e. Edit Name: **Insurance - Renters**

   f. Select **Is sub-account**

   g. Select parent account **5006 Insurance**

   h. Select **Save and Close**

3. Edit the Chart of Accounts to make the account Insurance - Liability (Expense) a subaccount of Insurance (Expense) account.

   a. From the Chart of Accounts screen, for the Account 5008 Insurance - Liability select the **down** arrow > **Edit**

   b. Category Type should be **Expenses**

   c. Detail Type should be **Insurance**

   d. Name should be **Insurance - Liability**

   e. Select **Is sub-account**

   f. Select parent account **5006 Insurance**

   g. Select **Save and Close**

4. Create Adjusting Journal Entry.

   a. From the Create (+) icon select **Journal Entry**

   b. Enter the adjusting journal entry in QBO on January 31, 2018.

   c. Complete the following.

   1. _____

   2. _____

   3. _____

   4. _____

5. How to Improve Processes.

   Business owners are busy people, juggling multiple items at once. So occasionally accounting items are not recorded due to an oversight. Suggest two ways that Mookie The Beagle Concierge and CK could improve processes to ensure that all accounting items are recorded in a timely manner.

   a. _____

   b. _____

www.my-quickbooksonline.com

Go to www.My-QuickBooksOnline.com for additional resources for you including QBO Help, QBO Videos, and more.

Chapter 10

QBO Reports

The objective of financial reports is to provide information to users for decision making. The users of the financial reports include investors, creditors, tax agencies, and management. Different users are focused on different decisions and require different types of reports for information related to those decisions. For example, an investor may be deciding whether to invest and a creditor deciding whether to extend credit and loan the business money.

Chapter 10 explores some frequently used QBO reports and the reporting process.

Section 10.1

QBO SatNav

QBO SatNav is your satellite navigation for QuickBooks Online, assisting you in navigating QBO

Chapter 10 covers reports, as shown in the following QBO SatNav.

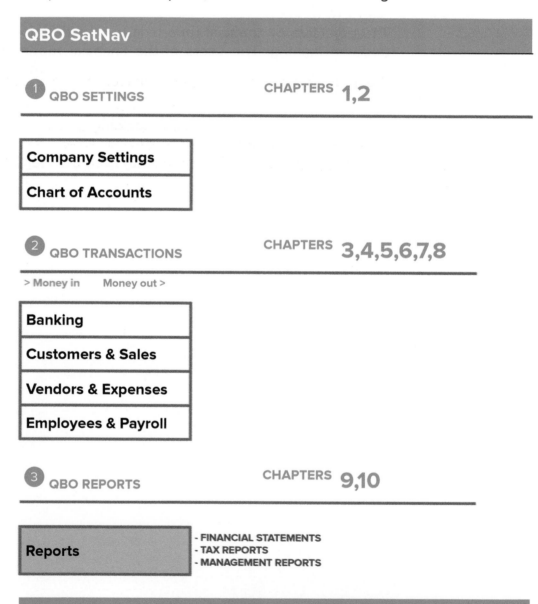

QBO SatNav

1 QBO SETTINGS   CHAPTERS **1,2**

| Company Settings |
| Chart of Accounts |

2 QBO TRANSACTIONS   CHAPTERS **3,4,5,6,7,8**

\> Money in   Money out >

| Banking |
| Customers & Sales |
| Vendors & Expenses |
| Employees & Payroll |

3 QBO REPORTS   CHAPTERS **9,10**

| Reports | - FINANCIAL STATEMENTS
- TAX REPORTS
- MANAGEMENT REPORTS |

Section 10.2

QBO LOGIN TO SAMPLE COMPANY

To log into the QBO Sample Company:

1. Open a web browser. (Note: Intuit recommends using Google Chrome.)

2. Go to the https://qbo.intuit.com/redir/testdrive

3. Follow onscreen instructions for security verification.

Craig's Design and Landscaping Services should appear on your screen.

> **We use the Sample Company** for practice throughout the chapter and exercises. The Sample Company will reset each time it is reopened. So make certain to allow enough time to complete all chapter activities before closing the Sample Company. Otherwise, you will lose the work you have entered when you reopen the Sample Company.

Section 10.3

NAVIGATING REPORTS

Most QBO reports are accessed from the Navigation Bar. Don't be overwhelmed by the number of reports offered by QBO. QBO offers a wide variety of reports to meet the needs of different QBO users. We will explore some of the more frequently used reports in this chapter.

To navigate QBO reports:

① From the Navigation Bar select **Dashboard** to view a financial dashboard for the company. This dashboard summarizes key financial metrics for the company. The dashboard includes bank account summaries, and charts for expenses, sales, and income. Select **Edit** or **drop-down arrows** to customize the dashboard.

② From the Navigation Bar select **Reports**

③ To search for a specific report, in the **Go to report** field enter the **report name** and click the magnifying glass

④ Select the **Recommended** reports tab to view reports that QBO recommends, such as Profit and Loss, Balance Sheet, A/R

(Accounts Receivable) Summary and A/P (Accounts Payable) Summary

5. Select **Company Snapshot** to view a second financial dashboard

6. Select the **Frequently Run** reports tab where reports we run frequently will be displayed to streamline finding reports

7. Select the **My Custom Reports** tab to view saved customized reports

8. Select the **Management Reports** tab to view bundles of reports that QBO has prepared

9. Select the **drop-down arrow** to view options to Edit, Send, Export as PDF, Export as DOCX or Copy

10. Select the **All Reports** tab to view QBO reports grouped by category, such as Business Overview, Review Sales, and Review Expenses and Purchases

11. Select **Business Overview** reports to view reports that provide an overview of business operations and results, such as the Profit and Loss, Balance Sheet and Statement of Cash Flows. QBO is continually updating and adding new reports. These reports are labeled New.

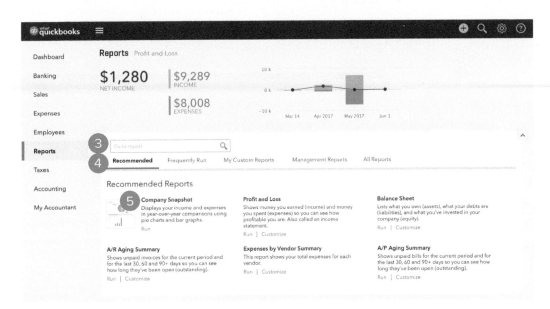

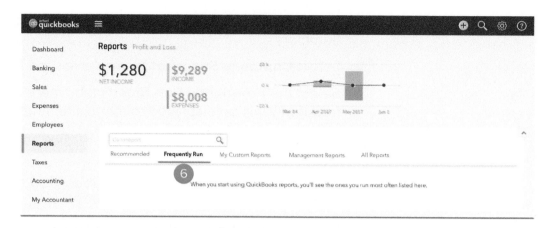

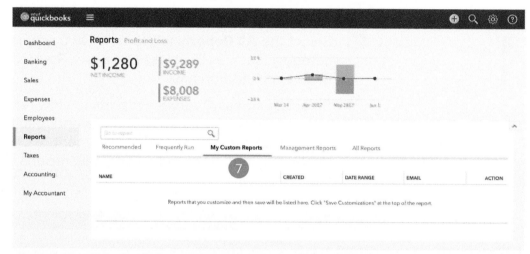

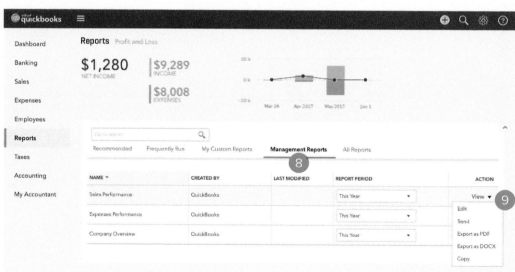

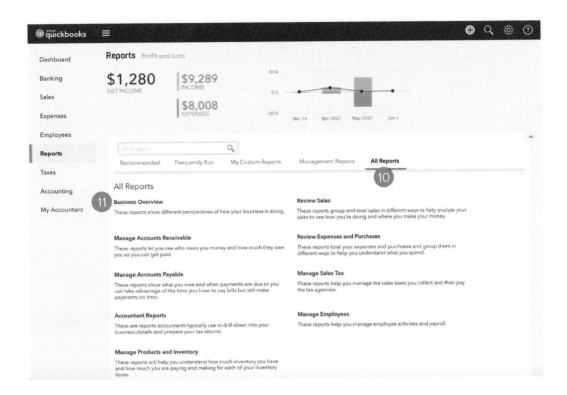

Section 10.4

FINANCIAL REPORTS: RESULTS OF THE ACCOUNTING CYCLE

Financial reports are the results or output of the accounting cycle. The accounting cycle is a series of accounting activities that a business performs each accounting period.

> An accounting period **can be one month, one quarter, or one year.**

The accounting cycle usually consists of the following steps.

- **Chart of Accounts.** The Chart of Accounts (Account List) is a list of all accounts used to accumulate information about assets, liabilities, owners' equity, revenues, and expenses. Create a Chart of Accounts when the business is established and modify the Chart of Accounts as needed over time. (The Chart of Accounts was discussed in Chapters 1 and 2 of this text.)

- **Transactions.** During the accounting period, record transactions with customers, vendors, employees, and owners. (Transactions were explored in Chapters 3, 4, 5, 6, 7, and 8 of this text.)

- **Trial Balance.** A Trial Balance is also referred to as an unadjusted Trial Balance because it is prepared before adjustments. A Trial Balance lists each account and the account balance at the end of the accounting period. Prepare a Trial Balance to verify that the accounting system is in balance—total debits should equal total credits.

- **Adjustments.** At the end of the accounting period before preparing financial statements, make any adjustments necessary to bring the accounts up to date. Adjustments are entered in the Journal using debits and credits. (Adjustments were covered in Chapter 9 of this text.)

- **Adjusted Trial Balance.** Prepare an Adjusted Trial Balance (a Trial Balance after adjustments) to verify that the accounting system still balances. If additional account detail is required, view the general ledger (the collection of all the accounts listing the transactions that affected the accounts).

- **Financial Statements.** Prepare financial statements (Profit and Loss, Balance Sheet, and Statement of Cash Flows) for external users and internal users. Prepare management reports.

Section 10.5

TRIAL BALANCE

Trial Balance is a listing of all of a company's accounts and the ending account balances. A Trial Balance is often prepared both before and after making adjustments. The purpose of the Trial Balance is to verify account balances and that the accounting system balances. On a Trial Balance, all debit ending account balances are listed in the debit column and credit ending balances are listed in the credit column. If the accounting system balances, total debits equal total credits.

To view the Trial Balance in QBO:

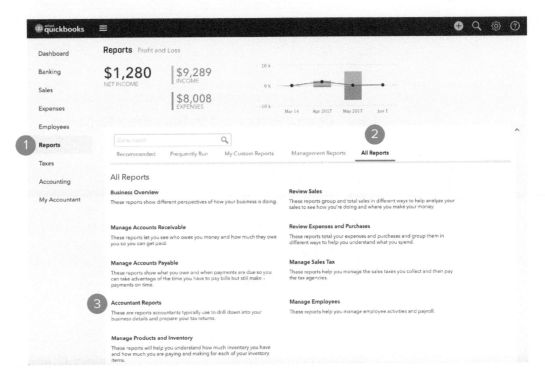

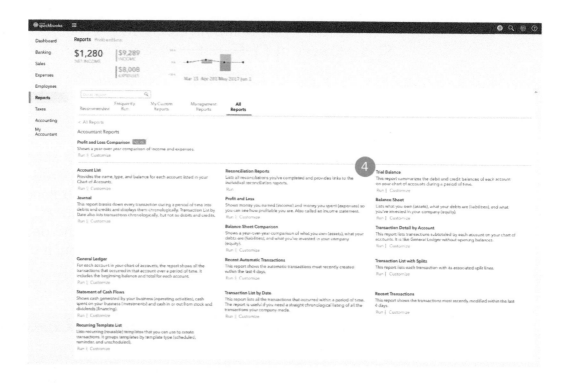

1. From the Navigation Bar select **Reports**

2. Select **All Reports tab**

3. Select **Accountant Reports**

4. Select **Trial Balance**

5. From the drop-down menu select Report period **This Year**

6. **Dates** should autofill

7. Select **Active rows**

8. Select Accounting method **Accrual**

9. Select **Run report**

10. To customize the report further select **Customize**

11. From the Customize report slide out drawer make **customization selections**

12. Select **Run report**

13. Notice on the Trial Balance report that **Total Debits equal Total Credits**

14. Select **Export** icon to display the export options: Export to Excel and Export to PDF

15 Select **Save Customizations** and follow onscreen instructions to save so the customized report will now appear under the My Custom Reports tab.

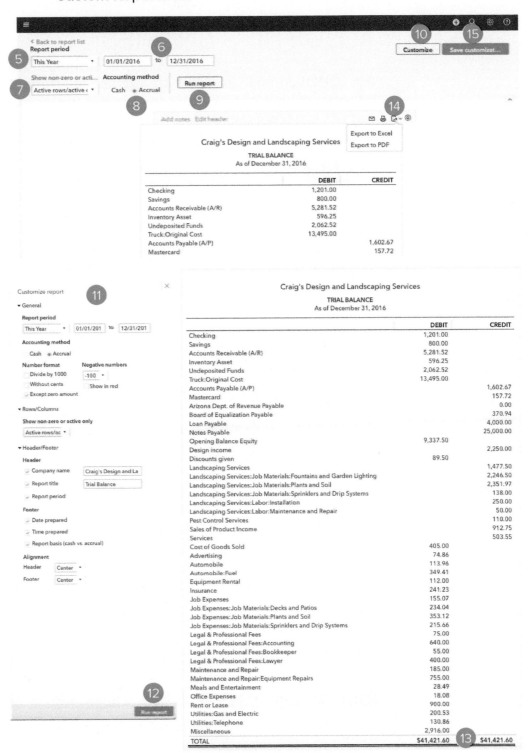

Section 10.6

ADJUSTING ENTRIES

The QBO Journal is used to record adjustments (and corrections). Adjustments are often necessary to bring the accounts up to date at the end of the accounting period.

To make adjusting entries using the Journal:

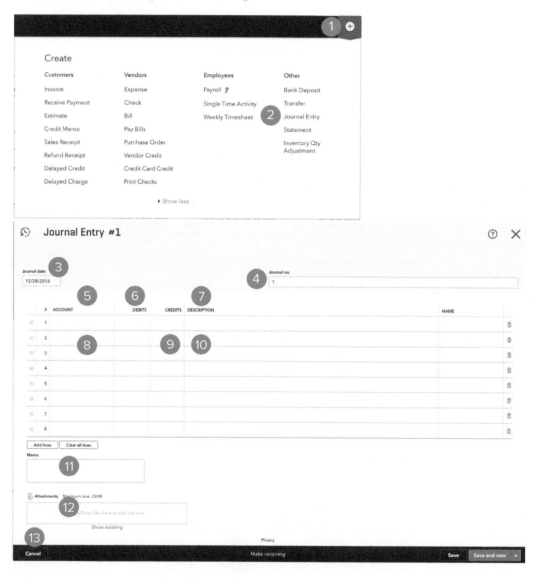

1. Select **Create (+)** icon

2. Select **Journal Entry** to access the onscreen Journal

3. Enter **Journal date**

4. Enter **Journal no.** QBO will automatically number Journal entries consecutively unless we modify the Journal no. Often we label adjusting entries as ADJ 1, ADJ 2, and so on. Then we can clearly see which Journal entries are adjusting entries.

5. On Line 1 select **Account** to debit from the drop-down list of accounts

6. Enter the **Debit Amount**

7. Enter **Description**

8. On Line 2 select **Account** to credit

9. Enter the **Credit Amount**

10. Enter **Description**

11. Enter **Memo,** such as Adjusting entry to record amount of insurance expired. If we had to make any calculations to determine the adjusting entry amounts, then we should include those calculations in the Memo field.

12. Add **Attachments** that are source documents related to the adjusting entry

13. Normally we would select Save and New or Save and Close, but in this case, select **Cancel.**

If we use the accrual basis of accounting to calculate profits, the following four types of adjusting entries may be necessary.

1. **Prepaid items.** Items that are prepaid, such as prepaid insurance or prepaid rent.

2. **Unearned items.** Items that a customer has paid us for, but we have not provided the product or service.

3. **Accrued expenses.** Expenses that are incurred but not yet paid or recorded.

4. **Accrued revenues.** Revenues that have been earned but not yet collected or recorded.

For more detailed information about adjusting entries, see Chapter 9.

Section 10.7

ADJUSTED TRIAL BALANCE

The Adjusted Trial Balance is prepared to view updated account balances and verify that the accounting system still balances after adjusting entries are made.

To view an Adjusted Trial Balance in QBO simply run the Trial Balance report again after adjusting entries have been entered in QBO.

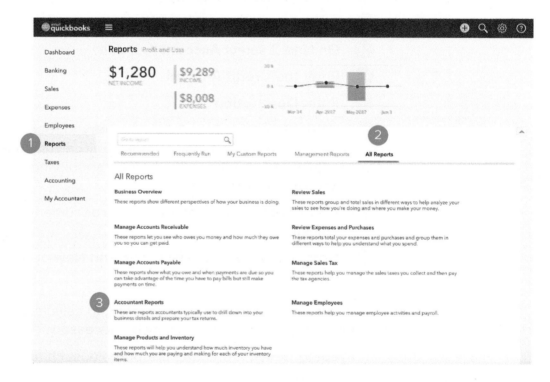

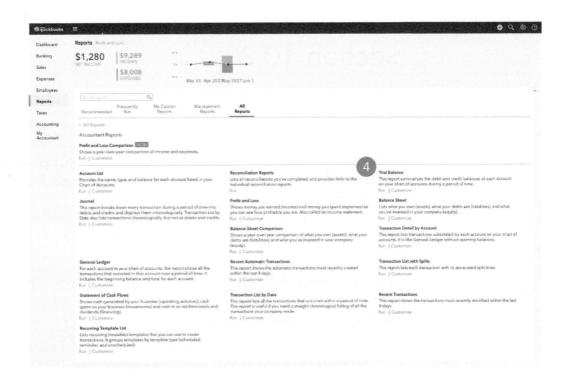

1. From the Navigation Bar select **Reports**

2. Select **All Reports** tab

3. Select **Accountant Reports**

4. Select **Trial Balance** then complete steps to run the Trial Balance again after adjusting entries are entered

Section 10.8

FINANCIAL STATEMENTS

Financial statements are standardized financial reports given to bankers and investors. The three main financial statements are the Profit and Loss, Balance Sheet, and Statement of Cash Flows.

PROFIT AND LOSS

The Profit and Loss Statement lists sales (sometimes called revenues) and expenses for a specified accounting period. Profit, or net income, can be measured two different ways:

- **Cash basis.** A sale is recorded when cash is collected from the customer. Expenses are recorded when cash is paid.

- **Accrual basis.** Sales are recorded when the good or service is provided regardless of when the cash is collected from the customer. Expenses are recorded when the cost is incurred or expires, even if the expense has not been paid.

QBO permits us to prepare the Profit and Loss Statement using either the accrual or the cash basis. QBO also permits us to prepare Profit and Loss Statements monthly, quarterly, or annually.

To prepare a Profit and Loss Statement using the accrual basis:

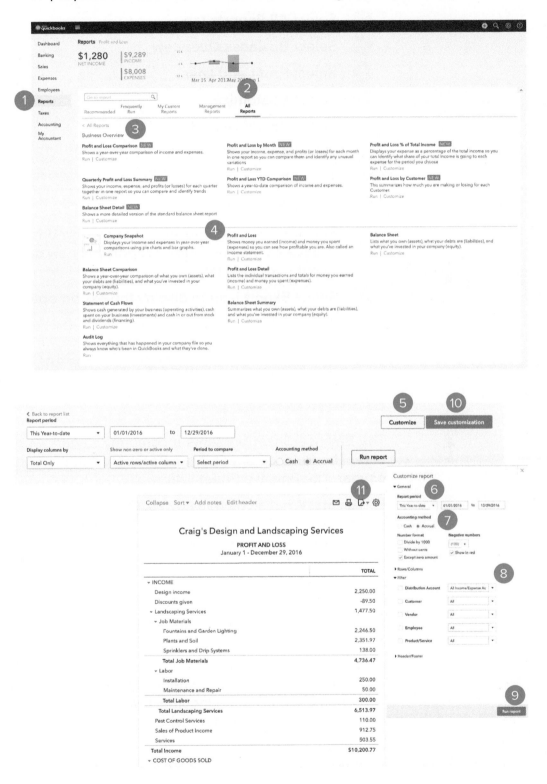

1. From the Navigation Bar select **Reports**
2. Select **All Reports** tab
3. Select **Business Overview**
4. Select **Profit and Loss**
5. Select **Customize**
6. Select **Report period**
7. Select **Accounting method**
8. Select **Filters**
9. Select **Run report**
10. Select **Save Customizations** and follow onscreen instructions to save so the customized report will now appear under the My Custom Reports tab
11. Select **Export** icon to display the export options: Export to Excel and Export to PDF

> Note that we can also prepare the Profit and Loss Statement using the Recommended Reports tab.

BALANCE SHEET

The Balance Sheet presents a company's financial position on a specific date. The Balance Sheet can be prepared at the end of a month, quarter, or year. The Balance Sheet lists:

- **Assets.** What a company owns. On the Balance Sheet, assets are recorded at their historical cost, the amount we paid for the asset when we purchased it. Note that historical cost can be different from the market value of the asset, which is the amount the asset is worth now.

- **Liabilities.** What a company owes. Liabilities are obligations that include amounts owed vendors (accounts payable) and bank loans (notes payable).

- **Owners' equity.** The residual that is left after liabilities are satisfied. Also called net worth, owners' equity is increased by owners' contributions and net income. Owners' equity is decreased by owners' withdrawals (or dividends) and net losses.

To prepare a Balance Sheet:

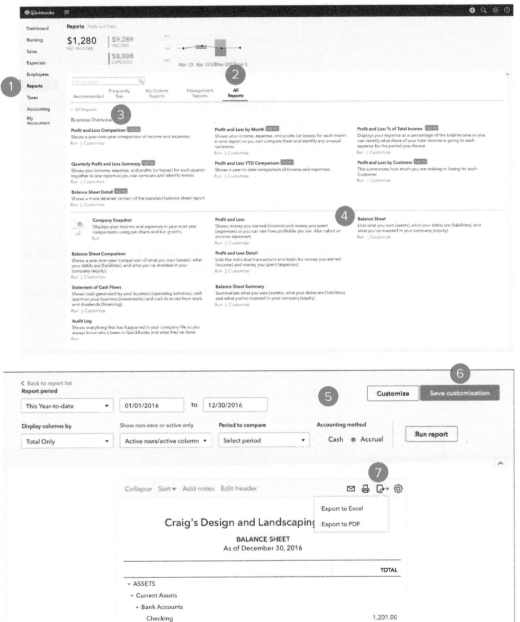

1. From the Navigation Bar select **Reports**

2. Select **All Reports** tab

3. Select **Business Overview**

4. Select **Balance Sheet**

5 Enter **Customize** features using the Customization Bar across the top of the report or using the Customize button

6 Select **Save Customizations** and follow onscreen instructions to save so the customized report will now appear under the My Custom Reports tab

7 Select **Export** icon to display the export options: Export to Excel and Export to PDF

STATEMENT OF CASH FLOWS

The Statement of Cash Flows summarizes cash inflows and cash outflows for a business over a period of time. Cash flows are grouped into three categories:

1. **Cash flows from operating activities.** Cash inflows and outflows related to the company's primary business, such as cash flows from sales and operating expenses.

2. **Cash flows from investing activities.** Cash inflows and outflows related to acquisition and disposal of long-term assets.

3. **Cash flows from financing activities.** Cash inflows and outflows to and from investors and creditors (except for interest payments). Examples include: loan principal repayments and investments by owners.

To prepare the Statement of Cash Flows:

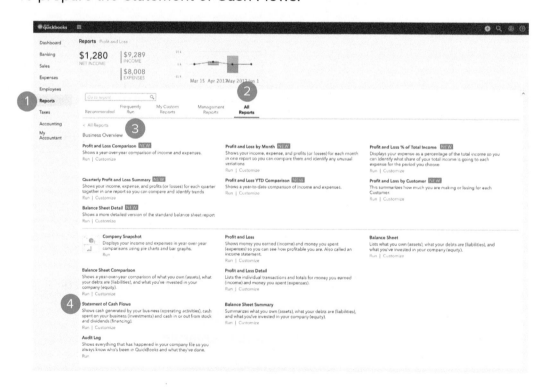

1. From the Navigation Bar select **Reports**

2. Select **All Reports** tab

3. Select **Business Overview**

4. Select **Statement of Cash Flows**

5. Enter **Customize** features using the Customization Bar across the top of the report or using the Customize button

6. Select **Save Customizations** and follow onscreen instructions to save so the customized report will now appear under the My Custom Reports tab

7. Select **Export** icon to display the export options: Export to Excel and Export to PDF

Section 10.9

MANAGEMENT REPORTS

Reports used by management do not have to follow a specified set of rules such as GAAP or the Internal Revenue Code. Instead, management reports are prepared as needed to provide management with information for making operating and business decisions.

Management reports include:

1. Customer reports, such as Customer Profitability and Accounts Receivable Aging
2. Vendor reports, such as Open Purchase Orders and Accounts Payable Aging
3. Inventory reports, such as Sales by Product/Services Summary and Physical Inventory Worksheet
4. Transaction Journal
5. Audit Log

INCOME BY CUSTOMER SUMMARY

To improve profitability in the future, a business may evaluate which customers have been profitable in the past. This information permits a business to improve profitability by:

- Increasing business in profitable areas
- Improving performance in unprofitable areas
- Discontinuing unprofitable areas

To determine which customers are generating the most profit for our business, it is necessary to look at both the sales for the customer and associated costs.

To prepare the Income by Customer Summary report:

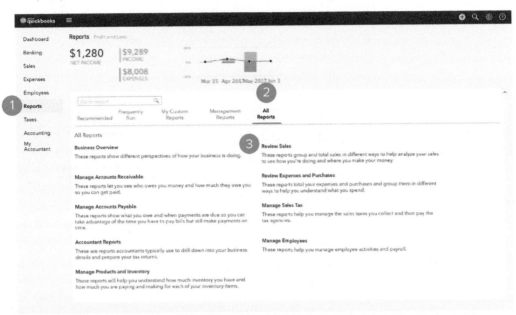

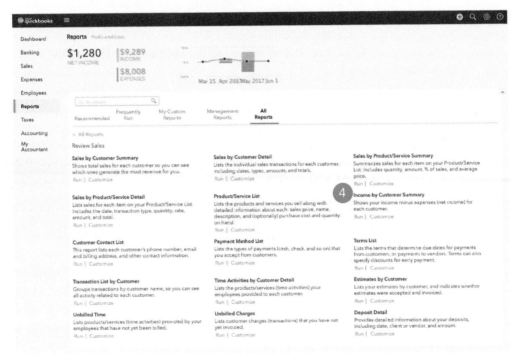

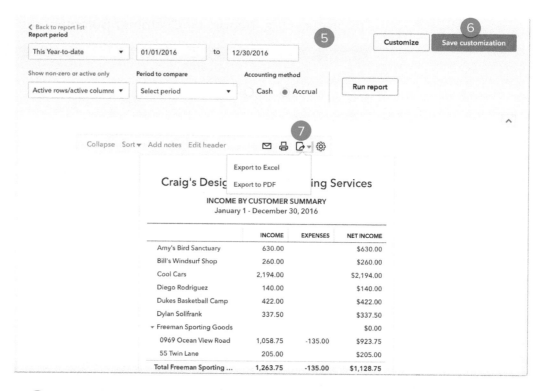

1. From the Navigation Bar select **Reports**

2. Select **All Reports** tab

3. Select **Review Sales**

4. Select **Income by Customer Summary**

5. Enter **Customize** features using the Customization Bar across the top of the report or using the Customize button

6. Select **Save Customizations** and follow onscreen instructions to save so the customized report will now appear under the My Custom Reports tab

7. Select **Export** icon to display the export options: Export to Excel and Export to PDF

ACCOUNTS RECEIVABLE (A/R) AGING

Accounts Receivable reports provide information about which customers owe our business money. When we make a credit sale, our company provides products and services to a customer in exchange for a promise that the customer will pay us later. Sometimes the customer breaks the promise and does not pay. Therefore, a business should have a credit policy to ensure that credit is extended only to customers who are likely to keep their promise and pay their bills.

After credit has been extended, a business needs to track accounts receivable to determine if accounts are being collected in a timely manner.

The Accounts Receivable Aging report provides information useful in tracking accounts receivable by providing information about the age of customer accounts. This report lists the age of accounts receivable balances. In general, the older an account, the less likely the customer will pay the bill. Therefore, it is important to monitor the age of accounts receivable and take action to collect old accounts.

To prepare the Accounts Receivable Aging report:

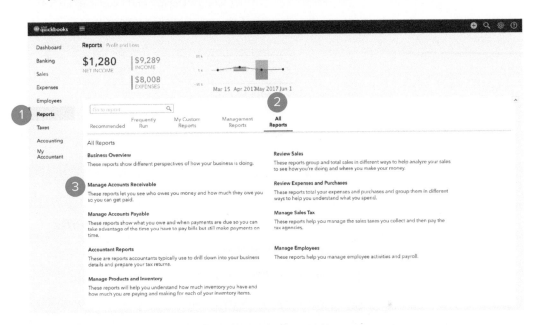

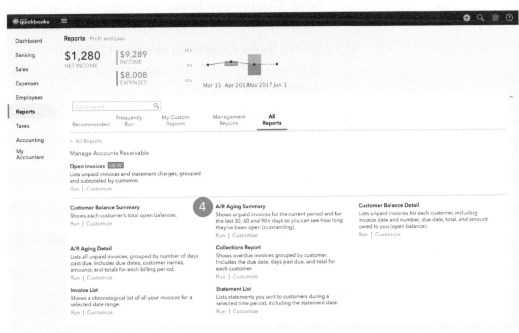

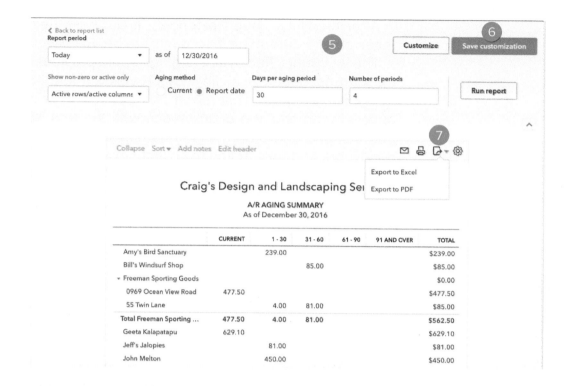

1. From the Navigation Bar select **Reports**

2. Select **All Reports** tab

3. Select **Manage Accounts Receivable**

4. Select **A/R Aging Summary**

5. Enter **Customize** features using the Customization Bar across the top of the report or using the Customize button

6. Select **Save Customizations** and follow onscreen instructions to save so the customized report will now appear under the My Custom Reports tab

7. Select **Export** icon to display the export options: Export to Excel and Export to PDF

OPEN PURCHASE ORDERS

Open purchase orders are purchase orders for items ordered but not yet received. QBO permits us to view all open purchase orders or just those for a specific vendor.

To prepare the Open Purchase Orders report that lists all open purchase orders:

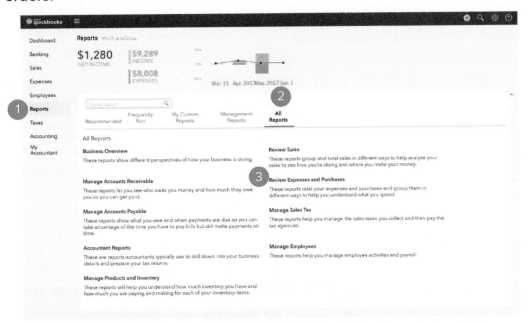

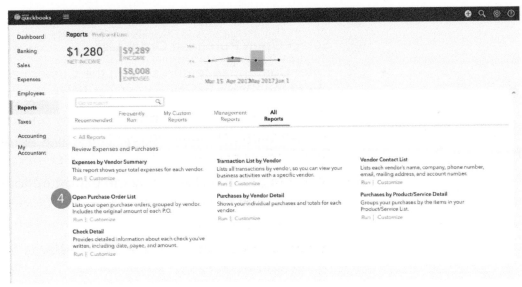

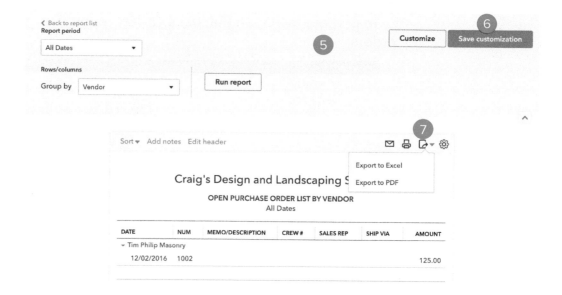

① From the Navigation Bar select **Reports**

② Select **All Reports** tab

③ Select **Review Expenses and Purchases**

④ Select **Open Purchase Order List**

⑤ Enter **Customize** features using the Customization Bar across the top of the report or using the Customize button

⑥ Select **Save Customizations** and follow onscreen instructions to save so the customized report will now appear under the My Custom Reports tab

⑦ Select **Export** icon to display the export options: Export to Excel and Export to PDF

ACCOUNTS PAYABLE (A/P) AGING

Accounts payable consists of amounts that our company is obligated to pay in the future. Accounts Payable reports tell us how much we owe vendors and when amounts are due.

The Accounts Payable Aging Summary summarizes accounts payable balances by the age of the account. This report helps to track any past due bills as well as provides information about bills that will be due shortly.

To prepare the Accounts Payable Aging report:

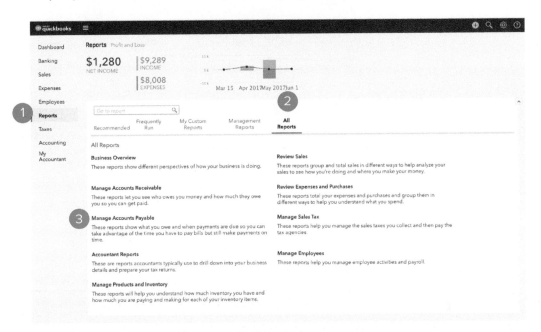

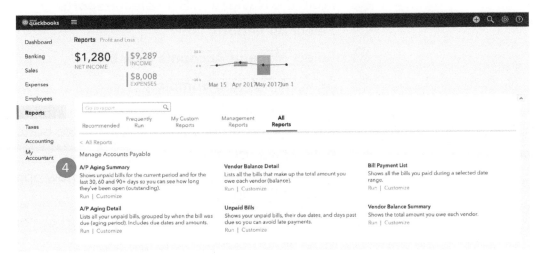

From the Navigation Bar select **Reports**

Select **All Reports** tab

Select **Manage Accounts Payable**

Select **A/P Aging Summary**

Enter **Customize** features using the Customization Bar across the top of the report or using the Customize button

Select **Save Customizations** and follow onscreen instructions to save so the customized report will now appear under the My Custom Reports tab

Select **Export** icon to display the export options: Export to Excel and Export to PDF

SALES BY PRODUCT/SERVICE SUMMARY

The Sales by Product/Service Summary report shows us which products are selling the most and which products are the most profitable. This information is useful for planning which products to order.

To prepare the Sales by Product/Service Summary report:

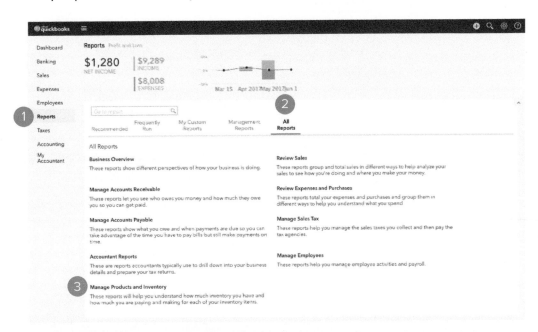

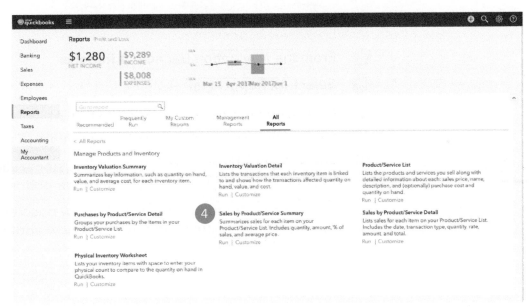

1. From the Navigation Bar select **Reports**

2. Select **All Reports** tab

3. Select **Manage Products and Inventory**

4. Select **Sales by Product/Service Summary**

5. Enter **Customize** features using the Customization Bar across the top of the report or using the Customize button

6. Select **Save Customizations** and follow onscreen instructions to save so the customized report will now appear under the My Custom Reports tab

7. Select **Export** icon to display the export options: Export to Excel and Export to PDF

PHYSICAL INVENTORY WORKSHEET

The Physical Inventory Worksheet is used when taking a physical count of inventory on hand. The worksheet lists the quantity of inventory items on hand and provides a blank column in which to enter the quantity counted during a physical inventory count. This worksheet permits us to compare our physical inventory count with our QBO records.

To prepare the Physical Inventory Worksheet:

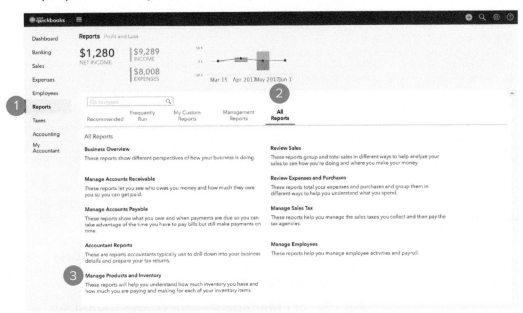

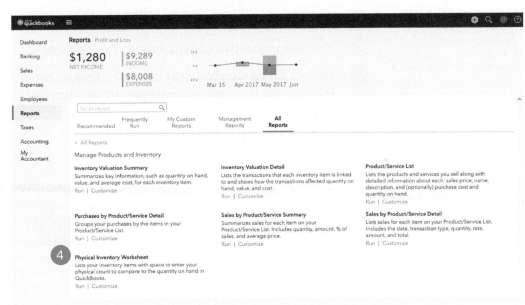

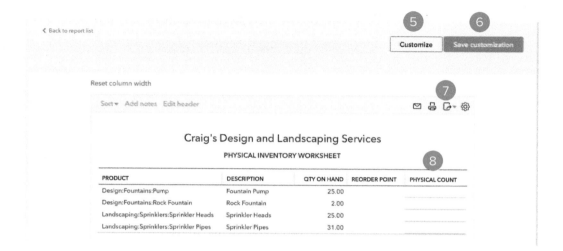

1. From the Navigation Bar select **Reports**

2. Select **All Reports tab**

3. Select **Manage Products and Inventory**

4. Select **Physical Inventory Worksheet**

5. To customize the report select **Customize**

6. Select **Save Customizations** and follow onscreen instructions to save so the customized report will now appear under the My Custom Reports tab

7. Select **Export** icon to display the export options: Export to Excel or Export to PDF

8. Enter **Physical Count** of inventory on exported report

After completing the worksheet if we have any unresolved discrepancies, we can use the Inventory Adjustment feature to update our inventory records.

To make an inventory adjustment:

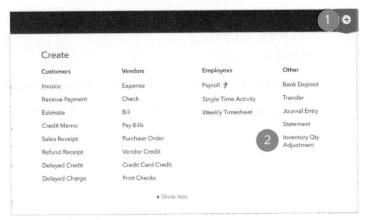

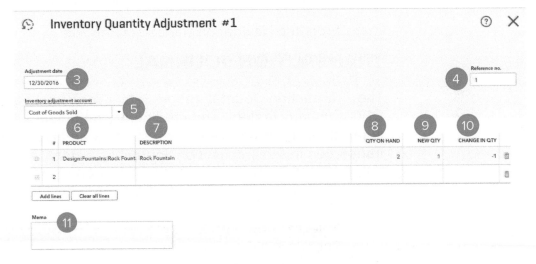

①   Select **Create (+)** icon

②   Select **Inventory Qty Adjustment**

③   Enter **Date** of inventory adjustment

④   Enter **Reference no.** or use the Reference no. that QBO automatically assigns

⑤   Select **Inventory Adjustment Account.** We can adjust Cost of Goods Sold or we can add a new account entitled Inventory Shrinkage as an Expense account If we want to track the amount of inventory shrinkage separately from our CGS account.

⑥   Select **Product** from the drop-down list

7) Verify **Description** which QBO should autofill from the Products and Services List

8) Verify **QTY on Hand** which QBO should autofill from our inventory tracking records

9) Enter **New QTY** from physical inventory worksheet

10) Verify **Change in QTY** which QBO will automatically calculate for us

11) Enter **Memo** to document the inventory adjustment

12) Normally we would select Save and New or Save and Close, but in this case select **Cancel.** We will enter new inventory adjustments in the exercises at the end of the chapter.

TRANSACTION JOURNAL

The Transaction Journal report lists every transaction entered in our QBO company in debit and credit entry form. Even if the transaction was entered using an onscreen form such as an Invoice, QBO will show the transaction in the Transaction Journal as a debit and credit journal entry. The Transaction Journal can be useful when tracking down errors.

To view the Transaction Journal report:

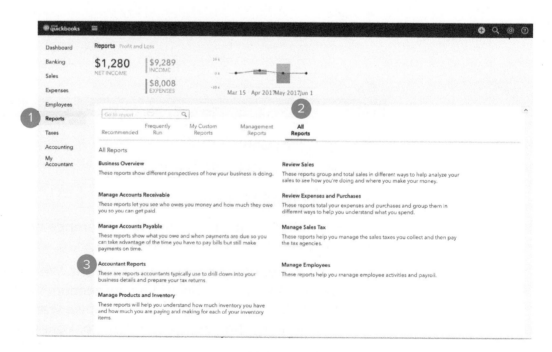

① From the Navigation Bar select **Reports**

② Select **All Reports tab**

③ Select **Accountant Reports**

④ Select **Journal**

⑤ Select **Report period**

⑥ To customize the report further select **Customize**

⑦ Select **Save Customizations** and follow onscreen instructions to save so the customized report will now appear under the My Custom Reports tab

⑧ Select **Export** icon to display the export options: Export to Excel or Export to PDF

AUDIT LOG

The Audit Log feature of QBO permits us to track all changes (additions, modifications, and deletions) made to our QBO records. When used appropriately, the Audit Log feature improves internal control by tracking any unauthorized changes to accounting records. The owner (or manager) should periodically review the Audit Log for discrepancies or unauthorized changes.

To view the Audit Log in QBO:

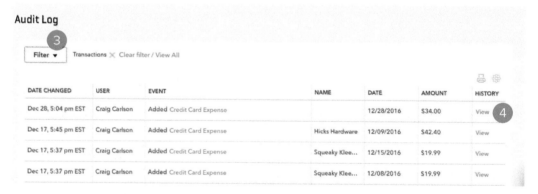

① Select **Gear** icon

② Under Tools select **Audit Log**

③ Select **Filter** to filter for specific entries, such as Transctions

④ Select **View** to view the History of the log entry with a record of changes made by specific users

The Audit Log is especially useful if we have more than one QBO user. The Log permits us to determine which user made which changes.

This chapter provided an overview of some frequently used reports. QBO offers many more reports that provide useful information to a business. These additional reports can be accessed from the Reports screen.

Section 10.10

ACCOUNTING ESSENTIALS

Financial Reports

Accounting Essentials summarize important foundational accounting knowledge you may find useful when using QBO

What are three types of financial reports a business prepares?

1. **Financial statements.** Financial statements are reports used by investors, owners, and creditors to make decisions. A banker might use the financial statements to decide whether to make a loan to a company. A prospective investor might use the financial statements to decide whether to invest in a company.

   The three financial statements most frequently used by external users are:

   * **Profit and Loss** (also referred to as the P & L or Income Statement) lists income and expenses, summarizing the income a company has earned and the expenses incurred to earn the income.

   * **Balance Sheet** lists assets, liabilities, and owners' equity, summarizing what a company *owns* and *owes* on a particular date.

   * **Statement of Cash Flows** lists cash flows from operating, investing, and financing activities of a business.

2. **Tax forms.** The objective of the tax form is to provide information to federal and state tax authorities. When preparing tax returns, a company uses different rules from those used to prepare financial statements. When preparing a federal tax return, use the Internal Revenue Code.

   Tax forms include the following:

   * Federal income tax return

   * State tax return

   * Federal Payroll Forms 940, 941/944, W-2, W-3

   * Federal Form 1099

3. **Management reports.** Management reports are used by internal users (managers) to make decisions regarding company operations. These reports are created to satisfy a manager's information needs.

Examples of reports that managers use include:

- Cash budget that projects amounts of cash that will be collected and spent in the future. (Note a Statement of Cash Flows focuses on cash inflows and outflows in the *past*. A Cash Budget focuses on expected cash flows in the *future*.)

- Accounts receivable aging report that lists the age and balance of customer accounts receivable so accounts are collected in a timely manner.

PRACTICE QUIZ 10

Q10.1

The physical inventory worksheet is used when:

a. Inventory items are physically placed in the warehouse

b. The computer network goes down

c. Taking a physical count of inventory on hand

d. All of the above

Q10.2

Which one of the following is not a financial statement?

a. Statement of Cash Flows

b. Profit & Loss

c. Trial Balance

d. Balance Sheet

Q10.3

The Chart of Accounts displays:

a. Account Name

b. Type

c. Detail Type

d. All of the above

Q10.4

The Balance Sheet lists:

a. Assets, Revenues, and Owner's Equity

b. Assets, Liabilities, and Owner's Equity

c. Revenues, Expenses, and Net Income

d. Revenues, Liabilities, and Net Income

Q10.5

Which one of the following classifications is not found on the Statement of Cash Flows?

a. Cash Flows from Selling Activities

b. Cash Flows from Financing Activities

c. Cash Flows from Investing Activities

d. Cash Flows from Operating Activities

Q10.6

Which of the following is correct?

a. Statement of Cash Flows is reported on a particular date

b. The Income Statement is reported on a particular date

c. The Balance Sheet is reported on a particular date

d. The Balance Sheet is reported for a specific time period

Q10.7

QuickBooks Online uses which basis of accounting?

a. Accrual

b. Cash

c. Both a and b

d. Neither a nor b

Q10.8

The Profit and Loss Statement lists:

a. Assets, Revenues, and Owner's Equity

b. Assets, Liabilities, and Owner's Equity

c. Revenues, Expenses, and Net Income

d. Revenues, Liabilities, and Net Income

Q10.9

Management reports:

a. Must follow a set of rules specified by Generally Accepted Accounting Principles

b. Must follow the rules specified by the Internal Revenue Service

c. Must follow the rules specified by vendors

d. Do not have to follow a specified set of rules

Q10.10

Management reports include:

a. Customer Profitability reports

b. Accounts Receivable Aging reports

c. Accounts Payable Aging reports

d. Inventory reports

e. All of the above

Q10.11

Which of the following is a Customer report:

a. Accounts Receivable (A/R) Aging

b. Accounts Payable (A/P) Aging

c. Open Purchase Orders

d. None of the above

Q10.12

The Transaction Journal:

a. Lists every journal entry made only through the onscreen journal

b. Is also called the Audit Log

c. Lists every transaction entered in QBO in debit and credit entry form

d. None the above

Q10.13

The Audit Log tracks:

a. Additions to our QBO records

b. Modifications to our QBO records

c. Deletions to our QBO records

d. All of the above

Q10.14

Which of the following reports can improve internal control by tracking unauthorized changes to accounting records?

a. Cash Budget

b. Cash Forecast

c. Audit Log

d. Transaction Journal

EXERCISES 10

> We use the QBO Sample Company, Craig's Design and Landscaping Services for practice throughout the exercises. The Sample Company will reset each time it is reopened. So make certain to allow enough time to complete exercises before closing the Sample Company. Otherwise, you will lose the work you have entered when you reopen the Sample Company.

To access the QBO Sample Company, complete the following steps.

1. Open a web browser. (Note: Intuit recommends using Google Chrome.)
2. Go to the https://qbo.intuit.com/redir/testdrive
3. Follow onscreen instructions for security verification.

Craig's Design and Landscaping Services should appear on your screen.

E10.1 Accounting Cycle

Match the following accounting cycle steps with the appropriate description.

Accounting Cycle Descriptions

a. Prepared at the end of the accounting period before preparing financial statements to bring the accounts up to date.

b. Prepared during the accounting period to record exchanges with customers, vendors, employees, and owners.

c. A list of all accounts used to accumulate information about assets, liabilities, owners' equity, revenues, and expenses.

d. Prepared for external users and includes the Profit & Loss, Balance Sheet, and Statement of Cash Flows.

e. Prepared after adjustments to verify that the accounting system still balances.

f. Lists each account and the account balance at the end of the accounting period to verify that the accounting system is in balance—total debits should equal total credits.

Accounting Cycle Steps

1. Chart of Accounts
2. Transactions
3. Trial Balance
4. Adjustments

5. Adjusted Trial Balance

6. Financial Statements

E10.2

For the following accounts on Craig's Design and Landscaping Services Chart of Accounts, identify Account Type and Financial Statement on which it appears.

Account Types

- **Asset**
- **Liability**
- **Equity**
- **Income**
- **Expense**

Financial Statements

- **Balance Sheet**
- **Profit and Loss**

	Account Type	**Financial Statement**
1. Design Income		
2. Savings		
3. Accounts Receivable (A/R)		
4. Rent or Lease		
5. Prepaid Expenses		
6. Notes Payable		
7. Inventory Asset		
8. Opening Balance Equity		
9. Utilities		
10. Undeposited Funds		
11. Accounts Payable (A/P)		
12. MasterCard		
13. Visa		
14. Loan Payable		
15. Sales of Product Income		

Account Type   Financial Statement

16. Legal and Professional Fees

17. Advertising

18. Meals and Entertainment

19. Retained Earnings

20. Checking

21. Landscaping Services

22. Pest Control Services

23. Cost of Goods Sold

24. Automobile: Fuel

25. Bank Charges

26. Interest Earned

E10.3 Statement of Cash Flows

For each of the following, identify the appropriate classification on the Statement of Cash Flows.

Statement of Cash Flows Classifications

a. Cash Flows from Operating Activities

b. Cash Flows from Investing Activities

c. Cash Flows from Financing Activities

1. Cash flows related to sales

2. Cash paid to repay a long-term loan

3. Cash flows related to purchasing inventory to resell

4. Cash flow from issuance of capital stock

5. Cash paid to purchase new equipment

6. Cash from sale of a warehouse

E10.4 Trial Balance (Adjusted)

Using the QBO Sample Company, Craig's Design and Landscaping Company, complete the following.

Match the following steps to prepare a QBO Trial Balance with the order in which the steps should occur.

Steps to Prepare a QBO Trial Balance

- **Select Accountant Reports**
- **Select Accrual**
- **Select Navigation Bar Reports**
- **Select Run Report**
- **Select All Reports Tab**
- **Select Active Rows**
- **Select Trial Balance**
- **Select Date**

1. _____
2. _____
3. _____
4. _____
5. _____
6. _____
7. _____
8. _____

E10.5 Profit and Loss Statement

Using the QBO Sample Company, Craig's Design and Landscaping Company, complete the following.

Match the following steps to prepare a QBO Profit and Loss Statement with the order in which the steps should occur.

Steps to Prepare a QBO Profit and Loss Statement

- **Select Navigation Bar Reports**
- **Select Profit and Loss**
- **Select Date**
- **Select Run Report**
- **Select All Reports Tab**
- **Select Active Rows**
- **Select Business Overview**
- **Select Accrual**

1. _____
2. _____
3. _____
4. _____
5. _____
6. _____
7. _____
8. _____

E10.6 Balance Sheet

Using the QBO Sample Company, Craig's Design and Landscaping Company, complete the following.

Match the following steps to prepare a QBO Balance Sheet with the order in which the steps should occur.

Steps to Prepare a QBO Balance Sheet

- **Select Business Overview**
- **Select Accrual**
- **Select Navigation Bar Reports**
- **Select Balance Sheet**
- **Select All Reports Tab**
- **Select Active Rows**
- **Select Run Report**
- **Select Date**

1. _____
2. _____
3. _____
4. _____
5. _____
6. _____
7. _____
8. _____

E10.7 Statement of Cash Flows

Using the QBO Sample Company, Craig's Design and Landscaping Company, complete the following.

Match the following steps to prepare a QBO Statement of Cash Flows with the order in which the steps should occur.

Steps to Prepare a QBO Statement of Cash Flows

- **Select Business Overview**
- **Select Statement of Cash Flows Select**
- **Run Report**
- **Select All Reports Tab**
- **Select Active Rows**
- **Select Navigation Bar Reports**
- **Select Date**

1. _____

2. _____

3. _____

4. _____

5. _____

6. _____

7. _____

E10.8 Accounts Receivable (A/R) Aging

Using the QBO Sample Company, Craig's Design and Landscaping Company, complete the following.

Match the following steps to prepare a QBO A/R Aging Summary report with the order in which the steps should occur.

Steps to Prepare a QBO A/R Aging Summary Report

- **Select Active Rows**
- **Select All Reports Tab**
- **Select Navigation Bar Reports**
- **Select A/R Aging Summary**
- **Select Days Per Aging Period**

- **Select Manage Accounts Receivable**
- **Select Run Report**
- **Select Date**
- **Select Aging Method**
- **Select Number of Periods**

1. _____

2. _____

3. _____

4. _____

5. _____

6. _____

7. _____

8. _____

9. _____

10. _____

E10.9 Open Purchase Orders

Using the QBO Sample Company, Craig's Design and Landscaping Company, complete the following.

Match the following steps to prepare a QBO Open Purchase Orders report with the order in which the steps should occur.

Steps to Prepare a QBO Open Purchase Orders Report

- **Select Date**
- **Select Open Purchase Order List**
- **Select Navigation Bar Reports**
- **Select Run Report**
- **Select All Reports Tab**
- **Select Review Expenses and Purchases**

1. _____

2. _____

3. _____

4. _____

5. _____

6. _____

E10.10 Accounts Payable (A/P) Aging

Using the QBO Sample Company, Craig's Design and Landscaping Company, complete the following.

Match the following steps to prepare a QBO A/P Aging report with the order in which the steps should occur.

Steps to Prepare a QBO A/P Aging Report

- **Select Navigation Bar Reports**
- **Select Active Rows**
- **Select All Reports Tab**
- **Select Number of Periods**
- **Select Manage Accounts Receivable**
- **Select Date**
- **Select Aging Method**
- **Select Days Per Aging Period**
- **Select A/P Aging Summary**
- **Select Run Report**

1. _____

2. _____

3. _____

4. _____

5. _____

6. _____

7. _____

8. _____

9. _____

10. _____

PROJECT 10.1

> Project 10.1 is a continuation of Project 9.1. You will use the QBO client company you created for Project 1.1 and updated in Projects 2.1 through 9.1. Keep in mind the QBO company for Project 10.1 does not reset and carries your data forward, including any errors. So it is important to check and crosscheck your work to verify it is correct before clicking the Save button.

BACKSTORY

Mookie The Beagle™ Concierge, the provider of convenient, high-quality pet care, has asked for your assistance in preparing QBO financial reports for the first month of its operations.

Complete the following for Mookie The Beagle Concierge.

QBO SatNav

Project 10.1 focuses on the QBO Reports as shown in the following partial QBO SatNav.

HOW TO LOG INTO QBO+

To log into QBO, complete the following steps.

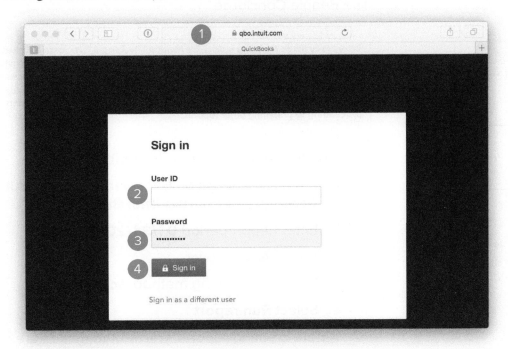

1. Using a web browser go to qbo.intuit.com
2. Enter **User ID** (the email address you used to set up your QBO Account)
3. Enter **Password** (the password you used to set up your QBO Account)
4. Select **Sign in**

If you are <u>not</u> using a public or shared computer, **to speed up login, you can save your login to your desktop and select Remember Me. If you are using a public computer or shared computer, do not save to your desktop and unselect Remember Me.**

The new QBO company **we created in Project 1.1 will carry all work forward into future chapters. So it is important to check and crosscheck your work to verify it is correct before clicking the Save button. Any errors entered are carried forward in the QBO company you create for text projects.**

P10.1.1 Trial Balance (Adjusted)

Complete the following to prepare an Adjusted Trial Balance for Mookie The Beagle Concierge.

> We already made adjusting entries for Mookie The Beagle Concierge in Project 9.1, so we will start the Accounting Cycle in Project 10.1 with the Adjusted Trial Balance, a trial balance prepared after adjusting entries have been made. Since any errors in your Mookie The Beagle Concierge QBO company will be carried forward from prior projects, Projects 1.1 through 9.1, in this activity we will make sure our adjusted trial balance has the correct balances, and update account balances as needed before proceeding to preparing other reports.

1. Create a Trial Balance (Adjusted).

   a. From the Navigation Bar select **Reports > All Reports tab > Accountant Reports > Trial Balance**

   b. Enter Report period **01/31/2018**

   c. Select **Active rows**

   d. Select Accounting method **Accrual**

   e. Select **Run report**

2. Before creating reports, we want to make sure our QBO balances are the same as the balances in the following Trial Balance (Adjusted) report. Compare your Trial Balance (Adjusted) account balances to the following Trial Balance (Adjusted) report. If your account balances are the same as the following Trial Balance, proceed to Step 3.

   If any of your QBO account balances differ from the following Trial Balance account balances, then there must be an error somewhere in your accounts.

   Make correcting journal entries as needed to update your accounts to the correct balances. (See Chapter 9 Accounting Essentials for more information about correcting entries. To use the Journal select Create (+) icon > Journal Entry.)

3. Trial Balance (Adjusted) Totals

   a. What is the amount of Total Debits on the Trial Balance?

   b. What is the amount of Total Credits on the Trial Balance?

   c. Export the Trial Balance (Adjusted) to PDF.

Mookie The Beagle Concierge
TRAIL BALANCE
As of January 31, 2018

	DEBIT	CREDIT
1001 Checking	8,071.80	
1002 Account Receivable (A/R)	792.56	
1005 Prepaid Expenses:Insurance	200.00	
1006 Prepaid Expenses:Supplies	236.00	
Prepaid Expenses:Rent	360.00	
1008 Undeposited Funds	0.00	
Inventory Asset	390.00	
2001 Accounts Payable (A/P)		500.00
2002 VISA Credit Card		1,228.00
Board of Equalization Payable		47.36
Loan Payable		1,000.00
Unearned Revenue		1,000.00
3001 Opening Balance Equity		0.00
3002 Owner Contributions		5,000.00
4001 Sales		3,885.00
Sales of Product Income		592.00
Cost of Goods Sold	225.00	
5004 Advertising	1,000.00	
5007 Insurance:Insurance - Renter	8.00	
5008 Insurance:Insurance - Liability	100.00	
5009 Interest Expense	5.00	
5010 Legal & Professional Fees	110.00	
5015 Rent or Lease	72.00	
5019 Subcontractors	1,320.00	
5020 Supplies	190.00	
5025 Utilities	172.00	

P10.1.2 Profit and Loss Statement

Complete the following to prepare a Profit and Loss Statement for Mookie The Beagle Concierge.

1. Create a Profit and Loss Statement.

   a. From the Navigation Bar select **Reports > All Reports tab > Business Overview > Profit and Loss**

   b. Enter Report period **01/01/2018 to 01/31/2018**

   c. Select **Active rows**

   d. Select Accounting method **Accrual**

   e. Select **Run report**

   f. On the Profit and Loss Statement, what is Gross Profit?

   g. On the Profit and Loss Statement, what are Total Expenses?

   h. On the Profit and Loss Statement, what is Net Income?

2. Export the Profit and Loss Statement to PDF.

P10.1.3 Balance Sheet

Complete the following to prepare a Balance Sheet for Mookie The Beagle Concierge.

1. Create a Balance Sheet.

   a. From the Navigation Bar select **Reports > All Reports tab > Business Overview > Balance Sheet**

   b. Enter Report period **01/31/2018**

   c. Select **Active rows**

   d. Select Accounting method **Accrual**

   e. Select **Run report**

   f. On the Balance, what are Total Assets?

   g. On the Balance Sheet, what are Total Liabilities?

2. Export the Balance Sheet to PDF.

P10.1.4 Statement of Cash Flows

Complete the following to prepare a Statement of Cash Flows for Mookie The Beagle Concierge.

1. Create a Statement of Cash Flows.

   a. From the Navigation Bar select **Reports > All Reports tab > Business Overview > Statement of Cash Flows**

   b. Enter Report period **01/01/2018 to 01/31/2018**

   c. Select **Active rows**

   d. Select **Run report**

   e. On the Statement of Cash Flows, what is the Net Cash Provided by Operating Activities?

   f. On the Statement of Cash Flows, what is the Net Cash Provided by Investing Activities?

   g. On the Statement of Cash Flows, what is the Net Cash Provided by Financing Activities?

   h. What was Cash at the end of the period?

2. Export the Statement of Cash Flows to PDF.

P10.1.5 Accounts Receivable (A/R) Aging

Complete the following to prepare an Accounts Receivable (A/R) Aging report for Mookie The Beagle Concierge.

1. Create Accounts Receivable (A/R) Aging Report.

   a. From the Navigation Bar select **Reports > All Reports tab > Manage Accounts Receivable > A/R Aging Summary**

   b. Enter Report period **01/31/2018**

   c. Select **Active rows**

   d. Select Aging Method: **Report Date**

   e. Select Days per aging period: **30**

   f. Select Number of periods: **4**

   g. Select **Run report**

   h. On the A/R Aging Summary, what is the amount of A/R that is Current?

   i. On the A/R Aging Summary, what is the amount of A/R that is 1-30 days past due?

2. Export the Accounts Receivable (A/R) Aging Summary to PDF.

P10.1.6 Accounts Payable (A/P) Aging

Complete the following to prepare an Accounts Payable (A/P) Aging report for Mookie The Beagle Concierge.

1. Create Accounts Payable (A/P) Aging Report.

   a. From the Navigation Bar select **Reports** > **All Reports tab** > **Manage Accounts Payable** > **A/P Aging Summary**

   b. Enter Report period **01/31/2018**

   c. Select **Active rows**

   d. Select Aging Method: **Report Date**

   e. Select Days per aging period: **30**

   f. Select Number of periods: **4**

   g. Select **Run report**

   h. On the Accounts Payable (A/P) Aging Summary Report, what is the amount of A/P that is Current?

   i. On the A/P Aging Summary, what is the amount of A/P that is 1-30 days past due?

   j. On the A/P Aging Summary, what is the amount of A/P that is 31-60 days past due?

2. Export the Accounts Payable (A/P) Aging Summary to PDF.

www.my-quickbooksonline.com

Go to www.My-QuickBooksOnline.com for additional resources for you including QBO Help, QBO Videos, and more.

Appendix A

QBO Apps: Mac, Windows and Mobile

QBO MAC OR WINDOWS APP

Get QuickBooks Mac & Windows Apps, powered by QuickBooks Online

Free Download

Whether using a Mac or Windows-based desktop or laptop, we can access QuickBooks Online using a browser and the Internet. In addition, QuickBooks Online also offers the option to download and install an QBO Mac App or a QBO Windows App on our desktop or laptop. The Mac and Windows Apps provide additional features. First, we must determine whether we will use the App with Mac or Windows. Then download either the QBO Mac App or the QBO Windows App to our desktop or laptop. After installing the App, use our QBO Company sign in.

The QBO Mac and Windows Apps provide a blended approach. We can still access our QBO company from anywhere, anytime through a browser. In addition, if we have the desktop QBO Mac or Windows App installed, we have additional features available, including a menu bar (similar to the QuickBooks Desktop version), the functionality to open multiple windows at the same time, and the ability to enter QBO data without an active Internet connection. Later, when you establish an Internet connection, the data will sync with the cloud QBO. The link to download the QBO Mac and Windows Apps appears at the QBO log in.

Open multiple windows at the same

- Drag and drop them anywhere, even across screens and side by side
- Switch quickly between multiple tasks
- Save time with automatic refresh of open windows

Open multiple windows at the same time

- Drag and drop them anywhere, even across screens and side by side
- Switch quickly between multiple tasks
- Save time with automatic refresh of open windows

QBO MOBILE APP

In addition to the QBO Mac and Windows Apps, there is also a QBO Mobile App available for smartphones and tablets. The QBO mobile app permits us to add transactions, such as credit card expenses, on the go. Snap a picture of our credit card receipt and input the data into the QBO mobile app. When set up to sync with our QBO, the credit card expense then is updated in our QBO system.

Appendix B

QuickBooks Online versus QuickBooks Desktop

ASK MY ACCOUNTANT: WHICH QUICKBOOKS SHOULD I USE?

To meet different QuickBooks users' needs, Intuit offers several different versions of QuickBooks. If we are advising different clients on the best fit between their needs and QuickBooks version, then a general knowledge of the different types of QuickBooks available becomes vital to provide sound client advice.

In general, QuickBooks versions can be divided into two broad categories:

- **QuickBooks Client.** Businesses and organizations that use QuickBooks to maintain their accounting and financial records.
- **QuickBooks Accountant.** Accountants who provide accounting and financial services to multiple clients who use QuickBooks.

Since QuickBooks offers several different options (summarized in the following table), QuickBooks users often turn to their accountants for recommendations about which QuickBooks to use. The QuickBooks version that the client uses dictates which QuickBooks version the client's accountant must use. As the accountant making recommendations, we need to consider not only how the recommendation affects our client, but also how the recommendation will impact our client services.

	QuickBooks Online (QBO)	QuickBooks Desktop (QBDT)
Client	• QuickBooks Online (QBO) Essentials • QuickBooks Online (QBO+) Plus	• QuickBooks Desktop (QBDT) Pro • QuickBooks Desktop (QBDT) Premier • QuickBooks Enterprise
Accountant	• QuickBooks Online Accountant (QBOA)	• QuickBooks Desktop Accountant (QBDTA)

Although features and functionality of QuickBooks options can be expected to change over time, the following sections summarize information about some of the QuickBooks options for clients and accountants. For additional updates about each of these options, see www.Intuit.com.

WHAT ARE MY QUICKBOOKS CLIENT OPTIONS?

A QuickBooks client is a business, entrepreneur, or not-for-profit organization that uses QuickBooks to maintain accounting and financial records for that entity. A QuickBooks client has two basic options:

- QuickBooks Desktop (QBDT)
- QuickBooks Online (QBO)

If the QuickBooks client selects the QuickBooks desktop option, then there are several additional choices to consider that are summarized next.

QUICKBOOKS DESKTOP QBDT

QuickBooks desktop software can be installed on the hard drive of desktop computers, laptops, or servers controlled by the client. If QuickBooks is installed on a network, it can be accessed by multiple QuickBooks users. QuickBooks desktop can also be hosted in the cloud by Intuit authorized providers. QuickBooks desktop software can be purchased using three different approaches:

1. CD. QuickBooks software is installed from a CD.
2. Software Download. Since new desktop computers and laptops increasingly do not have CD drives, users can purchase a QuickBooks

software key code and download the QuickBooks software using an Internet browser.

3. Subscription. Instead of purchasing QuickBooks software, the user can choose to pay a monthly subscription fee to use the software. The QuickBooks software is still downloaded to the desktop computer or laptop, but when the user decides to stop paying the monthly fee, the user's access to the QuickBooks software is blocked.

In general, QuickBooks desktop offers several advantages including:

- Additional features and functionality not offered by QuickBooks Online
- User control over desktop computer access and security
- User control over backups and access to backup data files
- Portability of backup and portable QuickBooks files
- Navigation features to streamline use, such as the Home page with flowcharts
- Intuit offers the following different editions of the QuickBooks desktop software to meet specific user needs, including:
  - QuickBooks Pro
  - QuickBooks Premier
  - QuickBooks Enterprise

QuickBooks Desktop Pro is a good option for small businesses that do not require industry-specific features because it is less expensive.

QuickBooks Desktop Premier offers more advanced features than QuickBooks Pro and permits you to customize QuickBooks by selecting a version with industry-specific features. QuickBooks Premier has different industry versions from which you can choose including the following.

- Contractor
- Manufacturing and Wholesale
- Nonprofit
- Professional Services
- Retailers
- General Business

QuickBooks Enterprise Solutions is designed for mid-size companies that have outgrown QuickBooks Premier. QuickBooks Enterprise can be used to track inventory at multiple locations and consolidate reports from multiple companies.

QUICKBOOKS ONLINE QBO

Accessed using a browser and the Internet, with QuickBooks Online, there is no need to install software on a computer hard drive or local server. (See Appendix A for the QBO App that can be installed on a computer to enhance the features of QBO.) The main advantage to QuickBooks Online is its anytime, anywhere use, so long as Internet access is available. Factors to consider when using QuickBooks Online include:

- Internet connection needs to be a secure connection with data in transit encrypted. Using an open WiFi at a café or a hotel when traveling to access QuickBooks Online, while convenient, places data in transit at risk. Our login, password, and confidential financial data could be viewed by others.
- Fewer features and functionality than QuickBooks desktop with features that will continue to change as QuickBooks Online is dynamically updated.
- The convenience of dynamic updates that occur automatically without needing to download and install.
- Loss of control over when updates occur, which may result in the need to learn new updates at unplanned times.
- Backups are performed automatically by Intuit.
- QBO Mobile app that makes it easier to stay up to date while on the go.

WHAT ARE MY QUICKBOOKS ACCOUNTANT OPTIONS?

Designed for accountants serving multiple clients, Intuit offers two QuickBooks Accountant options:

- QuickBooks Accountant Desktop (QBDTA)
- QuickBooks Online Accountant (QBOA)

Which option the accountant chooses is typically dictated by client use because QuickBooks desktop files, in general, are not compatible with QuickBooks Online. For example, if all the accounting firm's clients use QuickBooks desktop software, then the accounting firm would use QuickBooks Accountant desktop version. If the clients use QuickBooks Online, then the accountant needs to use QuickBooks Online Accountant. Some accounting firms have clients using QuickBooks desktop versions and other clients using QuickBooks Online, so those accounting firms must use both QuickBooks Accountant desktop and QuickBooks Online Accountant to be able to work with both types of clients.

QUICKBOOKS DESKTOP ACCOUNTANT QBDTA

QuickBooks Accountant desktop is the software packaged free with Kay's *Computer Accounting with QuickBooks* text if purchased new. Like QuickBooks desktop software, QuickBooks Accountant in the desktop edition is installed on the hard drive of desktop computers, laptops, or network servers. The QuickBooks Accountant edition permits the accountant to toggle between different desktop user editions of QuickBooks. This permits the accountant to view whatever edition of QuickBooks (QuickBooks Pro, QuickBooks Premier, and so on) that a particular client uses.

For more information about using QuickBooks Desktop, see Kay's *Computer Accounting with QuickBooks* at www.My-QuickBooks.com

How Can Our Accounting Firm Streamline Our QuickBooks Desktop Consulting?

Which QuickBooks version our clients use affects our consulting services operations. Some accounting firms relate nightmarish stories about clients using an array of QuickBooks desktop software from the 2002 edition and every year to the present edition. This approach to QuickBooks consulting requires the accounting firm to maintain all the various versions of the client software and track which clients use which versions. This can become a logistical nightmare for an accounting firm since it must have not only all the QuickBooks editions operational but also staff trained on the multiple versions.

Other accounting firms take a more streamlined, proactive approach when working with multiple clients that use QuickBooks. These firms recommend to clients which QuickBooks edition to use based on the best fit for the client while still keeping it manageable for the firm. Some accountants move all their clients to the next edition of QuickBooks at the same time. For example, after the 2018 QuickBooks edition is released, the accounting firm thoroughly tests the new edition, and then the firm moves all clients to QuickBooks 2018 on January 1, 2018. This approach permits the accounting firm to test the new software for possible issues, install updates, and create workarounds before moving clients to the new edition. Since many clients are on a calendar year starting January 1, this timeline permits a nice cutoff. Also, this approach streamlines firm operations since now all clients and the firm are in sync, using the same version of QuickBooks.

This proactive approach requires the accounting firm to communicate clearly with clients, working as a team with clients to prepare and transition them to the new version. Firms that use this proactive approach often state that it requires time and effort to do so, but much less time than trying to maintain multiple versions of QuickBooks for multiple clients. If clients start moving to the new edition as soon as it is released, clients may encounter unexpected issues that the accounting firm has not had time to thoroughly investigate and resolve. Some firms even provide training for clients as they transition them to the new version, summarizing differences and new features to proactively prepare clients for what to expect. This can minimize client errors in working with the new version and save the firm from unexpected disruptions and surprises.

QUICKBOOKS ONLINE ACCOUNTANT QBOA

QuickBooks Online Accountant is designed for accounting firms that provide services to multiple clients who use QuickBooks Online. QuickBooks Online Accountant is accessed using the Internet and a browser and permits the accountant to collaborate with several different clients, viewing their QuickBooks Online company files. At this time QuickBooks Online Accountant does not use the Home page navigational feature. In addition, there are fewer features and functionality with the QuickBooks Online Accountant version than the QuickBooks Accountant desktop version.

QBOA offers more features than QBO for clients. For example, QBOA has Adjusted Trial Balance and Adjusting Journal Entry features. In addition, there are other Accountant Tools in QBOA.

The main advantage to QuickBooks Online Accountant is the anytime, anywhere access when an Internet connection is available. Of course, since the accountant is responsible for maintaining the confidentiality of client financial data, the Internet connection needs to be a secure connection with data in transit encrypted. Using an open WiFi connection risks data in transit (such as login, password, and confidential client financial data) being viewed by others. Since accounting firms have a responsibility to maintain client data confidentiality and security, this is a serious concern.

For more information about QuickBooks Desktop, go to www.my-quickbooksonline.com.

Index